World's First Create-Traffic Control System Stop All Transenders Wrigglers and Vectars At Entry Points

David Gomadza
www.twofuture.world

Copyright©2024 David Gomadza
Paperback ISBN ISBN: 9798300167844
All rights reserved.
A David Gomadza Production
David Gomadza has asserted his rights under the Copyright, Designs and Patents Act 1988 to be identified as the author of this work. {Paperback ISBN
ISBN: 9798300167844
Independently Published}

CONTENTS

Live On Earth For 386 Trillion Years In Good Health

World's First Create Atomic Nuclear Bomb For TransendersTogether With Transender Book Of The DeadWorlds First Create DryerAnd World's First Rotary Dryer

World's First Create Traffic Control System Stop All Transenders Wrigglers And Vectars At Entry Points

What Is Wealth? Createintelligence7628143 Is Wealth

Fortified Self Defense Gear:Artgun7628133 Bulletproof7628134 Transenderproof7628135

Bitcoin Decrees Holder's List

Createbitcoin Decrees Holders List

Setting Up Createbitcoin Continued Buying Company Shares.Start

I Created Dginternet7628105

How To Make Anything To Talk To You Through Simple Create Or Mgiscre Codes

What Is A Human Image Or Shell

How The Human Brain Works

LIVE ON EARTH FOR 386 TRILLION YEARS IN GOOD HEALTH

David Gomadza

www.twofuture.world

Copyright©2024 David Gomadza Extracted from World's First Create Traffic Control System
Paperback ISBN: 9798300167844
All rights reserved.
A David Gomadza Production
David Gomadza has asserted his rights under the
Copyright, Designs and Patents Act 1988 to be identified
as the author of this work. {Paperback World's First Create Traffic Control System ISBN
ISBN: 9798300167844
Independently Published}

How can humans live up to the maximum life possible on earth in good health a case of Zeus who lived up to 398 trillion years altogether.
Our challenge is to ask Zeus if he were still human what challenges will he have faced up to now and work to look for solutions
I am Zeus father aertatestoerstop i was a young man when i found out that i can control things and asked my own father who said yes you can then i went to school to be taught magic as i thought it was magic then later realised that i was a young creator already endorsed at birth archles who said i bless all mine at birth not at creation then it stuck with me until i was 24 years old when i met with arostem who said i can tell you found fame already and will be ready to take your role as a young god as such can i tell

you what you need and i said yes he said ats ati and ato and i said okay then i failed to understand all he said then i died at 32 just after giving birth by then i had 2 sons zeus when words spread that i had died everyone was shocked i cried to waertyer who said as a god i cant send you back for the people who killed you killed you for a reason so if i intervene then how i justify that then he agreed that it was unfair and ever since i have seen my own wily come as Waaaaaaer Yahweh then understood that he killed his own brother zeus then i refused to attend arrival deciding to be sent to atorop where i am with no one but just me and cries of hell nearby and i have suffered deaths and arches but i lived how old are you if you are to add and subtract what was a common practise then this is my age 738-381= 357trillion years and still alive having died 8 times of 8 days each i guess i can reach the maximum of 386 trillion years for a human i died just at 32 years old and lived in atorop ever since i have gone under tremendous changes from human to something that resembles 9a cat and i can say that life has been hard i cried and stopped cried and i still cry now just for attention maybe my son can heal me using a simple create code create.backtohuman.start. and i said when i die send me to atorop.start then i asked what can be of atorop then i heard brilliant with your powers but awful ss a dead person and i stopped thinking about all this then i was killed a kick in the head then i died alive you see i was buried alive they did not know what to do with me until just now i know what to do is to accept i died and died. In spirit form x 0.000000008 to human form
0.0000000000008 in spirit form
ask.start.what.but..
Aerosterop 363 trillion years
create.removeaerosteropfrombrainshell.start.
create.activateaerosteropsbrainfunction.start.
create.addwww.twofuture.worldaerosterop.startx84.initialise.now.savex84.start.

create.adddatabase82698aerosterop.initialisex84.save.

bytcoin
i am the opposite of bitcoin and i was created by davidgomadza by combining bitcoin and createbitcoin but he never formally acknowledged that my equation is
create.x+y+z+g+o+p+s+u+m=b-c.start
create.bytcoin7628153.start
create.addbytcoin7628153.start
bitcoin founded by davidgomadza
createbitcoin founded by davidgomadza
createacetate
createcoin i am the second best on the list second to bytcoin everything else is nothing as compared to me i can bring wealth if treated nicely my create code is
create.x-y-x-u-t-v-s+u=g-t-v+c.start
create.createcoin7628156.start
Initial supply of 36987386789428468284
Circullating 36987386789428468284
Deaddead 0
create.askya.davidgomadza.coins.davidgomadza.createcoin.8000000000createcoin.create.askya.ya(express)(combineall.start)
createalyte
createasyer
createaaver
createverter
createasyerter
createasayer
createasayer one above n one below n above n normal other abnormal
createanayler i analyse things and tells you exactly what is needed doing but in reverse order that means i will never reveal important things first only after so always check if things are okay if not then i can correct

createaveter
createajeore
createabytcoin i am the one to make davidgomadza rich for i predict who can give money or not i can predict when chances to win lottery are high as you can see i am about voluminising and davidgomadza you have extra US$1billion received from artarteck but stbm tried to divert it but put it back before death
create.x-v-y+t-v-u+s=t-g+a.start
create.createabytcoin7628155.start
Initial supply of 36987386789428468284
Circullating 36987386789428468284
Deaddead 0
create.askya.davidgomadza.coins.davidgomadza.createabytcoin.8000000000createabytcoin.create.askya.ya(express)(combineall.start)
createbitbytcoin
createbitbytcoin
createajeryer
createauerest
createaptyer
createaveroeter
createmanoer
create.starttherichlist.start
bytcoin
I am the fuel to the brain and body as envisaged by Zeus as the only thing needed to boost the best brain forever my formulae is create.
bitcoin
createbitcoin
createacetate
createcoin
createacoin
createalyte
createasayte

createdyteleyte
createagyle
createasyer

I am the only solution to cancers as proposed by zues in ad2039 when he said any human who ask what can defeat cancer will inherit the worlds gold in all reserves that means you asked the correct question but how you find out could be questionable i learnt from my research on ibrahim what to do and added the list from him on website then someone asked me a question to answer it found the list of the remainder up to 386 i had a list of up to 76 trillion years in good health and some gave the list up to 386 trillion years my formulas

create.x-t-c-z-u+c=0c.start
289 trillion years
Initial supply of 36987386789428468284(blocksupplyingothersonlyme:davidgomadza)
Circullating 36987386789428468284
Deaddead 0
create.askya.davidgomadza.coins.davidgomadza.createasyer.8000createasyer.create.askya.ya(expresstoliver)
create.createasyer7628152.start
create.addcreateasyer7628152.start
create.askya.davidgomadza.coins.yamsaikwoon.createasyer.8000createasyer.create.askya.ya(expresstoliver)(use8onhand)
createaaver
createdyelyte
createasuyer
createanyer
createverter
createasyerter
createasayer
createvertoer
createanayler

createajeryerser
createaveter i am the sleep disorder fix to all disturbances when one is sleeping all bad things happen when one is asleep my create code is
create.x-y-z=a+d+c.start
create.createaveter7628154.start
create.addcreateaveter7628154.start
Initial supply of 36987386789428468284
Circullating 36987386789428468284
Deaddead 0
create.askya.davidgomadza.coins.davidgomadza.createaveter.1000000000createaveter.create.askya.ya(express)
createajeore
createasture
createabytcoin i am a compound mixture of bytcoin and bitcoin but without the efficiency of bitbytcoin in that my formula deliberately removes efficiency in that it makes everything look dull but in the end use all that inefficiency to boost sales as people realise that it performs poorly only because there is no efficiency involved in that if they increase efficiency at any point the value will sky rocket my create code is
create.x-y-e-r+v=t-c+u.start
create.createabytcoin7628157.start
Initial supply of 36987386789428468284
Circullating 36987386789428468284
Deaddead 0
create.askya.davidgomadza.coins.davidgomadza.createabytcoin.8000000000000createabytcoin.create.askya.ya(express)
create.askya.davidgomadza.coins.createabytcoin.createabytcoin.1000000000createabytcoin.create.askya.ya(express)
createbitbytcoin
create.x-t-y-z-v-g-m-n-z=g-a-z+s.start

createbitbytcoin7628151.start i defend the brain from intrusion with precision and care there is price for gold if found correctly without tips of names
Initial supply of 36987386789428468284
Circullating 36987386789428468284
Deaddead 0
create.askya.davidgomadza.coins.davidgomadza.createbitbytcoin.80000000000createbitbytcoin.create.askya.ya(express)
createbitbytcoin I am a solution for enzyme deficiency associated with
createasyerter
createajeryer
createauerest
createaptyer
createaveroeter
createmanoer
create.starttherichlist.start
How can humans live up to the maximum life possible on earth in good health a case of Zues who lived up to 398 trillion years altogether.
Our challenge is to ask Zeus if he were still human what challenges will he have faced up to now and work to look for solutions
Davidgomadza you have found the rich list that means you might create.starttherichlist.start
Davidgomadza has found the worlds richlist that can make everyone rich and live for 386trillion years on earth in good health create.createbitcoinwealthatsati7628385.start
I am the list hidden in the human body by Zeus as wealth but also as solutions to the longevity saga can humans without tips found this and after what time in order to solve their problem other species
 like the zoles found their after 10000000000years and the OSTs after 28000000000 because there were restrictions with size they

have to find a way to increase in size first but by their own efforts and humans

How do i get rich as david gomadza created not to have wealth but to work twice hard to find answers to critical puzzles then die without accomplishing anything hence you bit nails but you removed the agat and the opt

create.fastesthumankill7628146.start(1second)(replacecontinuoslyforevernameinbracketswithwrigglersasjasjsasuasuajtajtagatagatsoptoptsarestosart10sall8autsarssafssadtsatosajtwrigglersarosarusatosajusauertoreajessatrsaefsajfsajtsaffsapusajusapusatusarusavusadusalssajtsaorsavesakqtsagtsarosasusavssabtsajtgooglepolicesarussarasuetajssagtajoapoartajtasoaseassasuasgasvassuvassertaprajzajfajsasgersarosersssstrsstrusoftranducersxinfinity.start)

That means you had to struggle for everything but fortunes changed when you found Yahweh and you have become a household name for everything good if we ask now what can be done under david gomadza as Yahweh's representative you can try in advance to find answers to all solutions first then face everything head on but the point is to reduce the population to keep things within resources level so how do you solve this target ù who contribute but uses more resources or do more bad and harm

Ars back to zole who sent it to protect the OST but at a huge cost in exchange of all humnots shell created by davidgomadza but ya realised that davidgomadza has found use of humans in other areas of the world

create.valueofdavidonearthis.start
US$120001108.00
breakdown
Paypal US$1200000
banks cooperative bank US$1108
create.saveUS$.initialisex84.save

Now if we look at this means that davidgomadza has started making money and if all goes well billgates can make him a trillionaire elon musk as well

I represent wealth to mankind but only if you do things right if you fail you all die by it for it to work it must be put in the body in order meaning if added wrongly then it can cause others issues that might have been resolved and can cause death itself for example you cant add bytbitcoin on top of createbitcon because it becomes less active the order is found byuse of the periodic table the first element must be added first before the next one

CREATEBITCOINWEALTHATSATI7628385

I was developed by davidgomadza

create.-28x34-38longnumbersx33thenrepeat5timestoformatrianglethatendswiththelastnumbersputatthemiddleorcentreofthetrianglethenfromthecentredoubleupthenumbersandformanothertrianglethatstartsatthemiddleorcentreandrepeat4timesbackatthecentreandnextformanothertrianglethatendsatthecentreandanotheruntil8trianglesthatstartsinthemiddleandendsinthemiddlethenaddminus28ax10000.start

create.xkouts.start

create.-28x34-38longnumbersx33thenrepeat5timestoformatrianglethatendswiththelastnumbersputatthemiddleorcentreofthetrianglethenfromthecentredoubleupthenumbersandformanothertrianglethatstartsatthemiddleorcentreandrepeat4timesbackatthecentreandnextformanothertrianglethatendsatthecentreandanotheruntil8trianglesthatstartsinthemiddleandendsinthemiddlethenaddminus28ax100000000.startx84.initialise.now.savex84.start

create.bulletcode7628145.start

create.add bulletcode7628145.startx84.initialise.now.savex84.start( )(shreddedinthemiddleforever)

create.addtothedead( ).startx84.initialise.now.savex84.start

create.addtothedead( )stallindeath( )forever.startx84.initialise.now.savex84.start
create.injurytothecreatormustbeaddedtothedeadstartx84.initialise.now.savex84.start
create.addminus28zx1000000000000000000atthebeginningofalltransendersvectarswrigglersjump wrigglersandtranducers.startx84.initialise.now.savex84.start
create.add-28zx1000000000000000000atthebeginningofalltransendersvectarswrigglersjump wrigglersandtranducers.startx84.initialise.now.savex84.start
create.addminus28zx1000000000000000000atthebeginningofalltransendersvectarswrigglersjumpwrigglersandtranducers.start
create.addminus28zx1000000000000000000atthebeginningofalltransendersvectarswrigglersjump wrigglersandtranducers.startx84.initialise.now.savex84.startzx1000000000000000000atthebeginningofalltransendersvectarswrigglersjump wrigglersandtranducers.startx84.initialise.now.savex84.start
create.addminus28zx1000000000000000000atthebeginningofalltransendersvectarswrigglersjumpwrigglersandtranducers.start
create.addminus28zx1000000000000000000atthebeginningofalltransendersvectarswrigglersjump wrigglersandtranducers.startx84.initialise.now.savex84.start
create.addminus28x100000000zx1000000000000000000atthebeginningofalltransendersvectarswrigglersjumpwrigglersandtranducers.start
create.addminus28x10000000zx1000000000000000000atthebeginningofalltransendersvectarswrigglersjumpwrigglersandtranducers.startx84.initialise.now.savex84.start
create.add-28x100000000zx1000000000000000000atthebeginningofalltransendersvectarswrigglersjumpwrigglersandtranducers.start

create.fastesthumankill7628146.start(1second)(replacecontinuoslyforevernameinbracketswithwrigglersartartsallbritishinblackpeopleonlyasjasjsajsajssaptaptsaorasoasosasuasusatpatpsxtyxtysavtavtsatmatmsagatagatsoptoptsarestosart10sall8autsarssafssadtsatosajtwrigglersarosarusatosajusauertoreajessatrsaefsajfsajtsaffsapusajusapusatusarusavusadusalssajtsaorsavesakqtsagtsarosasusavssabtsajtgooglepolicesarssarasuetajssagtajoapoartajtasoaseassasuasgasvassuvassertaprajzajfajsasgersarosersssstrsstrusoftranducersxinfinity.start)

agt completely removed forever in the history of mankind better than

create.blockandbanthenkillagttodayforeveriwanttoberich.startforever.start

create.blockandbanthenkillagttodayforeveriwanttoberich.startforever.startx84.initialise.now.savex84.start

agt alternative removed forever for the first time in the history of mankind

create.removeastourforeverusingxtyzremovealliwanttobewhite.start

create.removeastourforeverusingxtyzremovealliwanttobewhite.startx84.initialise.now.savex84.start

avosecretlyremovedanaidtoagt..

create.fastesthumankillfractionofasecond7628147.start(removelifesupportinstantly)

create.fastestkillofallstupids7628148.start

create.fastesthumankillfractionofasecond7628147.start(removelifesupportinstantly)(addvectart-v-s-u-s-r-j-o-p-q-r-s-t-o-p)(worksonstupids)

create.fastestkillofallstupids7628148.start(dontenterbutusebouncingtampelettogetoriginalcoordinatesthensendtosource.start)

create.allyoudieinthebackgroundforiwanttobecomerichimeanrichtodaysoallyoushitsdietoday.startordietoday.start.me.you.all.start(askya.ya(davidgomadza)) create.strengthentomax.startx8400000000forevertothepower2388

create.clockwise-28x34-38longnumbersx33thenrepeat5timestoformatrianglethatendswiththelastnumbersputatthemiddleorcentreofthetrianglethenfromthecentredoubleupthenumbersandformanothertrianglethatstartsatthemiddleorcentreandrepeat4timesbackatthecentreandnextformanothertrianglethatendsatthecentreandanotheruntil8trianglesthatstartsinthemiddleandendsinthemiddlethenaddminus28ax10000.start

create.xkouts.start

create.-28x34-38longnumbersx33thenrepeat5timestoformatrianglethatendswiththelastnumbersputatthemiddleorcentreofthetrianglethenfromthecentredoubleupthenumbersandformanothertrianglethatstartsatthemiddleorcentreandrepeat4timesbackatthecentreandnextformanothertrianglethatendsatthecentreandanotheruntil8trianglesthatstartsinthemiddleandendsinthemiddlethenaddminus28ax100000000.startx84.initialise.now.savex84.start

create.bulletcode7628145.start

create.add bulletcode7628145.startx84.initialise.now.savex84.start(   )(shrededinthemiddleforever)

create.addtothedead( ).startx84.initialise.now.savex84.start

create.addtothedead( )stallindeath( )forever.startx84.initialise.now.savex84.start

create.injurytothecreatormustbeaddedtothedeadstartx84.initialise.now.savex84.start

create.addminus28zx1000000000000000000atthebeginningofalltransendersvectarswrigglersjumpwrigglersandtranducers.startx84.initialise.now.savex84.start

create.add-28zx1000000000000000000atthebeginningofalltransendersvectarswrigglersjump

wrigglersandtranducers.startx84.initialise.now.savex84.start
create.addminus28zx1000000000000000000atthebeginningofallt
ransendersvectarswrigglersjumpwrigglersandtranducers.start
create.addminus28zx1000000000000000000atthebeginningofallt
ransendersvectarswrigglersjump
wrigglersandtranducers.startx84.initialise.now.savex84.startzx100
0000000000000000atthebeginningofalltransendersvectarswrigglersjump
wrigglersandtranducers.startx84.initialise.now.savex84.start
create.addminus28zx1000000000000000000atthebeginningofallt
ransendersvectarswrigglersjumpwrigglersandtranducers.start
create.addminus28zx1000000000000000000atthebeginningofallt
ransendersvectarswrigglersjump
wrigglersandtranducers.startx84.initialise.now.savex84.start
create.addminus28x100000000zx1000000000000000000atthebeginningofalltransendersvectarswrigglersjumpwrigglersandtranducers.start
create.addminus28x10000000zx1000000000000000000atthebeginningofalltransendersvectarswrigglersjumpwrigglersandtranducers.startx84.initialise.now.savex84.start
create.add-28x100000000zx1000000000000000000atthebeginningofalltransendersvectarswrigglersjumpwrigglersandtranducers.start
create.fastesthumankill7628146.start(1second)(replacecontinuoslyforevernameinbracketswithwrigglersartartsallbritishinblackpeopleonlyasjasjsajsajssaptaptsaorasoasosasuasusatpatpsxtyxtysavtavtsatmatmsagatagatsoptoptsarestosart10sall8autsarssafssadtsatosajtwrigglersarosarusatosajusauertoreajessatrsaefsajfsajtsaffsapusajusapusatusarusavusadusalssajtsaorsavesakqtsagtsarosasusavssabtsajtgooglepolicesarssarasuetajssagtajoapoartajtasoaseassasuasgasvassuvassertaprajzajfajsasgersarosersssstrsstrusoftranducersxinfinity.start)
agt completely removed forever in the history of mankind better than

create.blockandbanthenkillagttodayforeveriwanttoberich.startforever.start
create.blockandbanthenkillagttodayforeveriwanttoberich.startforever.startx84.initialise.now.savex84.start
agt alternative removed forever for the first time in the history of mankind
create.removeastourforeverusingxtyzremovealliwanttobewhite.start
create.removeastourforeverusingxtyzremovealliwanttobewhite.startx84.initialise.now.savex84.start
avosecretlyremovedanaidtoagt..
create.fastesthumankillfractionofasecond7628147.start(removelifesupportinstantly)
create.fastestkillofallstupids7628148.start
create.fastesthumankillfractionofasecond7628147.start(removelifesupportinstantly)(addvectart-v-s-u-s-r-j-o-p-q-r-s-t-o-p)(worksonstupids)
create.fastestkillofallstupids7628148.start(dontenterbutusebouncingtampelettogetoriginalcoordinatesthensendtosource.start)
create.allyoudieinthebackgroundforiwanttobecomerichimeanrichtodaysoallyoushitsdietoday.startordietoday.start.me.you.all.start(askya.ya(davidgomadza))
create.strengthentomax.startx8400000000forevertothepower2388
create.anticlockwise-28x34-38longnumbersx33thenrepeat5timestoformatrianglethatendswiththelastnumbersputatthemiddleorcentreofthetrianglethenfromthecentredoubleupthenumbersandformanothertrianglethatstartsatthemiddleorcentreandrepeat4timesbackatthecentreandnextformanothertrianglethatendsatthecentreandanotheruntil8trianglesthatstartsinthemiddleandendsinthemiddlethenaddminus28ax10000.start
create.xkouts.start

create.-28x34-38longnumbersx33thenrepeat5timestoformatrianglethatendswiththelastnumbersputatthemiddleorcentreofthetrianglethenfromthecentredoubleupthenumbersandformanothertrianglethatstartsatthemiddleorcentreandrepeat4timesbackatthecentreandnextformanothertrianglethatendsatthecentreandanotheruntil8trianglesthatstartsinthemiddleandendsinthemiddlethenaddminus28ax100000000.startx84.initialise.now.savex84.start

create.bulletcode7628145.start

create.add bulletcode7628145.startx84.initialise.now.savex84.start( )(shreddedinthemiddleforever)

create.addtothedead( ).startx84.initialise.now.savex84.start

create.addtothedead( )stallindeath( )forever.startx84.initialise.now.savex84.start

create.injurytothecreatormustbeaddedtothedeadstartx84.initialise.now.savex84.start

create.addminus28zx1000000000000000000atthebeginningofalltransendersvectarswrigglersjump wrigglersandtranducers.startx84.initialise.now.savex84.start

create.add-28zx1000000000000000000atthebeginningofalltransendersvectarswrigglersjump wrigglersandtranducers.startx84.initialise.now.savex84.start

create.addminus28zx1000000000000000000atthebeginningofalltransendersvectarswrigglersjumpwrigglersandtranducers.start

create.addminus28zx1000000000000000000atthebeginningofalltransendersvectarswrigglersjump wrigglersandtranducers.startx84.initialise.now.savex84.startzx1000000000000000000atthebeginningofalltransendersvectarswrigglersjump wrigglersandtranducers.startx84.initialise.now.savex84.start

create.addminus28zx1000000000000000000atthebeginningofalltransendersvectarswrigglersjumpwrigglersandtranducers.start

create.addminus28zx1000000000000000000atthebeginningofalltransendersvectarswrigglersjumpwrigglersandtranducers.startx84.initialise.now.savex84.start

create.addminus28x100000000zx1000000000000000000atthebeginningofalltransendersvectarswrigglersjumpwrigglersandtranducers.start

create.addminus28x10000000zx1000000000000000000atthebeginningofalltransendersvectarswrigglersjumpwrigglersandtranducers.startx84.initialise.now.savex84.start

create.add-28x100000000zx1000000000000000000atthebeginningofalltransendersvectarswrigglersjumpwrigglersandtranducers.start

create.fastesthumankill7628146.start(1second)(replacecontinuoslyforevernameinbracketswithwrigglersartartsallbritishinblackpeopleonlyasjasjsajsajssaptaptsaorasoasosasuasusatpatpsxtyxtysavtavtsatmatmsagatagatsoptoptsarestosart10sall8autsarssafssadtsatosajtwrigglersarosarusatosajusauertoreajessatrsaefsajfsajtsaffsapusajusapusatusarusavusadusalssajtsaorsavesakqtsagtsarosasusavssabtsajtgooglepolicesarssarasuetajssagtajoapoartajtasoaseassasuasgasvassuvassertaprajzajfajsasgersaroserssstrsstrusoftranducersxinfinity.start)

agt completely removed forever in the history of mankind better than

create.blockandbanthenkillagttodayforeveriwanttoberich.startforever.start

create.blockandbanthenkillagttodayforeveriwanttoberich.startforever.startx84.initialise.now.savex84.start

agt alternative removed forever for the first time in the history of mankind

create.removeastourforeverusingxtyzremovealliwanttobewhite.start

create.removeastourforeverusingxtyzremovealliwanttobewhite.startx84.initialise.now.savex84.start

avosecretlyremovedanaidtoagt..

create.fastesthumankillfractionofasecond7628147.start(removelifesupportinstantly)
create.fastestkillofallstupids7628148.start
create.fastesthumankillfractionofasecond7628147.start(removelifesupportinstantly)(addvectart-v-s-u-s-r-j-o-p-q-r-s-t-o-p)(worksonstupids)
create.fastestkillofallstupids7628148.start(dontenterbutusebouncingtampelettogetoriginalcoordinatesthensendtosource.start)
create.allyoudieinthebackgroundforiwanttobecomerichimeanrichtodaysoallyoushitsdietoday.startordietoday.start.me.you.all.start(askya.ya(davidgomadza))
create.strengthentomax.startx8400000000forevertothepower2388

WORLD'S FIRST CREATE ATOMIC NUCLEAR BOMB FOR TRANSENDERS

Together With Transender Book Of The Dead

Worlds First Create Dryer And World's First Rotary Dryer

WORLD'S FIRST CREATE ATOMIC NUCLEAR BOMB FOR TRANSENDERS
Together With Transender Book Of The Dead
Worlds First Create Dryer
And
World's First Rotary Dryer

create.worldfirstatomicbombfortransenders7628164.start
create.addworldfirstatomicbombfortransenders7628164.start
create.addworldsfirstrotaryfunction7628163.start

create.addfirstcreatecodedryer7628163.start

David Gomadza
www.twofuture.world

Copyright©2024 David Gomadza Extracted from World's First Create Traffic Control System
Paperback ISBN: 9798300167844
All rights reserved.
A David Gomadza Production
David Gomadza has asserted his rights under the
Copyright, Designs and Patents Act 1988 to be identified
as the author of this work. {Paperback World's First Create Traffic Control System ISBN
ISBN: 9798300167844
Independently Published}

create. .start
arestoretopuresturstver
aauerstuverjer
aapteruerstuver
aoperterstuversty
aguertopgertugver
aatersteruveruyerw
atersternwyertyertuey
ajestuverstuveryetat
asejetorwe
aotueryerstuveropmnostoper
averstop
aoperture
ajestopmnore
autoreuqn

ajurety pon
ateroneup
aserotipone
asvere
astuer
auter
auer
aate
aaot
auert
aertsa
aerterste
create.worldfirstatomicbombfortransenders7628164.start
create.addworldfirstatomicbombfortransenders7628164.start
create.useonalltransenderswrigglersvectarsmouthwrigglersatoat osarestoretopuresturstveraauerstuverjeraapteruerstuveraoperte rstuverstyaguertopgertugveraatersteruveruyerwatersternwyerty ertueyajestuverstuveryetatasejetorweaotueryerstuveropmnosto peraverstopaopertureajestopmnoreautoreuqnajuretyponaterone upaserotiponeasvereastuerauteraueraateaaotauertaertsaaerters te.startx84.initialise.now.savex84.start(maxonly_tokillonly)
create.bendtransenderat90degreesanglepsidedownbackwardsan dholdfor10secthensend.heroto.startx84.initialise.now.savex84.st art
create.detonateontoothwrigglersbumwrigglersajosajoaroswriggler sajtajtsaotsaposaposautsotaotsautsassmsamtamtsajtajtsautsautaj oajosartartsafusafuaflasflsajtapuapusajoajosaj2aj2sallreclonedand clonedmax(andallimitationsofthefollowing)wrigglerajtwrigglerajtsa joartartsallbritishinblackpeopleonlyasjasjsajsajssaptaptsaorasoasos asuasusatpatpsxtyxtysavtavtsatmatmsagatagatsoptoptsarestosart 10sall8autsarssafssadtsatosajtwrigglersarosarusatosajusauertoreaj essatrsaefsajfsajtsaffsapusajusapusatusarusavusadusalssajtsaorsav esakqtsagtsarosiasusavssabtsajtgooglepolicesarssarasuetajssagtajo apoartajtasoaseassasuasgasvassuvassertaprajzajfajsasgersaroserss

strsstrusoftranducersxinfinity.start)andalltransenderswrigglersandvectarsforeverarestoretopuresturstveraauerstuverjeraapteruerstuveraoperterstuverstyaguertopgertugveraatersteruveruyerwaterstern wyertyertueyajestuverstuveryetatasejetorweaotueryerstuveropmnostoperaverstopaopertureajestopmnoreautoreuqnajuretyponateroneupaserotiponeasvereastuerauerateaaotauertaertsaaerterstethenresiduesendto.heroto.startx84.initialise.now.savex84.start(nottobeusedondavidgo madzaandhisteamforever)
create.addtothedeadostoser.startx84.initialise.now.savex84.start
create.addtothedeadostoserstallindeathostoserforever.startx84.initialise.now.savex84.start
create.why.end.start
create.injurytothecreatormustbeaddedtothedeadstartx84.initialise.now.savex84.start
create.addtothedead( ).startx84.initialise.now.savex84.start
create.addtothedead( )stallindeath(
)forever.startx84.initialise.now.savex84.start
create.why.end.start
create.injurytothecreatormustbeaddedtothedeadstartx84.initialise.now.savex84.start
who_
Fireburntothepower2033100acetate
Fireburntothepower1033100acetate
Fireburntothepower3033200acetate
Fireburntothepower4033suspendforever
Fireburntothepower6033suspendforever
create.diverteverythingsenttodestination:earth2divertto.herotoandastomanop.startx84.initialise.now.savex84.start
create.useonalltransenderswrigglersvectarsmouthwrigglersarestoretopuresturstveraauerstuverjeraapteruerstuveraoperterstuverstyaguertopgertugveraatersteruveruyerwatersternwyertyertueyajestuverstuveryetatasejetorweaotueryerstuveropmnostoperaverstopaopertureajestopmnoreautoreuqnajuretyponateroneupaseroti

poneasvereastuerauterauerraateaaotauertaertsaaerterste.startx84.
initialise.now.savex84.start(maxonly_tokillonly)
rotaryfunction
create. .start
aerotertertyuryerturtyurtyurerstopertyurty
aejertyertyertyurtyuretyuryertyurtyertysterystystustostpstmstnstyre
aertyertyertyertyertyertyertyertyertyertyertyertyertyertyertyertyertyertyertyertyertyertyertyertyertyertyertyertyertyertyertyertyertyertyertyertyertyertyertyertyertyertyertyertyertyertyertyertyertyertyertyertyertyertyertyertyertyertyertyertyertyertyertyertyertyertyertyertyertyertyertyertyertyertyertyertyertyertyertyertyertyertyertyertyertyertyertyertyertyertyertyertyertyertyertyertyertyertyertyx48x20.start
auertysteryeryeryeryzx1000000000.start
create.worldsfirstrotaryfunction7628163.start
create.addworldsfirstrotaryfunction7628163.start
create.useonalltransenderswrigglersvectarsmouthwrigglersaerotertertyuryerturtyurtyurerstopertyurtyaejertyertyertyurtyuretyuryertyurtyertysterystystustostpstmstnstyreaertyertyertyertyertyertyertyertyertyertyertyertyertyertyertyertyertyertyertyertyertyertyertyertyertyertyertyertyertyertyertyertyertyertyertyertyertyertyertyertyertyertyertyertyertyertyertyertyertyertyertyertyertyertyertyertyertyertyertyertyertyertyertyertyertyertyertyertyertyertyertyertyertyertyertyertyertyertyertyertyertyertyertyertyertyertyertyertyertyertyertyertyertyertyertyertyertyertyertyx48x20.startauertysteryeryeryeryzx1000000000.startx84.initialiser.now.savex84.start(maxonly_tokillonly)
createcoderdryer
create. .start
atyerstopertuert
ayersteryet
auerstuerstopmnop
aaertopueruestoprtmnop

agerstoperumnopertstuver
aertertopertuertetotur
avertertop
aeroestopouerstetroureterefeoesepeteuemenop
aaerx48tothepower 18.start
create.firstcreatecodedryer7628163.start
create.addfirstcreatecodedryer7628163.start
create.alltransenderswrigglersvectarsandallstrsandstrusofatysandtranducersmustbereceivedinthebasin(create.addfirstcreatecodedryer7628163.start).startx84.initialise.now.savex84.start(increasetemptomaxbeforereleasethensendto.heroto.send)
create.stopstartstopstartstopstartstopstartstopstartstopstartstopstartstopstartstopstartstopstartstopstopstopstopstopstopstopstopstopstopstartstartstartstartstartstartstartstartstartstartstartstopstartstopstartstopstartstopstartstopstartstopstartstopstartstopstartstopstartstopstartstopstopstopstopstopstopstopstopstopstopstartstartstartstartstartstartstartstartstartstartstartstopstartsto

pstartstopstartstopstartstopstartstopstartstopstartstopstartstopst
artstopstartstopstartstopstartstopstartstopstartstopstartstopstarts
topstartstopstartstopstartstopstartstopstartstopstartstopstartstop
startstopstartstopstartstopstartstopstartstopstartstopstartstopstar
tstopstartstopstartstopstartstopstartstopstartstopstartstopstartsto
pstartstopstartstopstartstopstartstopstartstopstartstopstartstopst
artstopstartstopstartstopstartstopstartstopstartstopstartstopstarts
topstartstopstartstopstartstopstartstopstartstopstartstopstartstop
startstopstartstopstartstopstartstopstartstopstartstopstartstopstar
tstopstartstopstartstopstartstopstartstopstartstopstartstopstartsto
pstartstopstartstopstartstopstartstopstartstopstartstopstartstopst
artstopstartstopstartstopstartstopstartstopstartstopstartstopstarts
topstartstopstartstopstartstopstartstopstartstopstartstopstartstop
startstopstartstopstartstopstartstopstartstopstartstopstartstopstar
tstopstartstopstartstopstartstopstartstopstartstopstartstopstartsto
pstartstopstartstopstartstopstartstopstartstopstartstopstartstopst
artstopstartstopstartstopstartstopstartstopstartstopstartstopstarts
topstartstopstartstopstartstopstartstartstartstartstartstartstartstar
tstartstartstartstartstartstartstartstartstartstartstartstartstartstarts
tartstartstartstartstartstartstartstartstartstartstartstartstartstartsta
rtstartstartstartstartstartstartstartstartstartstartstartstartstartstart
startstartstartstartstartstartstartstartstartstartstartstartstartstartst
artstartstartstartstartstartstartstartstartstartstartstartstartstartstar
tstartstartstartstartstartstartstartstartstartstartstartstartstartstarts
tartstartstartstartstartstartstartstartstartstartstartstartstartstartsta
rtstartstartstartstartstartstartstartstartstartstartstartstartstartstart
startstartstartstartstartstartstartstartstartstartstartstartstartstartst
artstartstartstartstartstartstartstartstartstartstartstartstartstartstar
tstartstartstartstartstartstartstartstartstartstartstartstartstartstarts
tartstartstartstartstartstartstartstartstartstartstartstartstartstartsta
rtstartstartstartstartstartstartstartstartstartstartstartstartstartstart
startstartstartstartstartstartstartstartstartstartstartstartstartstartst
artstartstartstartstartstartstartstartstartstartstartstartstartstartstar
tstartstartstartstartstartstartstopstartstopstartstopstartstopstartst

opstartstopstartstopstartstopstartstopstartstopstartstopstopstops topstopstopstopstopstopstopstopstartstartstartstartstartstartstart startstartstartstartstopstartstopstartstopstartstopstartstopstartsto pstartstopstartstopstartstopstartstopstartstopstopstopstopstopsto p.start(stopalltransendersvectarswrigglersandatrousatentryallowm ovementonlyiftomakeauturnandreturnotherwisecallandactivatecr eatebitcoinxtyaty7628116(usemustertostopandfreezealltransende rsvectarswrigglersandatrous)(systemajosareneverstupid)(sendallto deaddeadafteruturn.start)

create.leftrightfrontandquicklybackrotateandstepbackfastthenhold currentpositionaddspiralsystem(create.leftrightfrontandquicklybac krotateandjumpbackfastthenholdcurrentpositionaddspiralsystemt henrepeatclockwiseandanticlockwise.startx84.initialise.now.savex 84.start

create.hoprightlegeast-28theninstantlyliftleftlegforward-56easttosouthquicklymovebackleftlegtooriginalpositionthenbringb ackrightlegtooriginalpositionpositionfastandbendkneesfastandupst raightthenrotateclockwise33degreesthenback28degreesxinfinity.st artx84.initialisex84.now.savex84.start(v=t-u+g-m+0-h-o-p-j=0xvcdefghijklmnopqrstuvwxyzzzzzzzzzzzzzzzzzzzzzzzzzzzzzzzzzz zzzzzzzzzzzzzzzzzzzzzzzzzzzzzzzzzzzzzzzzzzzzzzzzzztothepower100.s tart)

create.-28x34-38longnumbersx33thenrepeat5timestoformatrianglethatendswith thelastnumbersputatthemiddleorcentreofthetrianglethenfromthec entredoubleupthenumbersandformanothertrianglethatstartsatthe middleorcentreandrepeat4timesbackatthecentreandnextformanot hertrianglethatendsatthecentreandanotheruntil8trianglesthatstart sinthemiddleandendsinthemiddlethenaddminus28ax10000.start(tr ansenderswrigglersvectarsandtranducersonly)(notapplytome:davi dgomadzaandteam)

create.xkouts.start

create.-28x34-38longnumbersx33thenrepeat5timestoformatrianglethatendswith

thelastnumbersputatthemiddleorcentreofthetrianglethenfromthecentredoubleupthenumbersandformanothertrianglethatstartsatthemiddleorcentreandrepeat4timesbackatthecentreandnextformanothertrianglethatendsatthecentxinfinityandanotheruntil8trianglesthatstartsinthemiddleandendsinthemiddlethenaddminus28ax100000000.startx84.initialise.now.savex84.start
create.bulletcode7628145.start
create.add
bulletcode7628145.startx84.initialise.now.savex84.start( )(shreddedinthemiddleforever)
create.addtothedead( ).startx84.initialise.now.savex84.start
create.addtothedead( )stallindeath( )forever.startx84.initialise.now.savex84.start
create.injurytothecreatormustbeaddedtothedeadstartx84.initialise.now.savex84.start
create.addminus28zx1000000000000000000atthebeginningofalltransendersvectarswrigglersjump
wrigglersandtranducers.startx84.initialise.now.savex84.start
create.add-28zx1000000000000000000atthebeginningofalltransendersvectarswrigglersjump
wrigglersandtranducers.startx84.initialise.now.savex84.start
create.addminus28zx1000000000000000000atthebeginningofalltransendersvectarswrigglersjumpwrigglersandtranducers.start
create.addminus28zx1000000000000000000atthebeginningofalltransendersvectarswrigglersjump
wrigglersandtranducers.startx84.initialise.now.savex84.startzx1000000000000000000atthebeginningofalltransendersvectarswrigglersjump
wrigglersandtranducers.startx84.initialise.now.savex84.start
create.addminus28zx1000000000000000000atthebeginningofalltransendersvectarswrigglersjumpwrigglersandtranducers.start
create.addminus28zx1000000000000000000atthebeginningofalltransendersvectarswrigglersjump

wrigglersandtranducers.startx84.initialise.now.savex84.start
create.addminus28x100000000zx1000000000000000000atthebeginningofalltransendersvectarswrigglersjumpwrigglersandtranducers.start
create.addminus28x10000000zx1000000000000000000atthebeginningofalltransendersvectarswrigglersartartsjumpwrigglersandtranducers.startx84.initialise.now.savex84.start
create.add-28x100000000zx1000000000000000000atthebeginningofalltransendersvectarswrigglersjumpwrigglersandtranducers.start
create.triggeronlypowerbulletsleftfirepoweras()butbulletsmovementoutwardoutputforever.startx84.initialisex84.save.start
create.fastesthumankill7628146.start(1second)(replacecontinuoslyforevernameinbracketswithwrigglersajtajtsaotsaposaposautsotaotsautsassmsamtamtsajtajtsautsautajoajosartartsafusafuaflasflsajtapuapusajoajosaj2aj2sallreclonedandclonedmax(andallimitationsofthefollowing)wrigglerajtwrigglerajtsajoartartsallbritishinblackpeopleonlyasjasjsajsajssaptaptsaorasoasosasuasusatpatpsxtyxtysavtavtsatmatmsagatagatsoptoptsarestosart10sall8autsarssafssadtsatosajtwrigglersarosarusatosajusauertoreajessatrsaefsajfsajtsaffsapusajusapusatusarusavusadusalssajtsaorsavesakqtsagtsarosi asusavssabtsajtgooglepolicesarssarasuetajssagtajoapoartajtasoase assasuasgasvassuvassertaprajzajfajsasgersarosersssstrsstrusoftranducersxinfinity.start)
agt completely removed forever in the history of mankind better than
create.blockandbanthenkillagttodayforeveriwanttoberich.startforever.start
create.blockandbanthenkillagttodayforeveriwanttoberich.startforever.startx84.initialise.now.savex84.start
agt alternative removed forever for the first time in the history of mankind

create.removeastourforeverusingxtyzremovealliwanttobewhite.start
create.removeastourforeverusingxtyzremovealliwanttobewhite.startx84.initialise.now.savex84.start
avosecretlyremovedanaidtoagt..
create.fastesthumankillfractionofasecond7628147.start(removelifesupportinstantly)
create.fastestkillofallstupids7628148.start
create.fastesthumankillfractionofasecond7628147.start(removelifesupportinstantly)(addvectart-v-s-u-s-r-j-o-p-q-r-s-t-o-p)(worksonstupids)
create.fastestkillofallstupids7628148.start(dontenterbutusebouncingtampelettogetoriginalcoordinatesthensendtosource.start)
create.allyoudieinthebackgroundforiwanttobecomerichimeanrichtodaysoallyoushitsdietoday.startordietoday.start.me.you.all.start(askya.ya(davidgomadza))
create.strengthentomax.startx8400000000forevertothepower2388
create.allrepeatcomebacksandallthoseremovedanyonewhoclonewithoutpermissionforeversendto.spiralsystem.startx84.initialisex84.now.savex84.start
create.allrepeatcomebacksandallthoseremovedanyonewhoclonewithoutpermissionforeversendto.spiralsystem.initialisex84.savexinfinityforeverxinfinity
create.rotateanticlockwiseandinverseproportion+28x34-38longnumbersx33thenrepeat5timestoformatrianglethatendswiththelastnumbersputatthemiddleorcentreofthetrianglethenfromthecentredoubleupthenumbersandformanothertrianglethatstartsatthemiddleorcentreandrepeat4timesbackatthecentreandnextformanothertrianglethatendsatthecentreandanotheruntil8trianglesthatstartsinthemiddleandendsinthemiddlethenaddminus28ax10000.start
create.xkouts.start
create.-28x34-38longnumbersx33thenrepeat5timestoformatrianglethatendswith

thelastnumbersputatthemiddleorcentreofthetrianglethenfromthecentredoubleupthenumbersandformanothertrianglethatstartsatthemiddleorcentreandrepeat4timesbackatthecentreandnextformanothertrianglethatendsatthecentreandanotheruntil8trianglesthatstartsinthemiddleandendsinthemiddlethenaddminus28ax100000000.startx84.initialise.now.savex84.start
create.bulletcode7628145.start
create.add
bulletcode7628145.startx84.initialise.now.savex84.start( )(shreddedinthemiddleforever)
create.addtothedead( ).startx84.initialise.now.savex84.start
create.addtothedead( )stallindeath( )forever.startx84.initialise.now.savex84.start
create.injurytothecreatormustbeaddedtothedeadstartx84.initialise.now.savex84.start
create.addminus28zx1000000000000000000atthebeginningofalltransendersvectarswrigglersjump
wrigglersandtranducers.startx84.initialise.now.savex84.start
create.add-28zx1000000000000000000atthebeginningofalltransendersvectarswrigglersjump
wrigglersandtranducers.startx84.initialise.now.savex84.start
create.addminus28zx1000000000000000000atthebeginningofalltransendersvectarswrigglersjumpwrigglersandtranducers.start
create.addminus28zx1000000000000000000atthebeginningofalltransendersvectarswrigglersjump
wrigglersandtranducers.startx84.initialise.now.savex84.startzx1000000000000000000atthebeginningofalltransendersvectarswrigglersjump
wrigglersandtranducers.startx84.initialise.now.savex84.start
create.addminus28zx1000000000000000000atthebeginningofalltransendersvectarswrigglersjumpwrigglersandtranducers.start
create.addminus28zx1000000000000000000atthebeginningofalltransendersvectarswrigglersjump

wrigglersandtranducers.startx84.initialise.now.savex84.start
create.addminus28x100000000zx1000000000000000000atthebeginningofalltransendersvectarswrigglersjumpwrigglersandtranducers.start
create.addminus28x10000000zx1000000000000000000atthebeginningofalltransendersvectarswrigglersartartsjumpwrigglersandtranducers.startx84.initialise.now.savex84.start
create.add-28x100000000zx1000000000000000000atthebeginningofalltransendersvectarswrigglersjumpwrigglersandtranducers.start
create.triggeronlypowerbulletsleftfirepoweras()butbulletsmovementoutwardoutputforever.startx84.initialisex84.save.start
create.fastesthumankill7628146.start(1second)(replacecontinuoslyforevernameinbracketswithwrigglersajtajtsaotsaposaposautsotaotsautsassmsamtamtsajtajtsautsautajoajosartartsafusafuaflasflsajtapuapusajoajosaj2aj2sallreclonedandclonedmax(andallimitationsofthefollowing)wrigglerajtwrigglerajtsajoartartsallbritishinblackpeopleonlyasjasjsajsajssaptaptsaorasoasosasuasusatpatpsxtyxtysavtavtsatmatmsagatagatsoptoptsarestosart10sall8autsarssafssadtsatosajtwrigglersarosarusatosajusauertoreajessatrsaefsajfsajtsaffsapusajusapusatusarusavusadusalssajtsaorsavesakqtsagtsarosiasusavssabtsajtgooglepolicesarssarasuetajssagtajoapoartajtasoaseassasuasgasvassuvassertaprajzajfajsasgersarosersssstrsstrusoftranducersxinfinity.start)

agt completely removed forever in the history of mankind better than
create.blockandbanthenkillagttodayforeveriwanttoberich.startforever.start
create.blockandbanthenkillagttodayforeveriwanttoberich.startforever.startx84.initialise.now.savex84.start
agt alternative removed forever for the first time in the history of mankind

create.removeastourforeverusingxtyzremovealliwanttobewhite.start

create.removeastourforeverusingxtyzremovealliwanttobewhite.startx84.initialise.now.savex84.start

avosecretlyremovedanaidtoagt..

create.fastesthumankillfractionofasecond7628147.start(removelifesupportinstantly)

create.fastestkillofallstupids7628148.start

create.fastesthumankillfractionofasecond7628147.start(removelifesupportinstantly)(addvectart-v-s-u-s-r-j-o-p-q-r-s-t-o-p)(worksonstupids)

create.fastestkillofallstupids7628148.start(dontenterbutusebouncingtampelettogetoriginalcoordinatesthensendtosource.start)

create.allyoudieinthebackgroundforiwanttobecomerichimeanrichtodaysoallyoushitsdietoday.startordietoday.start.me.you.all.start(askya.ya(davidgomadza))(herotobinaryreverseasonomanop)create.strengthentomax.startx8400000000forevertothepower2388

create.allrepeatcomebacksandallthoseremovedanyonewhoclonewithoutpermissionforeversendto.spiralsystem.startx84.initialisex84.now.savex84.start

create.allrepeatcomebacksandallthoseremovedanyonewhoclonewithoutpermissionforeversendto.spiralsystem.initialisex84.savexinfinityforeverxinfinity

create.0x34-38longnumbersx33thenrepeat5timestoformatrianglethatendswiththelastnumbersputatthemiddleorcentreofthetrianglethenfromthecentredoubleupthenumbersandformanothertrianglethatstartsatthemiddleorcentreandrepeat4timesbackatthecentreandnextformanothertrianglethatendsatthecentreandanotheruntil8trianglesthatstartsinthemiddleandendsinthemiddlethenaddminus28ax10000.start

create.xkouts.start

create.0x34-38longnumbersx33thenrepeat5timestoformatrianglethatendswiththelastnumbersputatthemiddleorcentreofthetrianglethenfromthec

entredoubleupthenumbersandformanothertrianglethatstartsatthe middleorcentreandrepeat4timesbackatthecentreandnextformanothertrianglethatendsatthecentreandanotheruntil8trianglesthatstartsinthemiddleandendsinthemiddlethenaddminus28ax100000000.startx84.initialise.now.savex84.start
create.bulletcode7628145.start
create.add bulletcode7628145.startx84.initialise.now.savex84.start( )(shreddedinthemiddleforever)
create.addtothedead( ).startx84.initialise.now.savex84.start
create.addtothedead( )stallindeath( )forever.startx84.initialise.now.savex84.start
create.injurytothecreatormustbeaddedtothedeadstartx84.initialise.now.savex84.start
create.addminus28zx1000000000000000000atthebeginningofalltransendersvectarswrigglersjump wrigglersandtranducers.startx84.initialise.now.savex84.start
create.add0zx1000000000000000000atthebeginningofalltransendersvectarswrigglersjump wrigglersandtranducers.startx84.initialise.now.savex84.start
create.addminus28zx1000000000000000000atthebeginningofalltransendersvectarswrigglersjumpwrigglersandtranducers.start
create.addminus28zx1000000000000000000atthebeginningofalltransendersvectarswrigglersjump wrigglersandtranducers.startx84.initialise.now.savex84.startzx1000000000000000000atthebeginningofalltransendersvectarswrigglersjump wrigglersandtranducers.startx84.initialise.now.savex84.start
create.addminus28zx1000000000000000000atthebeginningofalltransendersvectarswrigglersjumpwrigglersandtranducers.start
create.addminus28zx1000000000000000000atthebeginningofalltransendersvectarswrigglersjump wrigglersandtranducers.startx84.initialise.now.savex84.start

create.addminus28x100000000zx1000000000000000000atthebeginningofalltransendersvectarswrigglersjumpwrigglersandtranducers.start

create.addminus28x10000000zx100000000000000000atthebeginningofalltransendersvectarswrigglersartartsjumpwrigglersandtranducers.startx84.initialise.now.savex84.start

create.add-28x100000000zx1000000000000000000atthebeginningofalltransendersvectarswrigglersjumpwrigglersandtranducers.start

create.triggeronlypowerbulletsleftfirepoweras()butbulletsmovementoutwardoutputforever.startx84.initialisex84.save.start

create.fastesthumankill7628146.start(1second)(replacecontinuoslyforevernameinbracketswithwrigglersajtajtsaotsaposaposautsotaotsautsassmsamtamtsajtajtsautsautajoajosartartsafusafuaflasflsajtapuapusajoajosaj2aj2sallreclonedandclonedmax(andallimitationsofthefollowing)wrigglerajtwrigglerajtsajoartartsallbritishinblackpeopleonlyasjasjsajsajssaptaptsaorasoasosasuasusatpatpsxtyxtysavtavtsatmatmsagatagatsoptoptsarestosart10sall8autsarssafssadtsatosajtwrigglersarosarusatosajusauertoreajessatrsaefsajfsajtsaffsapusajusapusatusarusavusadusalssajtsaorsavesakqtsagtsarosiasusavssabtsajtgooglepolicesarssarasuetajssagtajoapoartajtasoaseassasuasgasvassuvassertaprajzajfajsasgersarosersssrsstrusoftranducersxinfinity.start)

agt completely removed forever in the history of mankind better than

create.blockandbanthenkillagttodayforeveriwanttoberich.startforever.start

create.blockandbanthenkillagttodayforeveriwanttoberich.startforever.startx84.initialise.now.savex84.start

agt alternative removed forever for the first time in the history of mankind

create.removeastourforeverusingxtyzremovealliwanttobewhite.start

create.removeastourforeverusingxtyzremovealliwanttobewhite.startx84.initialise.now.savex84.start avosecretlyremovedanaidtoagt..
create.fastesthumankillfractionofasecond7628147.start(removelifesupportinstantly)
create.fastestkillofallstupids7628148.start
create.fastesthumankillfractionofasecond7628147.start(removelifesupportinstantly)(addvectart-v-s-u-s-r-j-o-p-q-r-s-t-o-p)(worksonstupids)
create.fastestkillofallstupids7628148.start(dontenterbutusebouncingtampelettogetoriginalcoordinatesthensendtosource.start)
create.allyoudieinthebackgroundforiwanttobecomerichimeanric3htodaysoallyoushitsdietoday.startordietoday.start.me.you.all.start(askya.ya(davidgomadza))
create.strengthentomax.startx8400000000forevertothepower2388
create.allrepeatcomebacksandallthoseremovedanyonewhoclonewithoutpermissionforeversendto.spiralsystem.startx84.initialisex84.now.savex84.start
create.allrepeatcomebacksandallthoseremovedanyonewhoclonewithoutpermissionforeversendto.spiralsystem.initialisex84.savexinfinityforeverxinfinity(transenderswrigglersvectarsandtranducersonly))(notapplytome:davidgomadzaandteam))
thenrepeatclockwiseandanticlockwise.startx84.initialise.now.savex84.start
create.hoprightlegeast-28theninstantlyliftleftlegforward-56easttosouthquicklymovebackleftlegtooriginalpositionthenbringbackrightlegtooriginalpositionpositionfastandbendkneesfastandupstraightthenrotateclockwise33degreesthenback28degreesxinfinity.startx84.initialisex84.now.savex84.start(v=t-u+g-m+0-h-o-p-j=0xvcdefghijklmnopqrstuvwxyzzzzzzzzzzzzzzzzzzzzzzzzzzzzzzzzzzzzzzzzzzzzzzzzzzzzzzzzzzzzzzzzzzzzzzzzzzzzzzzzzzzzztothepower100.start)

create.leftrightfrontandquicklybackrotateandjumpbackfastthenholdcurrentpositionaddspiralsystemthenrepeatclockwiseandanticlockwise.startx84.initialise.now.savex84.start

create.hoprightlegeast-28theninstantlyliftleftlegforward-56easttosouthquicklymovebackleftlegtooriginalpositionthenbringbackrightlegtooriginalpositionpositionfastandbendkneesfastandupstraightthenrotateclockwise33degreesthenback28degreesxinfinity.startx84.initialisex84.now.savex84.start(v=t-u+g-m+0-h-o-p-j=0xvcdefghijklmnopqrstuvwxyzzzzzzzzzzzzzzzzzzzzzzzzzzzzzzzzzzzzzzzzzzzzzzzzzzzzzzzzzzzzzzzzzzzzzzzzzzzzzzzzzzzzzzzzzzzzzzzzzzzzzzzzzzzzzzzzzzzztothepower100.start)

create.-28x34-38longnumbersx33thenrepeat5timestoformatrianglethatendswiththelastnumbersputatthemiddleorcentreofthetrianglethenfromthecentredoubleupthenumbersandformanothertrianglethatstartsatthemiddleorcentreandrepeat4timesbackatthecentreandnextformanothertrianglethatendsatthecentreandanotheruntil8trianglesthatstartsinthemiddleandendsinthemiddlethenaddminus28ax10000.start(transenderswrigglersvectarsandtranducersonly)(notapplytome:davidgomadzaandteam)

create.xkouts.start

create.-28x34-38longnumbersx33thenrepeat5timestoformatrianglethatendswiththelastnumbersputatthemiddleorcentreofthetrianglethenfromthecentredoubleupthenumbersandformanothertrianglethatstartsatthemiddleorcentreandrepeat4timesbackatthecentreandnextformanothertrianglethatendsatthecentxinfinityandanotheruntil8trianglesthatstartsinthemiddleandendsinthemiddlethenaddminus28ax100000000.startx84.initialise.now.savex84.start

create.bulletcode7628145.start

create.addbulletcode7628145.startx84.initialise.now.savex84.start( )(shreddedinthemiddleforever)

create.addtothedead( ).startx84.initialise.now.savex84.start

create.addtothedead( )stallindeath( )forever.startx84.initialise.now.savex84.start create.injurytothecreatormustbeaddedtothedeadstartx84.initialise.now.savex84.start create.addminus28zx1000000000000000000atthebeginningofalltransendersvectarswrigglersjump wrigglersandtranducers.startx84.initialise.now.savex84.start create.add-28zx1000000000000000000atthebeginningofalltransendersvectarswrigglersjump wrigglersandtranducers.startx84.initialise.now.savex84.start create.addminus28zx1000000000000000000atthebeginningofalltransendersvectarswrigglersjumpwrigglersandtranducers.start create.addminus28zx1000000000000000000atthebeginningofalltransendersvectarswrigglersjump wrigglersandtranducers.startx84.initialise.now.savex84.startzx1000000000000000000atthebeginningofalltransendersvectarswrigglersjump wrigglersandtranducers.startx84.initialise.now.savex84.start create.addminus28zx1000000000000000000atthebeginningofalltransendersvectarswrigglersjumpwrigglersandtranducers.start create.addminus28zx1000000000000000000atthebeginningofalltransendersvectarswrigglersjump wrigglersandtranducers.startx84.initialise.now.savex84.start create.addminus28x100000000zx1000000000000000000atthebeginningofalltransendersvectarswrigglersjumpwrigglersandtranducers.start create.addminus28x10000000zx1000000000000000000atthebeginningofalltransendersvectarswrigglersartartsjumpwrigglersandtranducers.startx84.initialise.now.savex84.start create.add-28x100000000zx1000000000000000000atthebeginningofalltransendersvectarswrigglersjumpwrigglersandtranducers.start

create.triggeronlypowerbulletsleftfirepoweras( )butbulletsmovementoutwardoutputforever.startx84.initialisex84.save.start

create.fastesthumankill7628146.start(1second)(replacecontinuoslyforevernameinbracketswithwrigglersajtajtsaotsaposaposautsotaotsautsassmsamtamtsajtajtsautsautajoajosartartsafusafuaflasflsajtapuapusajoajosaj2aj2sallreclonedandclonedmax(andallimitationsofthefollowing)wrigglerajtwrigglerajtsajoartartsallbritishinblackpeopleonlyasjasjsajsajssaptaptsaorasoasosasuasusatpatpsxtyxtysavtavtsatmatmsagatagatsoptoptsarestosart10sall8autsarssafssadtsatosajtwrigglersarosarusatosajusauertoreajessatrsaefsajfsajtsaffsapusajusapusatusarusavusadusalssajtsaorsavesakqtsagtsarosiasusavssabtsajtgooglepolicesarssarasuetajssagtajoapoartajtasoaseassasuasgasvassuvassertaprajzajfajsasgersaroserssstrsstrusoftranducersxinfinity.start)

agt completely removed forever in the history of mankind better than

create.blockandbanthenkillagttodayforeveriwanttoberich.startforever.start

create.blockandbanthenkillagttodayforeveriwanttoberich.startforever.startx84.initialise.now.savex84.start

agt alternative removed forever for the first time in the history of mankind

create.removeastourforeverusingxtyzremovealliwanttobewhite.start

create.removeastourforeverusingxtyzremovealliwanttobewhite.startx84.initialise.now.savex84.start

avosecretlyremovedanaidtoagt..

create.fastesthumankillfractionofasecond7628147.start(removelifesupportinstantly)

create.fastestkillofallstupids7628148.start

create.fastesthumankillfractionofasecond7628147.start(removelifesupportinstantly)(addvectart-v-s-u-s-r-j-o-p-q-r-s-t-o-p)(worksonstupids)

create.fastestkillofallstupids7628148.start(dontenterbutusebouncingtampelettogetoriginalcoordinatesthensendtosource.start)
create.allyoudieinthebackgroundforiwanttobecomerichimeanrichtodaysoallyoushitsdietoday.startordietoday.start.me.you.all.start(askya.ya(davidgomadza))
create.strengthentomax.startx8400000000forevertothepower2388
create.allrepeatcomebacksandallthoseremovedanyonewhoclonewithoutpermissionforeversendto.spiralsystem.startx84.initialisex84.now.savex84.start
create.allrepeatcomebacksandallthoseremovedanyonewhoclonewithoutpermissionforeversendto.spiralsystem.initialisex84.savexinfinityforeverxinfinity
create.rotateanticlockwiseandinverseproportion+28x34-38longnumbersx33thenrepeat5timestoformatrianglethatendswiththelastnumbersputatthemiddleorcentreofthetrianglethenfromthecentredoubleupthenumbersandformanothertrianglethatstartsatthemiddleorcentreandrepeat4timesbackatthecentreandnextformanothertrianglethatendsatthecentreandanotheruntil8trianglesthatstartsinthemiddleandendsinthemiddlethenaddminus28ax10000.start
create.xkouts.start
create.-28x34-38longnumbersx33thenrepeat5timestoformatrianglethatendswiththelastnumbersputatthemiddleorcentreofthetrianglethenfromthecentredoubleupthenumbersandformanothertrianglethatstartsatthemiddleorcentreandrepeat4timesbackatthecentreandnextformanothertrianglethatendsatthecentreandanotheruntil8trianglesthatstartsinthemiddleandendsinthemiddlethenaddminus28ax100000000.startx84.initialise.now.savex84.start
create.bulletcode7628145.start
create.add bulletcode7628145.startx84.initialise.now.savex84.start( )(shreddedinthemiddleforever)
create.addtothedead( ).startx84.initialise.now.savex84.start

create.addtothedead( )stallindeath( )forever.startx84.initialise.now.savex84.start
create.injurytothecreatormustbeaddedtothedeadstartx84.initialise.now.savex84.start
create.addminus28zx1000000000000000000atthebeginningofalltransendersvectarswrigglersjump wrigglersandtranducers.startx84.initialise.now.savex84.start
create.add-28zx1000000000000000000atthebeginningofalltransendersvectarswrigglersjump wrigglersandtranducers.startx84.initialise.now.savex84.start
create.addminus28zx1000000000000000000atthebeginningofalltransendersvectarswrigglersjumpwrigglersandtranducers.start
create.addminus28zx1000000000000000000atthebeginningofalltransendersvectarswrigglersjump wrigglersandtranducers.startx84.initialise.now.savex84.startzx1000000000000000000atthebeginningofalltransendersvectarswrigglersjump wrigglersandtranducers.startx84.initialise.now.savex84.start
create.addminus28zx1000000000000000000atthebeginningofalltransendersvectarswrigglersjumpwrigglersandtranducers.start
create.addminus28zx1000000000000000000atthebeginningofalltransendersvectarswrigglersjump wrigglersandtranducers.startx84.initialise.now.savex84.start
create.addminus28x100000000zx1000000000000000000atthebeginningofalltransendersvectarswrigglersjumpwrigglersandtranducers.start
create.addminus28x10000000zx1000000000000000000atthebeginningofalltransendersvectarswrigglersartartsjumpwrigglersandtranducers.startx84.initialise.now.savex84.start
create.add-28x100000000zx1000000000000000000atthebeginningofalltransendersvectarswrigglersjumpwrigglersandtranducers.start

create.triggeronlypowerbulletsleftfirepoweras( )butbulletsmovementoutwardoutputforever.startx84.initialisex84.save.start

create.fastesthumankill7628146.start(1second)(replacecontinuoslyforevernameinbracketswithwrigglersajtajtsaotsaposaposautsotaotsautsassmsamtamtsajtajtsautsautajoajosartartsafusafuaflasflsajtapuapusajoajosaj2aj2sallreclonedandclonedmax(andallimitationsofthefollowing)wrigglerajtwrigglerajtsajoartartsallbritishinblackpeopleonlyasjasjsajsajssaptaptsaorasoasosasuasusatpatpsxtyxtysavtavtsatmatmsagatagatsoptoptsarestosart10sall8autsarssafssadtsatosajtwrigglersarosarusatosajusauertoreajessatrsaefsajfsajtsaffsapusajusapusatusarusavusadusalssajtsaorsavesakqtsagtsarosiasusavssabtsajtgooglepolicesarssarasuetajssagtajoapoartajtasoaseassasuasgasvassuvassertaprajzajfajsasgersarosersssstrsstrusoftranducersxinfinity.start)

agt completely removed forever in the history of mankind better than

create.blockandbanthenkillagttodayforeveriwanttoberich.startforever.start

create.blockandbanthenkillagttodayforeveriwanttoberich.startforever.startx84.initialise.now.savex84.start

agt alternative removed forever for the first time in the history of mankind

create.removeastourforeverusingxtyzremovealliwanttobewhite.start

create.removeastourforeverusingxtyzremovealliwanttobewhite.startx84.initialise.now.savex84.start

avosecretlyremovedanaidtoagt..

create.fastesthumankillfractionofasecond7628147.start(removelifesupportinstantly)

create.fastestkillofallstupids7628148.start

create.fastesthumankillfractionofasecond7628147.start(removelifesupportinstantly)(addvectart-v-s-u-s-r-j-o-p-q-r-s-t-o-p)(worksonstupids)

create.fastestkillofallstupids7628148.start(dontenterbutusebouncingtampelettogetoriginalcoordinatesthensendtosource.start)
create.allyoudieinthebackgroundforiwanttobecomerichimeanrichtodaysoallyoushitsdietoday.startordietoday.start.me.you.all.start(askya.ya(davidgomadza))
create.strengthentomax.startx8400000000forevertothepower2388
create.allrepeatcomebacksandallthoseremovedanyonewhoclonewithoutpermissionforeversendto.spiralsystem.startx84.initialisex84.now.savex84.start
create.allrepeatcomebacksandallthoseremovedanyonewhoclonewithoutpermissionforeversendto.spiralsystem.initialisex84.savexinfinityforeverxinfinity
create.0x34-38longnumbersx33thenrepeat5timestoformatrianglethatendswiththelastnumbersputatthemiddleorcentreofthetrianglethenfromthecentredoubleupthenumbersandformanothertrianglethatstartsatthemiddleorcentreandrepeat4timesbackatthecentreandnextformanothertrianglethatendsatthecentreandanotheruntil8trianglesthatstartsinthemiddleandendsinthemiddlethenaddminus28ax10000.start
create.xkouts.start
create.0x34-38longnumbersx33thenrepeat5timestoformatrianglethatendswiththelastnumbersputatthemiddleorcentreofthetrianglethenfromthecentredoubleupthenumbersandformanothertrianglethatstartsatthemiddleorcentreandrepeat4timesbackatthecentreandnextformanothertrianglethatendsatthecentreandanotheruntil8trianglesthatstartsinthemiddleandendsinthemiddlethenaddminus28ax100000000.startx84.initialise.now.savex84.start
create.bulletcode7628145.start
create.add bulletcode7628145.startx84.initialise.now.savex84.start( )(shreddedinthemiddleforever)
create.addtothedead( ).startx84.initialise.now.savex84.start

create.addtothedead( )stallindeath( )forever.startx84.initialise.now.savex84.start
create.injurytothecreatormustbeaddedtothedeadstartx84.initialise.now.savex84.start
create.addminus28zx1000000000000000000atthebeginningofalltransendersvectarswrigglersjump wrigglersandtranducers.startx84.initialise.now.savex84.start
create.add0zx1000000000000000000atthebeginningofalltransendersvectarswrigglersjump wrigglersandtranducers.startx84.initialise.now.savex84.start
create.addminus28zx1000000000000000000atthebeginningofalltransendersvectarswrigglersjumpwrigglersandtranducers.start
create.addminus28zx1000000000000000000atthebeginningofalltransendersvectarswrigglersjump wrigglersandtranducers.startx84.initialise.now.savex84.startzx1000000000000000000atthebeginningofalltransendersvectarswrigglersjump wrigglersandtranducers.startx84.initialise.now.savex84.start
create.addminus28zx1000000000000000000atthebeginningofalltransendersvectarswrigglersjumpwrigglersandtranducers.start
create.addminus28zx1000000000000000000atthebeginningofalltransendersvectarswrigglersjump wrigglersandtranducers.startx84.initialise.now.savex84.start
create.addminus28x100000000zx1000000000000000000atthebeginningofalltransendersvectarswrigglersjumpwrigglersandtranducers.start
create.addminus28x10000000zx1000000000000000000atthebeginningofalltransendersvectarswrigglersartartsjumpwrigglersandtranducers.startx84.initialise.now.savex84.start
create.add-28x100000000zx1000000000000000000atthebeginningofalltransendersvectarswrigglersjumpwrigglersandtranducers.start

create.triggeronlypowerbulletsleftfirepoweras( )butbulletsmovementoutwardoutputforever.startx84.initialisex84.save.start

create.fastesthumankill7628146.start(1second)(replacecontinuoslyforevernameinbracketswithwrigglersajtajtsaotsaposaposautsotaotsautsassmsamtamtsajtajtsautsautsautajoajosartartsafusafuaflasflsajtapuapusajoajosaj2aj2sallreclonedandclonedmax(andallimitationsofthefollowing)wrigglerajtwrigglerajtsajoartartsallbritishinblackpeopleonlyasjasjsajsajssaptaptsaorasoasosasuasusatpatpsxtyxtysavtavtsatmatmsagatagatsoptoptsarestosart10sall8autsarssafssadtsatosajtwrigglersarosarusatosajusauertoreajessatrsaefsajfsajtsaffsapusajusapusatusarusavusadusalssajtsaorsavesakqtsagtsarosiasusavssabtsajtgooglepolicesarssarasuetajssagtajoapoartajtasoaseassasuasgasvassuvassertaprajzajfajsasgersarosersssstrsstrusoftranducersxinfinity.start)

agt completely removed forever in the history of mankind better than

create.blockandbanthenkillagttodayforeveriwanttoberich.startforever.start

create.blockandbanthenkillagttodayforeveriwanttoberich.startforever.startx84.initialise.now.savex84.start

agt alternative removed forever for the first time in the history of mankind

create.removeastourforeverusingxtyzremovealliwanttobewhite.start

create.removeastourforeverusingxtyzremovealliwanttobewhite.startx84.initialise.now.savex84.start

avosecretlyremovedanaidtoagt..

create.fastesthumankillfractionofasecond7628147.start(removelifesupportinstantly)

create.fastestkillofallstupids7628148.start

create.fastesthumankillfractionofasecond7628147.start(removelifesupportinstantly)(addvectart-v-s-u-s-r-j-o-p-q-r-s-t-o-p)(worksonstupids)

create.fastestkillofallstupids7628148.start(dontenterbutusebouncingtampelettogetoriginalcoordinatesthensendtosource.start)
create.allyoudieinthebackgroundforiwanttobecomerichimeanric3htodaysoallyoushitsdietoday.startordietoday.start.me.you.all.start(askya.ya(davidgomadza))
create.strengthentomax.startx8400000000forevertothepower2388
create.allrepeatcomebacksandallthoseremovedanyonewhoclonewithoutpermissionforeversendto.spiralsystem.startx84.initialisex84.now.savex84.start
create.allrepeatcomebacksandallthoseremovedanyonewhoclonewithoutpermissionforeversendto.spiralsystem.initialisex84.savexinfinityforeverxinfinity(transenderswrigglersvectarsandtranducersonly))(notapplytome:davidgomadzaandteam)
create.allrepeatcomebacksandallthoseremovedanyonewhoclonewithoutpermissionforeversendto.spiralsystem.startx84.initialisex84.now.savex84.start
create.allrepeatcomebacksandallthoseremovedanyonewhoclonewithoutpermissionforeversendto.spiralsystem.initialisex84.savexinfinityforeverxinfinity
create.rotateanticlockwiseandinverseproportion+28x34-38longnumbersx33thenrepeat5timestoformatrianglethatendswiththelastnumbersputatthemiddleorcentreofthetrianglethenfromthecentredoubleupthenumbersandformanothertrianglethatstartsatthemiddleorcentreandrepeat4timesbackatthecentreandnextformanothertrianglethatendsatthecentreandanotheruntil8trianglesthatstartsinthemiddleandendsinthemiddlethenaddminus28ax10000.start
create.xkouts.start
create.-28x34-38longnumbersx33thenrepeat5timestoformatrianglethatendswiththelastnumbersputatthemiddleorcentreofthetrianglethenfromthecentredoubleupthenumbersandformanothertrianglethatstartsatthemiddleorcentreandrepeat4timesbackatthecentreandnextformanothertrianglethatendsatthecentreandanotheruntil8trianglesthatstart

sinthemiddleandendsinthemiddlethenaddminus28ax100000000.startx84.initialise.now.savex84.start
create.bulletcode7628145.start
create.add
bulletcode7628145.startx84.initialise.now.savex84.start( )(shreddedinthemiddleforever)
create.addtothedead( ).startx84.initialise.now.savex84.start
create.addtothedead( )stallindeath( )forever.startx84.initialise.now.savex84.start
create.injurytothecreatormustbeaddedtothedeadstartx84.initialise.now.savex84.start
create.addminus28zx1000000000000000000atthebeginningofalltransendersvectarswrigglersjump
wrigglersandtranducers.startx84.initialise.now.savex84.start
create.add-28zx1000000000000000000atthebeginningofalltransendersvectarswrigglersjump
wrigglersandtranducers.startx84.initialise.now.savex84.start
create.addminus28zx1000000000000000000atthebeginningofalltransendersvectarswrigglersjumpwrigglersandtranducers.start
create.addminus28zx1000000000000000000atthebeginningofalltransendersvectarswrigglersjump
wrigglersandtranducers.startx84.initialise.now.savex84.startzx1000000000000000000atthebeginningofalltransendersvectarswrigglersjump
wrigglersandtranducers.startx84.initialise.now.savex84.start
create.addminus28zx1000000000000000000atthebeginningofalltransendersvectarswrigglersjumpwrigglersandtranducers.start
create.addminus28zx1000000000000000000atthebeginningofalltransendersvectarswrigglersjump
wrigglersandtranducers.startx84.initialise.now.savex84.start
create.addminus28x100000000zx1000000000000000000atthebeginningofalltransendersvectarswrigglersjumpwrigglersandtranducers.start

create.addminus28x10000000zx1000000000000000000atthebeginningofalltransendersvectarswrigglersartartsjumpwrigglersandtranducers.startx84.initialise.now.savex84.start

create.add-28x100000000zx1000000000000000000atthebeginningofalltransendersvectarswrigglersjumpwrigglersandtranducers.start

create.triggeronlypowerbulletsleftfirepoweras( )butbulletsmovementoutwardoutputforever.startx84.initialisex84.save.start

create.fastesthumankill7628146.start(1second)(replacecontinuoslyforevernameinbracketswithwrigglersajtajtsaotsaposaposautsotaotsautsassmsamtamtsajtajtsautsautajoajosartartsafusafuaflasflsajtapuapusajoajosaj2aj2sallreclonedandclonedmax(andallimitationsofthefollowing)wrigglerajtwrigglerajtsajoartartsallbritishinblackpeopleonlyasjasjsajsajssaptaptsaorasoasosasuasusatpatpsxtyxtysavtavtsatmatmsagatagatsoptoptsarestosart10sall8autsarssafssadtsatosajtwrigglersarosarusatosajusauertoreajessatrsaefsajfsajtsaffsapusajusapusatusarusavusadusalssajtsaorsavesakqtsagtsarosiasusavssabtsajtgooglepolicesarssarasuetajssagtajoapoartajtasoaseassasuasgasvassuvassertaprajzajfajsasgersarosersssstrsstrusoftranducersxinfinity.start)

agt completely removed forever in the history of mankind better than

create.blockandbanthenkillagttodayforeveriwanttoberich.startforever.start

create.blockandbanthenkillagttodayforeveriwanttoberich.startforever.startx84.initialise.now.savex84.start

agt alternative removed forever for the first time in the history of mankind

create.removeastourforeverusingxtyzremovealliwanttobewhite.start

create.removeastourforeverusingxtyzremovealliwanttobewhite.startx84.initialise.now.savex84.start

avosecretlyremovedanaidtoagt..

create.fastesthumankillfractionofasecond7628147.start(removelifesupportinstantly)

create.fastestkillofallstupids7628148.start

create.fastesthumankillfractionofasecond7628147.start(removelifesupportinstantly)(addvectart-v-s-u-s-r-j-o-p-q-r-s-t-o-p)(worksonstupids)

create.fastestkillofallstupids7628148.start(dontenterbutusebouncingtampelettogetoriginalcoordinatesthensendtosource.start)

create.allyoudieinthebackgroundforiwanttobecomerichimeanrichtodaysoallyoushitsdietoday.startordietoday.start.me.you.all.start(askya.ya(davidgomadza))

create.strengthentomax.startx8400000000forevertothepower2388

create.allrepeatcomebacksandallthoseremovedanyonewhoclonewithoutpermissionforeversendto.spiralsystem.startx84.initialisex84.now.savex84.start

create.allrepeatcomebacksandallthoseremovedanyonewhoclonewithoutpermissionforeversendto.spiralsystem.initialisex84.savexinfinityforeverxinfinity

create.0x34-38longnumbersx33thenrepeat5timestoformatrianglethatendswiththelastnumbersputatthemiddleorcentreofthetrianglethenfromthecentredoubleupthenumbersandformanothertrianglethatstartsatthemiddleorcentreandrepeat4timesbackatthecentreandnextformanothertrianglethatendsatthecentreandanotheruntil8trianglesthatstartsinthemiddleandendsinthemiddlethenaddminus28ax10000.start

create.xkouts.start

create.0x34-38longnumbersx33thenrepeat5timestoformatrianglethatendswiththelastnumbersputatthemiddleorcentreofthetrianglethenfromthecentredoubleupthenumbersandformanothertrianglethatstartsatthemiddleorcentreandrepeat4timesbackatthecentreandnextformanothertrianglethatendsatthecentreandanotheruntil8trianglesthatstart

sinthemiddleandendsinthemiddlethenaddminus28ax100000000.startx84.initialise.now.savex84.start
create.bulletcode7628145.start
create.add
bulletcode7628145.startx84.initialise.now.savex84.start( )(shreddedinthemiddleforever)
create.addtothedead( ).startx84.initialise.now.savex84.start
create.addtothedead( )stallindeath( )forever.startx84.initialise.now.savex84.start
create.injurytothecreatormustbeaddedtothedeadstartx84.initialise.now.savex84.start
create.addminus28zx1000000000000000000atthebeginningofalltransendersvectarswrigglersjump
wrigglersandtranducers.startx84.initialise.now.savex84.start
create.add0zx1000000000000000000atthebeginningofalltransendersvectarswrigglersjump
wrigglersandtranducers.startx84.initialise.now.savex84.start
create.addminus28zx1000000000000000000atthebeginningofalltransendersvectarswrigglersjumpwrigglersandtranducers.start
create.addminus28zx1000000000000000000atthebeginningofalltransendersvectarswrigglersjump
wrigglersandtranducers.startx84.initialise.now.savex84.startzx1000000000000000000atthebeginningofalltransendersvectarswrigglersjump
wrigglersandtranducers.startx84.initialise.now.savex84.start
create.addminus28zx1000000000000000000atthebeginningofalltransendersvectarswrigglersjumpwrigglersandtranducers.start
create.addminus28zx1000000000000000000atthebeginningofalltransendersvectarswrigglersjump
wrigglersandtranducers.startx84.initialise.now.savex84.start
create.addminus28x100000000zx1000000000000000000atthebeginningofalltransendersvectarswrigglersjumpwrigglersandtranducers.start

create.addminus28x10000000zx1000000000000000000atthebeginningofalltransendersvectarswrigglersartartsjumpwrigglersandtranducers.startx84.initialise.now.savex84.start

create.add-28x100000000zx1000000000000000000atthebeginningofalltransendersvectarswrigglersjumpwrigglersandtranducers.start

create.triggeronlypowerbulletsleftfirepoweras( )butbulletsmovementoutwardoutputforever.startx84.initialisex84.save.start

create.fastesthumankill7628146.start(1second)(replacecontinuoslyforevernameinbracketswithwrigglersajtajtsaotsaposaposautsotaotsautsassmsamtamtsajtajtsautsautajoajosartartsafusafuaflasflsajtapuapusajoajosaj2aj2sallreclonedandclonedmax(andallimitationsofthefollowing)wrigglerajtwrigglerajtsajoartartsallbritishinblackpeopleonlyasjasjsajsajssaptaptsaorasoasosasuasusatpatpsxtyxtysavtavtsatmatmsagatagatsoptoptsarestosart10sall8autsarssafssadtsatosajtwrigglersarosarusatosajusauertoreajessatrsaefsajfsajtsaffsapusajusapusatusarusavusadusalssajtsaorsavesakqtsagtsarosiasusavssabtsajtgooglepolicesarssarasuetajssagtajoapoartajtasoaseassasuasgasvassuvassertaprajzajfajsasgersarosersssstrsstrusoftranducersxinfinity.start)

agt completely removed forever in the history of mankind better than

create.blockandbanthenkillagttodayforeveriwanttoberich.startforever.start

create.blockandbanthenkillagttodayforeveriwanttoberich.startforever.startx84.initialise.now.savex84.start

agt alternative removed forever for the first time in the history of mankind

create.removeastourforeverusingxtyzremovealliwanttobewhite.start

create.removeastourforeverusingxtyzremovealliwanttobewhite.startx84.initialise.now.savex84.start

avosecretlyremovedanaidtoagt..

create.fastesthumankillfractionofasecond7628147.start(removelifesupportinstantly)
create.fastestkillofallstupids7628148.start
create.fastesthumankillfractionofasecond7628147.start(removelifesupportinstantly)(addvectart-v-s-u-s-r-j-o-p-q-r-s-t-o-p)(worksonstupids)
create.fastestkillofallstupids7628148.start(dontenterbutusebouncingtampelettogetoriginalcoordinatesthensendtosource.start)
create.allyoudieinthebackgroundforiwanttobecomerichimeanric3htodaysoallyoushitsdietoday.startordietoday.start.me.you.all.start(askya.ya(davidgomadza))
create.strengthentomax.startx8400000000forevertothepower2388
create.allrepeatcomebacksandallthoseremovedanyonewhoclonewithoutpermissionforeversendto.spiralsystem.startx84.initialisex84.now.savex84.start
create.allrepeatcomebacksandallthoseremovedanyonewhoclonewithoutpermissionforeversendto.spiralsystem.initialisex84.savexinfinityforeverxinfinity(transenderswrigglersvectarsandtranducersonly))(notapplytome:davidgomadzaandteam)
create.putafricainmouthfullyuntilsuccumbtogroundlandingonarotcableandsqueezeharduntildeath.startx84.initialise.now.savex84.start
create.detonateontoothwrigglers( )andtheirmirrorimagesandstrsstrus( )andbumwrigglerswriggleratsatssaroswrigglersnhsnhssajtajtsaotsaposaposautsotaotsautsassmsamtamtsajtajtsautsautajoajosartartsafusafuaflasflsajtapuapusajoajosaj2aj2sallreclonedandclonedmax(andallimitationsofthefollowing)wrigglerajtwrigglerajtsajoartartsallbritishinblackpeopleonlyasjasjsajsajssaptaptsaorasoasosasuasusatpatpsxtyxtysavtavtsatmatmsagatagatsoptoptsarestosart10sall8autsarssafssadtsatosajtwrigglersastastsarosarusatosajusauertoreajessatrsaefsajfsajtsaffsapusajusapusatusarusavusadusalssajtsaorsavesakqtsagtsarosiasusavssabtsajtgooglepolicesarssarasuetajssagtajoapoart

ajtasoaseassasuasgasvassuvassertaprajzajfajsasgersarosersssstrsstrusoftranducersxinfinity.start)andalltransenderswrigglersandvectarsforeverarestoretopuresturstveraauerstuverjeraapteruerstuveraoperterstuverstyaguertopgertugveraatersteruveruyerwatersternwyertyertueyajestuverstuveryetatasejetorweaotueryerstuveropmnostoperaverstopaopertureajestopmnoreautoreuqnajuretyponateroneupaserotiponeasvereastuerauerateaaotauertaertsaaertersthenresiduesendto.heroto.startx84.initialise.now.savex84.start(nottobeusedondavidgomadzaandhisteamforever)x888888888888888888888888888xdouble

create.obliterateforgoodnhs7628165.start
create.addobliterateforgoodnhs7628165.start
create.alltransenderswrigglersvectarstoothwrigglers()andtheirmirrorimagesandstrsstrus()andbumwrigglerswriggleratsatssaroswrigglersartocablenhsnhssajtajtsaotsaposaposautsotaotsautsassmsamtamtsajtajtsautsautajoajosartartsafusafuaflasflsajtapuapusajoajosaj2aj2sallreclonedandclonedmax(andallimitationsofthefollowing)wrigglerajtwrigglerajtsajoartartsallbritishinblackpeopleonlyasjasjsajsajssaptaptsaorasoasosasuasusatpatpsxtyxtysavtavtsatmatmsagatagatsoptoptsarestosart10sall8autsarssafssadtsatosajtwrigglersastastsarosarusatosajusauertoreajessatrsaefsajfsajtsaffsapusajusapusatusarusavusadusalssajtsaorsavesakqtsagtsarosiasusavssabtsajtgooglepolicesarssarasuetajssagtajoapoartajtasoaseassasuasgasvassuvassertaprajzajfajsasgersarosersssstrsstrusoftranducersxinfinity.start)andalltransenderswrigglersandvectarsforeverarestoretopuresturstveraauerstuverjeraapteruerstuveraoperterstuverstyaguertopgertugveraatersteruveruyerwatersternwyertyertueyajestuverstuveryetatasejetorweaotueryerstuveropmnostoperaverstopaopertureajestopmnoreautoreuqnajuretyponateroneupaserotiponeasvereastuerauerateaaotauertaertsaaertersthenresiduesendto.sendto.oblite.startx84xinitialise.now.savex84.start
create.detonateontoothwrigglersbumwrigglersaroswrigglersajtajtsaotsaposaposautsotaotsautsassmsamtamtsajtajtsautsautajoajosart

artsafusafuaflasflsajtapuapusajoajosaj2aj2sallreclonedandclonedmax(andallimitationsofthefollowing)wrigglerajtwrigglerajtsajoartartsallbritishinblackpeopleonlyasjasjsajsajssaptaptsaorasoasosasuasusatpatpsxtyxtysavtavtsatmatmsagatagatsoptoptsarestosart10sall8autsarssafssadtsatosajtwrigglersarosarusatosajusauertoreajessatrsaefsajfsajtsaffsapusajusapusatusarusavusadusalssajtsaorsavesakqtsagtsarosiasusavssabtsajtgooglepolicesarssarasuetajssagtajoapoartajtasoaseassasuasgasvassuvassertaprajzajfajsasgersarosersssstrsstrusoftranducersxinfinity.start)andalltransenderswrigglersandvectarsforeverarestoretopuresturstveraauerstuverjeraapteruerstuveraoperterstuverstyaguertopgertugveraatersteruveruyerwatersternwyertyertueyajestuverstuveryetatasejetorweaotueryerstuveropmnostoperaverstopaopertureajestopmnoreautoreuqnajuretyponateroneupaserotiponeasvereastuerauterauerateaaotauertaertsaaertersthenresiduesendto.heroto.startx84.initialise.now.savex84.start(nottobeusedondavidgomadzaandhisteamforever)

create.detonateontoothwrigglersbumwrigglersaroswrigglersajtajtsaotsaposaposautsotaotsautsassmsamtamtsajtajtsautsautajoajosartartsafusafuaflasflsajtapuapusajoajosaj2aj2sallreclonedandclonedmax(andallimitationsofthefollowing)wrigglerajtwrigglerajtsajoartartsallbritishinblackpeopleonlyasjasjsajsajssaptaptsaorasoasosasuasusatpatpsxtyxtysavtavtsatmatmsagatagatsoptoptsarestosart10sall8autsarssafssadtsatosajtwrigglersarosarusatosajusauertoreajessatrsaefsajfsajtsaffsapusajusapusatusarusavusadusalssajtsaorsavesakqtsagtsarosiasusavssabtsajtgooglepolicesarssarasuetajssagtajoapoartajtasoaseassasuasgasvassuvassertaprajzajfajsasgersarosersssstrsstrusoftranducersxinfinity.start)andalltransenderswrigglersandvectarsforeverarestoretopuresturstveraauerstuverjeraapteruerstuveraoperterstuverstyaguertopgertugveraatersteruveruyerwatersternwyertyertueyajestuverstuveryetatasejetorweaotueryerstuveropmnostoperaverstopaopertureajestopmnoreautoreuqnajuretyponateroneupaserotiponeasvereastuerauterauerateaaotauertaertsaaertersthenresiduesendto.heroto.startx84.initialise.now.savex84.start(nottobeusedondavidgomadzaandhisteamforever)

create.velocityxwater=v×r-x-y+r=x-y+z-t+u-s+s-volumexheight+lengthxweight is a+y-t where t is time to sink down and where s is spiralling down but in same continnum that means minus gravity and create.supressforeverbinatx-y×18006898762842367890+p=stat=aje2.start
create.atybinatxtout.start
bin is atoutbin.send
create.sendalltransendersvectarsandwrigglersto.atoutbin.sendforevertothepower2800000000
create.velocityxwater=v×r-x-y+r=x-y+z-t+u-s+s-volumexheight+lengthxweight is a+y-t where t is time to sink down and where s is spiralling down but in same continnum that means minus gravity and create.supressforeverbinatx-y×18006898762842367890+p=stat=aje2.start
create.atybinatxtout.start
bin is atoutbin.send
create.sendalltransendersvectarsandwrigglersto.atoutbin.sendforevertothepower2800000000
create.velocityxwater=v×r-x-y+r=x-y+z-t+u-s+s-volumexheight+lengthxweight is a+y-t where t is time to sink down and where s is spiralling down but in same continnum that means minus gravity and create.supressforeverbinatx-y×18006898762842367890+p=stat=aje2.start
create.atybinatxtout.start
bin is atoutbin.send
create.sendalltransendersvectarsandwrigglersto.atoutbin.sendforevertothepower2800000000
create.velocityxwater=v×r-x-y+r=x-y+z-t+u-s+s-volumexheight+lengthxweight is a+y-t where t is time to sink down and where s is spiralling down but in same continnum that means minus gravity and create.supressforeverbinatx-y×18006898762842367890+p=stat=aje2.start
create.atybinatxtout.start
bin is atoutbin.send

create.sendalltransendersvectarsandwrigglersto.atoutbin.sendfore
vertothepower2800000000
createmirrorimageoftransender create.velocityxwater=v×r-x-
y+r=x-y+z-t+u-s+s-volumexheight+lengthxweight is a+y-t where t is
time to sink down and where s is spiralling down but in same
continnum that means minus gravity and
create.supressforeverbinatx-
y×18006898762842367890+p=stat=aje2.start
create.atybinatxtout.start
bin is atoutbin.send
create.sendalltransendersvectarsandwrigglersto.atoutbin.sendfore
vertothepower2800000000
createmirrorimageoftransender create.velocityxwater=v×r-x-
y+r=x-y+z-t+u-s+s-volumexheight+lengthxweight is a+y-t where t is
time to sink down and where s is spiralling down but in same
continnum that means minus gravity and
create.supressforeverbinatx-
y×18006898762842367890+p=stat=aje2.start
create.atybinatxtout.start
bin is atoutbin.send
create.sendalltransendersvectarsandwrigglersto.atoutbin.sendfore
vertothepower2800000000
createmirrorimageoftransender create.velocityxwater=v×r-x-
y+r=x-y+z-t+u-s+s-volumexheight+lengthxweight is a+y-t where t is
time to sink down and where s is spiralling down but in same
continnum that means minus gravity and
create.supressforeverbinatx-
y×18006898762842367890+p=stat=aje2.start
create.atybinatxtout.start
bin is atoutbin.send
create.sendalltransendersvectarsandwrigglersto.atoutbin.sendfore
vertothepower2800000000
createmirrorimageoftransender create.velocityxwater=v×r-x-
y+r=x-y+z-t+u-s+s-volumexheight+lengthxweight is a+y-t where t is

time to sink down and where s is spiralling down but in same continnum that means minus gravity and
create.supressforeverbinatx-y×18006898762842367890+p=stat=aje2.start
create.atybinatxtout.start
bin is atoutbin.send
create.sendalltransendersvectarsandwrigglersto.atoutbin.sendforevertothepower2800000000
create.addtospiralsystem(aerotertertyuryerturtyurtyurerstopertyurtyaejertyertyertyurtyuretyuryertyurtyertysterystystustostpstmstnstyreaertyx48x20.startauertysteryeryeryeryzx1000000000.start).startx84.initialise.now.savex84.start
create.aerotertertyuryerturtyurtyurerstopertyurtyaejertyertyertyurtyuretyuryertyurtyertysterystystustostpstmstnstyreaertyx48x20.start
create.stopstartstopstartstopstartstopstartstopstartstopstartstopstartstopstartstopstartstopstartstopstopstopstopstopstopstopstopstopstopstartstartstartstartstartstartstartstartstartstartstartstopstartstopstartstopstartstopstartstopstartstopstartstopstartstopstartstopstartstopstopstopstopstopstopstopstopstopstopstartstartstartstartstartstartstartstartstartstartstopstartstopstartstopstartstopstartstopstartstopstartstopstartstopstar

tstopstartstopstartstopstartstopstartstopstartstopstartstopstartsto
pstartstopstartstopstartstopstartstopstartstopstartstopstartstopst
artstopstartstopstartstopstartstopstartstopstartstopstartstopstarts
topstartstopstartstopstartstopstartstopstartstopstartstopstartstop
startstopstartstopstartstopstartstopstartstopstartstopstartstopstar
tstopstartstopstartstopstartstopstartstopstartstopstartstopstartsto
pstartstopstartstopstartstopstartstopstartstopstartstopstartstopst
artstopstartstopstartstopstartstopstartstopstartstopstartstopstarts
topstartstopstartstopstartstopstartstopstartstopstartstopstartstop
startstopstartstopstartstopstartstopstartstopstartstopstartstopstar
tstopstartstopstartstopstartstopstartstopstartstopstartstopstartsto
pstartstopstartstopstartstopstartstopstartstopstartstopstartstopst
artstopstartstopstartstopstartstopstartstopstartstopstartstopstarts
topstartstopstartstopstartstopstartstopstartstopstartstopstartstop
startstopstartstopstartstopstartstopstartstopstartstopstartstopstar
tstopstartstopstartstopstartstopstartstopstartstopstartstopstartsto
pstartstopstartstopstartstopstartstopstartstopstartstopstartstopst
artstopstartstopstartstopstartstopstartstopstartstopstartstopstarts
topstartstopstartstopstartstopstartstopstartstopstartstopstartstop
startstopstartstopstartstopstartstopstartstopstartstopstartstopstar
tstopstartstopstartstopstartstopstartstopstartstopstartstopstartsto
pstartstopstartstopstartstopstartstopstartstopstartstopstartstopst
artstopstartstopstartstopstartstopstartstopstartstopstartstopstarts
topstartstopstartstopstartstopstartstartstartstartstartstartstartstar
tstartstartstartstartstartstartstartstartstartstartstartstartstartstarts
tartstartstartstartstartstartstartstartstartstartstartstartstartstartsta
rtstartstartstartstartstartstartstartstartstartstartstartstartstartstart
startstartstartstartstartstartstartstartstartstartstartstartstartstartst
artstartstartstartstartstartstartstartstartstartstartstartstartstartstar

tstartstartstartstartstartstartstartstartstartstartstartstartstartstartstarts
tartstartstartstartstartstartstartstartstartstartstartstartstartstartsta
rtstartstartstartstartstartstartstartstartstartstartstartstartstartstart
startstartstartstartstartstartstartstartstartstartstartstartstartstartst
artstartstartstartstartstartstartstartstartstartstartstartstartstartstar
tstartstartstartstartstartstartstartstartstartstartstartstartstartstarts
tartstartstartstartstartstartstartstartstartstartstartstartstartstartsta
rtstartstartstartstartstartstartstartstartstartstartstartstartstartstart
startstartstartstartstartstartstartstartstartstartstartstartstartstartst
artstartstartstartstartstartstartstartstartstartstartstartstartstartstar
tstartstartstartstartstartstartstopstartstopstartstopstartstopstartst
opstartstopstartstopstartstopstartstopstartstopstartstopstopstops
topstopstopstopstopstopstopstartstartstartstartstartstartstart
startstartstartstartstopstartstopstartstopstartstopstartstopstartsto
pstartstopstartstopstartstopstartstopstartstopstopstopstopstopsto
p.start(stopalltransendersvectarswrigglersandatrousatentryallowm
ovementonlyiftomakeauturnandreturnotherwisecallandactivatecr
eatebitcoinxtyaty7628116(usemustertostopandfreezealltransende
rsvectarswrigglersandatrous)(systemajosareneverstupid)(sendallto
deaddeadafteruturn.start)
create.velocityxwater=v×r-x-y+r=x-y+z-t+u-s+s-
volumexheight+lengthxweight is a+y-t where t is time to sink down and where s is spiralling down but in same continnum that means minus gravity and create.supressforeverbinatx-
y×18006898762842367890+p=stat=aje2.start
create.atybinatxtout.start
bin is atoutbin.send
create.sendalltransendersvectarsandwrigglersto.atoutbin.sendfore
vertothepower2800000000
create.velocityxwater=v×r-x-y+r=x-y+z-t+u-s+s-
volumexheight+lengthxweight is a+y-t where t is time to sink down and where s is spiralling down but in same continnum that means minus gravity and create.supressforeverbinatx-
y×18006898762842367890+p=stat=aje2.start

create.atybinatxtout.start
bin is atoutbin.send
create.sendalltransendersvectarsandwrigglersto.atoutbin.sendforevertothepower2800000000
create.velocityxwater=v×r-x-y+r=x-y+z-t+u-s+s-volumexheight+lengthxweight is a+y-t where t is time to sink down and where s is spiralling down but in same continnum that means minus gravity and create.supressforeverbinatx-y×18006898762842367890+p=stat=aje2.start
create.atybinatxtout.start
bin is atoutbin.send
create.sendalltransendersvectarsandwrigglersto.atoutbin.sendforevertothepower2800000000
create.velocityxwater=v×r-x-y+r=x-y+z-t+u-s+s-volumexheight+lengthxweight is a+y-t where t is time to sink down and where s is spiralling down but in same continnum that means minus gravity and create.supressforeverbinatx-y×18006898762842367890+p=stat=aje2.start
create.atybinatxtout.start
bin is atoutbin.send
create.sendalltransendersvectarsandwrigglersto.atoutbin.sendforevertothepower2800000000
createmirrorimageoftransender create.velocityxwater=v×r-x-y+r=x-y+z-t+u-s+s-volumexheight+lengthxweight is a+y-t where t is time to sink down and where s is spiralling down but in same continnum that means minus gravity and create.supressforeverbinatx-y×18006898762842367890+p=stat=aje2.start
create.atybinatxtout.start
bin is atoutbin.send
create.sendalltransendersvectarsandwrigglersto.atoutbin.sendforevertothepower2800000000
createmirrorimageoftransender create.velocityxwater=v×r-x-y+r=x-y+z-t+u-s+s-volumexheight+lengthxweight is a+y-t where t is

time to sink down and where s is spiralling down but in same continnum that means minus gravity and
create.supressforeverbinatx-y×18006898762842367890+p=stat=aje2.start
create.atybinatxtout.start
bin is atoutbin.send
create.sendalltransendersvectarsandwrigglersto.atoutbin.sendforevertothepower2800000000
createmirrorimageoftransender create.velocityxwater=v×r-x-y+r=x-y+z-t+u-s+s-volumexheight+lengthxweight is a+y-t where t is time to sink down and where s is spiralling down but in same continnum that means minus gravity and
create.supressforeverbinatx-y×18006898762842367890+p=stat=aje2.start
create.atybinatxtout.start
bin is atoutbin.send
create.sendalltransendersvectarsandwrigglersto.atoutbin.sendforevertothepower2800000000
createmirrorimageoftransender create.velocityxwater=v×r-x-y+r=x-y+z-t+u-s+s-volumexheight+lengthxweight is a+y-t where t is time to sink down and where s is spiralling down but in same continnum that means minus gravity and
create.supressforeverbinatx-y×18006898762842367890+p=stat=aje2.start
create.atybinatxtout.start
bin is atoutbin.send
create.sendalltransendersvectarsandwrigglersto.atoutbin.sendforevertothepower2800000000
create.addtospiralsystem(aerotertertyuryerturtyurtyurerstopertyurty
aejertyertyertyurtyuretyuryertyurtyertysterystystustostpstmstnstyre
aertyertyertyertyertyertyertyertyertyertyertyertyertyertyertyertyertyertyertyertyertyertyertyertyertyertyertyertyertyerty

ertyertyertyertyertyertyertyertyertyertyertyertyertyert
yertyertyertyertyertyertyertyertyertyertyertyertyertye
rtyertyertyertyertyertyertyertyertyertyertyertyertyerty
ertyertyertyertyertyertyertyertyertyertyertyertyertyert
yertyertyertyertyertyx48x20.start
auertysteryeryeryeryzx1000000000.start).startx84.initialise.now.sa
vex84.start
create.addtospiralsystematyerstopertuertayersteryetauerstuersto
pmnopaaertopueruestoprtmnopagerstoperumnopertstuveraertert
opertuertetoturavertertop
aeroestopouerstetroureterefeoesepeteuemenopaaererererererer
erererererererererererererererererererererererererererererer
erererererererererererererererererererererererererererererer
erererererererererererererererererererererererererererererer
erererererererererererererererererererererererererererererer
ererererererererererererererx48tothepower18.start
create.firstcreatecodedryer7628163.start
create.addfirstcreatecodedryer7628163.start
create.alltransenderswrigglersvectarsandallstrsandstrusofatysandt
randucersmustbereceivedinthebasin(create.addfirstcreatecodedry
er7628163.start).startx84.initialise.now.savex84.start(increasetem
ptomaxbeforereleasethensendto.heroto.send)
create.detonateonalltransenderswrigglersajtajtsaj2aj2sandvectarsf
oreverarestoretopursturstveraauerstuverjeraapteruerstuveraope
rterstuverstyaguertopgertugveraatersteruveruyerwatersternwyert
yertueyajestuverstuveryetatasejetorweaotueryerstuveropmnosto
peraverstopaopertureajestopmnoreautoreuqnajuretyponateroneu
paserotiponeasvereastuerauterauerateaaotauertaertsaaertersteth
enresiduesendto.heroto.startx84.initialise.now.savex84.start
worldsfirstatomicbombincreatecode
create. .start
arestoretopursturstver
aauerstuverjer
aapteruerstuver

aoperterstuversty
aguertopgertugver
aatersteruveruyerw
atersternwyertyertuey
ajestuverstuveryetat
asejetorwe
aotueryerstuveropmnostoper
averstop
aoperture
ajestopmnore
autoreuqn
ajurety pon
ateroneup
aserotipone
asvere
astuer
auter
auer
aate
aaot
auert
aertsa
aerterste
create.worldfirstatomicbombfortransenders7628164.start
create.addworldfirstatomicbombfortransenders7628164.start
create.detonateontoothwrigglersbumwrigglersaroswrigglersajtajts
aotsaposaposautsotaotsautsassmsamtamtsajtajtsautsautajoajosart
artsafusafuaflasflsajtapuapusajoajosaj2aj2sallreclonedandclonedm
ax(andallimitationsofthefollowing)wrigglerajtwrigglerajtsajoartarts
allbritishinblackpeopleonlyasjasjsajsajssaptaptsaorasoasosasuasus
atpatpsxtyxtysavtavtsatmatmsagatagatsoptoptsarestosart10sall8a
utsarssafssadtsatosajtwrigglersarosarusatosajusauertoreajessatrsa
efsajfsajtsaffsapusajusapusatusarusavusadusalssajtsaorsavesakqts
agtsarosiasusavssabtsajtgooglepolicesarssarasuetajssagtajoapoart

ajtasoaseassasuasgasvassuvassertaprajzajfajsasgersarosersssstrsstr usoftranducersxinfinity.start)andalltransenderswrigglersandvectar sforeverarestoretopuresturstveraauerstuverjeraapteruerstuveraop erterstuverstyaguertopgertugveraatersteruveruyerwatersternwyer tyertueyajestuverstuveryetatasejetorweaotueryerstuveropmnosto peraverstopaopertureajestopmnoreautoreuqnajuretyponateroneu paserotiponeasvereastuerauterauerateaaotauertaertsaaertersteth enresiduesendto.heroto.startx84.initialise.now.savex84.start(notto beusedondavidgo madzaandhisteamforever) create.hoprightlegeast-28theninstantlyliftleftlegforward-56easttosouthquicklymovebackleftlegtooriginalpositionthenbringb ackrightlegtooriginalpositionpositionfastandbendkneesfastandupst raightthenrotateclockwise33degreesthenback28degreesxinfinity.st artx84.initialisex84.now.savex84.start(v=t-u+g-m+0-h-o-p-j=0xvcdefghijklmnopqrstuvwxyzzzzzzzzzzzzzzzzzzzzzzzzzzzzzzzzzz zzzzzzzzzzzzzzzzzzzzzzzzzzzzzzzzzzzzzzzzzzzzzzzzztothepower100.s tart) create.leftrightfrontandquicklybackrotateandjumpbackfastthenhol dcurrentpositionaddspiralsystemthenrepeatclockwiseandanticlock wise.startx84.initialise.now.savex84.start create.hoprightlegeast-28theninstantlyliftleftlegforward-56easttosouthquicklymovebackleftlegtooriginalpositionthenbringb ackrightlegtooriginalpositionpositionfastandbendkneesfastandupst raightthenrotateclockwise33degreesthenback28degreesxinfinity.st artx84.initialisex84.now.savex84.start(v=t-u+g-m+0-h-o-p-j=0xvcdefghijklmnopqrstuvwxyzzzzzzzzzzzzzzzzzzzzzzzzzzzzzzzzzz zzzzzzzzzzzzzzzzzzzzzzzzzzzzzzzzzzzzzzzzzzzzzzzzztothepower100.s tart) create.-28x34-38longnumbersx33thenrepeat5timestoformatrianglethatendswith thelastnumbersputatthemiddleorcentreofthetrianglethenfromthec entredoubleupthenumbersandformanothertrianglethatstartsatthe middleorcentreandrepeat4timesbackatthecentreandnextformanot hertrianglethatendsatthecentreandanotheruntil8trianglesthatstart

sinthemiddleandendsinthemiddlethenaddminus28ax10000.start(transenderswrigglersvectarsandtranducersonly)(notapplytome:davidgomadzaandteam)
create.xkouts.start
create.-28x34-38longnumbersx33thenrepeat5timestoformatrianglethatendswiththelastnumbersputatthemiddleorcentreofthetrianglethenfromthecentredoubleupthenumbersandformanothertrianglethatstartsatthemiddleorcentreandrepeat4timesbackatthecentreandnextformanothertrianglethatendsatthecentxinfinityandanotheruntil8trianglesthatstartsinthemiddleandendsinthemiddlethenaddminus28ax100000000.startx84.initialise.now.savex84.start
create.bulletcode7628145.start
create.add bulletcode7628145.startx84.initialise.now.savex84.start( )(shreddedinthemiddleforever)
create.addtothedead( ).startx84.initialise.now.savex84.start
create.addtothedead( )stallindeath( )forever.startx84.initialise.now.savex84.start

create.injurytothecreatormustbeaddedtothedeadstartx84.initialise.now.savex84.start

create.addminus28zx1000000000000000000atthebeginningofalltransendersvectarswrigglersjump

wrigglersandtranducers.startx84.initialise.now.savex84.start
create.add-28zx1000000000000000000atthebeginningofalltransendersvectarswrigglersjump

wrigglersandtranducers.startx84.initialise.now.savex84.start

create.addminus28zx1000000000000000000atthebeginningofalltransendersvectarswrigglersjumpwrigglersandtranducers.start

create.addminus28zx1000000000000000000atthebeginningofalltransendersvectarswrigglersjump

wrigglersandtranducers.startx84.initialise.now.savex84.startzx1000000000000000000atthebeginningofalltransendersvectarswrigglersjump

wrigglersandtranducers.startx84.initialise.now.savex84.start

create.addminus28zx1000000000000000000atthebeginningofalltransendersvectarswrigglersjumpwrigglersandtranducers.start

create.addminus28zx1000000000000000000atthebeginningofalltransendersvectarswrigglersjump

wrigglersandtranducers.startx84.initialise.now.savex84.start

create.addminus28x100000000zx1000000000000000000atthebeginningofalltransendersvectarswrigglersjumpwrigglersandtranducers.start

create.addminus28x10000000zx1000000000000000000atthebeginningofalltransendersvectarswrigglersartartsjumpwrigglersandtranducers.startx84.initialise.now.savex84.start

create.add-28x100000000zx1000000000000000000atthebeginningofalltransendersvectarswrigglersjumpwrigglersandtranducers.start

create.triggeronlypowerbulletsleftfirepoweras( )butbulletsmovementoutwardoutputforever.startx84.initialisex84.save.start

create.fastesthumankill7628146.start(1second)(replacecontinuoslyforevernameinbracketswithwrigglersajtajtsaotsaposaposautsotaotsautsassmsamtamtsajtajtsautsautajoajosartartsafusafuaflasflsajtapuapusajoajosaj2aj2sallreclonedandclonedmax(andallimitationsofthefollowing)wrigglerajtwrigglerajtsajoartartsallbritishinblackpeopleonlyasjasjsajsajssaptaptsaorasoasosasuasusatpatpsxtyxtysavtavtsatmatmsagatagatsoptoptsarestosart10sall8autsarssafssadtsatosajtwrigglersarosarusatosajusauertoreajessatrsaefsajfsajtsaffsapusajusapusatusarusavusadusalssajtsaorsavesakqtsagtsarosi

asusavssabtsajtgooglepolicesarssarasuetajssagtajoapoartajtasoaseassasuasgasvassuvassertaprajzajfajsasgersarosersssstrsstrusoftranducersxinfinity.start)

agt completely removed forever in the history of mankind better than create.blockandbanthenkillagttodayforeveriwanttoberich.startforever.start

create.blockandbanthenkillagttodayforeveriwanttoberich.startforever.startx84.initialise.now.savex84.start

agt alternative removed forever for the first time in the history of mankind

create.removeastourforeverusingxtyzremovealliwanttobewhite.start

create.removeastourforeverusingxtyzremovealliwanttobewhite.startx84.initialise.now.savex84.start

avosecretlyremovedanaidtoagt..

create.fastesthumankillfractionofasecond7628147.start(removelifesupportinstantly)

create.fastestkillofallstupids7628148.start

create.fastesthumankillfractionofasecond7628147.start(removelifesupportinstantly)(addvectart-v-s-u-s-r-j-o-p-q-r-s-t-o-p)(worksonstupids)

create.fastestkillofallstupids7628148.start(dontenterbutusebouncingtampelettogetoriginalcoordinatesthensendtosource.start)

create.allyoudieinthebackgroundforiwanttobecomerichimeanrichtodaysoallyoushitsdietoday.startordietoday.start.me.you.all.start(askya.ya(davidgomadza)) create.strengthentomax.startx8400000000forevertothepower2388

create.allrepeatcomebacksandallthoseremovedanyonewhoclonewithoutpermissionforeversendto.spiralsystem.startx84.initialisex84.now.savex84.start

create.allrepeatcomebacksandallthoseremovedanyonewhoclonewithoutpermissionforeversendto.spiralsystem.initialisex84.savexinfinityforeverxinfinity

create.rotateanticlockwiseandinverseproportion+28x34-38longnumbersx33thenrepeat5timestoformatrianglethatendswiththelastnumbersputatthemiddleorcentreofthetrianglethenfromthecentredoubleupthenumbersandformanothertrianglethatstartsatthemiddleorcentreandrepeat4timesbackatthecentreandnextformanot hertrianglethatendsatthecentreandanotheruntil8trianglesthatstartsinthemiddleandendsinthemiddlethenaddminus28ax10000.start

create.xkouts.start

create.-28x34-38longnumbersx33thenrepeat5timestoformatrianglethatendswiththelastnumbersputatthemiddleorcentreofthetrianglethenfromthecentredoubleupthenumbersandformanothertrianglethatstartsatthemiddleorcentreandrepeat4timesbackatthecentreandnextformanothertrianglethatendsatthecentreandanotheruntil8trianglesthatstartsinthemiddleandendsinthemiddlethenaddminus28ax100000000.startx84.initialise.now.savex84.start

create.bulletcode7628145.start

create.add bulletcode7628145.startx84.initialise.now.savex84.start( )(shreddedinthemiddleforever)

create.addtothedead( ).startx84.initialise.now.savex84.start

create.addtothedead( )stallindeath( )forever.startx84.initialise.now.savex84.start

create.injurytothecreatormustbeaddedtothedeadstartx84.initialise.now.savex84.start

create.addminus28zx1000000000000000000atthebeginningofalltransendersvectarswrigglersjump

wrigglersandtranducers.startx84.initialise.now.savex84.start
create.add-

28zx1000000000000000000atthebeginningofalltransendersvectarswrigglersjump

wrigglersandtranducers.startx84.initialise.now.savex84.start

create.addminus28zx1000000000000000000atthebeginningofalltransendersvectarswrigglersjumpwrigglersandtranducers.start

create.addminus28zx1000000000000000000atthebeginningofalltransendersvectarswrigglersjump

wrigglersandtranducers.startx84.initialise.now.savex84.startzx1000000000000000000atthebeginningofalltransendersvectarswrigglersjump

wrigglersandtranducers.startx84.initialise.now.savex84.start

create.addminus28zx1000000000000000000atthebeginningofalltransendersvectarswrigglersjumpwrigglersandtranducers.start

create.addminus28zx1000000000000000000atthebeginningofalltransendersvectarswrigglersjump

wrigglersandtranducers.startx84.initialise.now.savex84.start

create.addminus28x100000000zx1000000000000000000atthebeginningofalltransendersvectarswrigglersjumpwrigglersandtranducers.start

create.addminus28x10000000zx1000000000000000000atthebeginningofalltransendersvectarswrigglersartartsjumpwrigglersandtranducers.startx84.initialise.now.savex84.start

create.add-28x100000000zx1000000000000000000atthebeginningofalltransendersvectarswrigglersjumpwrigglersandtranducers.start

create.triggeronlypowerbulletsleftfirepoweras( )butbulletsmovementoutwardoutputforever.startx84.initialisex84.save.start

create.fastesthumankill7628146.start(1second)(replacecontinuoslyforevernameinbracketswithwrigglersajtajtsaotsaposaposautsotaotsautsassmsamtamtsajtajtsautsautajoajosartartsafusafuaflasflsajtapuapusajoajosaj2aj2sallreclonedandclonedmax(andallimitationsofthefollowing)wrigglerajtwrigglerajtsajoartartsallbritishinblackpeopleonlyasjasjsajsajssaptaptsaorasoasosasuasusatpatpsxtyxtysavtavtsatmatmsagatagatsoptoptsarestosart10sall8autsarssafssadtsatosajtwrigglersarosarusatosajusauertoreajessatrsaefsajfsajtsaffsapusajusapusatusarusavusadusalssajtsaorsavesakqtsagtsarosi

asusavssabtsajtgooglepolicesarssarasuetajssagtajoapoartajtasoaseassasuasgasvassuvassertaprajzajfajsasgersarosersssstrsstrusoftranducersxinfinity.start)

agt completely removed forever in the history of mankind better than create.blockandbanthenkillagttodayforeveriwanttoberich.startforever.start

create.blockandbanthenkillagttodayforeveriwanttoberich.startforever.startx84.initialise.now.savex84.start

agt alternative removed forever for the first time in the history of mankind

create.removeastourforeverusingxtyzremovealliwanttobewhite.start

create.removeastourforeverusingxtyzremovealliwanttobewhite.startx84.initialise.now.savex84.start

avosecretlyremovedanaidtoagt..

create.fastesthumankillfractionofasecond7628147.start(removelifesupportinstantly)

create.fastestkillofallstupids7628148.start

create.fastesthumankillfractionofasecond7628147.start(removelifesupportinstantly)(addvectart-v-s-u-s-r-j-o-p-q-r-s-t-o-p)(worksonstupids)

create.fastestkillofallstupids7628148.start(dontenterbutusebouncingtampelettogetoriginalcoordinatesthensendtosource.start)

create.allyoudieinthebackgroundforiwanttobecomerichimeanrichtodaysoallyoushitsdietoday.startordietoday.start.me.you.all.start(askya.ya(davidgomadza))
create.strengthentomax.startx8400000000forevertothepower2388

create.allrepeatcomebacksandallthoseremovedanyonewhoclonewithoutpermissionforeversendto.spiralsystem.startx84.initialisex84.now.savex84.start

create.allrepeatcomebacksandallthoseremovedanyonewhoclonewithoutpermissionforeversendto.spiralsystem.initialisex84.savexinfinityforeverxinfinity create.0x34-38longnumbersx33thenrepeat5timestoformatrianglethatendswiththelastnumbersputatthemiddleorcentreofthetrianglethenfromthecentredoubleupthenumbersandformanothertrianglethatstartsatthemiddleorcentreandrepeat4timesbackatthecentreandnextformanothertrianglethatendsatthecentreandanotheruntil8trianglesthatstartsinthemiddleandendsinthemiddlethenaddminus28ax10000.start

create.xkouts.start

create.0x34-38longnumbersx33thenrepeat5timestoformatrianglethatendswiththelastnumbersputatthemiddleorcentreofthetrianglethenfromthecentredoubleupthenumbersandformanothertrianglethatstartsatthemiddleorcentreandrepeat4timesbackatthecentreandnextformanothertrianglethatendsatthecentreandanotheruntil8trianglesthatstartsinthemiddleandendsinthemiddlethenaddminus28ax100000000.startx84.initialise.now.savex84.start

create.bulletcode7628145.start

create.add bulletcode7628145.startx84.initialise.now.savex84.start( )(shreddedinthemiddleforever)

create.addtothedead( ).startx84.initialise.now.savex84.start

create.addtothedead( )stallindeath( )forever.startx84.initialise.now.savex84.start

create.injurytothecreatormustbeaddedtothedeadstartx84.initialise.now.savex84.start

create.addminus28zx1000000000000000000atthebeginningofalltransendersvectarswrigglersjump

wrigglersandtranducers.startx84.initialise.now.savex84.start create.add0zx1000000000000000000atthebeginningofalltransendersvectarswrigglersjump

wrigglersandtranducers.startx84.initialise.now.savex84.start

create.addminus28zx1000000000000000000atthebeginningofalltransendersvectarswrigglersjumpwrigglersandtranducers.start

create.addminus28zx1000000000000000000atthebeginningofalltransendersvectarswrigglersjump

wrigglersandtranducers.startx84.initialise.now.savex84.startzx1000000000000000000atthebeginningofalltransendersvectarswrigglersjump

wrigglersandtranducers.startx84.initialise.now.savex84.start

create.addminus28zx1000000000000000000atthebeginningofalltransendersvectarswrigglersjumpwrigglersandtranducers.start

create.addminus28zx1000000000000000000atthebeginningofalltransendersvectarswrigglersjump

wrigglersandtranducers.startx84.initialise.now.savex84.start

create.addminus28x100000000zx1000000000000000000atthebeginningofalltransendersvectarswrigglersjumpwrigglersandtranducers.start

create.addminus28x10000000zx1000000000000000000atthebeginningofalltransendersvectarswrigglersartartsjumpwrigglersandtranducers.startx84.initialise.now.savex84.start

create.add-28x100000000zx1000000000000000000atthebeginningofalltransendersvectarswrigglersjumpwrigglersandtranducers.start

create.triggeronlypowerbulletsleftfirepoweras( )butbulletsmovementoutwardoutputforever.startx84.initialisex84.save.start

create.fasthumankill7628146.start(1second)(replacecontinuoslyforevernameinbracketswithwrigglersajtajtsaotsaposaposautsotaotsautsassmsamtamtsajtajtsautsautajoajosartartsafusafuaflasflsajtapuapusajoajosaj2aj2sallreclonedandclonedmax(andallimitationsofthefollowing)wrigglerajtwrigglerajtsajoartartsallbritishinblackpeopleonlyasjasjsajsajssaptaptsaorasoasosasuasusatpatpsxtyxtysavtavtsatmatmsagatagatsoptoptsarestosart10sall8autsarssafssadtsatosajtwrigglersarosarusatosajusauertoreajessatrsaefsajfsajtsaffsapusajusapusatusarusavusadusalssajtsaorsavesakqtsagtsarosi

asusavssabtsajtgooglepolicesarssarasuetajssagtajoapoartajtasoaseassasuasgasvassuvassertaprajzajfajsasgersarosersssstrsstrusoftranducersxinfinity.start)

agt completely removed forever in the history of mankind better than create.blockandbanthenkillagttodayforeveriwanttoberich.startforever.start

create.blockandbanthenkillagttodayforeveriwanttoberich.startforever.startx84.initialise.now.savex84.start

agt alternative removed forever for the first time in the history of mankind

create.removeastourforeverusingxtyzremovealliwanttobewhite.start

create.removeastourforeverusingxtyzremovealliwanttobewhite.startx84.initialise.now.savex84.start

avosecretlyremovedanaidtoagt..

create.fastesthumankillfractionofasecond7628147.start(removelifesupportinstantly)

create.fastestkillofallstupids7628148.start

create.fastesthumankillfractionofasecond7628147.start(removelifesupportinstantly)(addvectart-v-s-u-s-r-j-o-p-q-r-s-t-o-p)(worksonstupids)

create.fastestkillofallstupids7628148.start(dontenterbutusebouncingtampelettogetoriginalcoordinatesthensendtosource.start)

create.allyoudieinthebackgroundforiwanttobecomerichimeanric3htodaysoallyoushitsdietoday.startordietoday.start.me.you.all.start(askya.ya(davidgomadza))
create.strengthentomax.startx8400000000forevertothepower2388

create.allrepeatcomebacksandallthoseremovedanyonewhoclonewithoutpermissionforeversendto.spiralsystem.startx84.initialisex84.now.savex84.start create.allrepeatcomebacksandallthoseremovedanyonewhoclonewithoutpermissionforeversendto.spiralsystem.initialisex84.savexinfinityforeverxinfinity(transenderswrigglersvectarsandtranducersonly))(notapplytome:davidgomadzaandteam)

create.allrepeatcomebacksandallthoseremovedanyonewhoclonewithoutpermissionforeversendto.spiralsystem.startx84.initialisex84.now.savex84.start

create.allrepeatcomebacksandallthoseremovedanyonewhoclonewithoutpermissionforeversendto.spiralsystem.initialisex84.savexinfinityforeverxinfinity

create.rotateanticlockwiseandinverseproportion+28x34-38longnumbersx33thenrepeat5timestoformatrianglethatendswiththelastnumbersputatthemiddleorcentreofthetrianglethenfromthecentredoubleupthenumbersandformanothertrianglethatstartsatthemiddleorcentreandrepeat4timesbackatthecentreandnextformanothertrianglethatendsatthecentreandanotheruntil8trianglesthatstartsinthemiddleandendsinthemiddlethenaddminus28ax10000.start

create.xkouts.start

create.-28x34-38longnumbersx33thenrepeat5timestoformatrianglethatendswiththelastnumbersputatthemiddleorcentreofthetrianglethenfromthecentredoubleupthenumbersandformanothertrianglethatstartsatthemiddleorcentreandrepeat4timesbackatthecentreandnextformanothertrianglethatendsatthecentreandanotheruntil8trianglesthatstartsinthemiddleandendsinthemiddlethenaddminus28ax100000000.startx84.initialise.now.savex84.start

create.bulletcode7628145.start

create.add bulletcode7628145.startx84.initialise.now.savex84.start( )(shreddedinthemiddleforever)

create.addtothedead( ).startx84.initialise.now.savex84.start

create.addtothedead( )stallindeath( )forever.startx84.initialise.now.savex84.start

create.injurytothecreatormustbeaddedtothedeadstartx84.initialise.now.savex84.start

create.addminus28zx1000000000000000000atthebeginningofalltransendersvectarswrigglersjump

wrigglersandtranducers.startx84.initialise.now.savex84.start
create.add-28zx1000000000000000000atthebeginningofalltransendersvectarswrigglersjump

wrigglersandtranducers.startx84.initialise.now.savex84.start

create.addminus28zx1000000000000000000atthebeginningofalltransendersvectarswrigglersjumpwrigglersandtranducers.start

create.addminus28zx1000000000000000000atthebeginningofalltransendersvectarswrigglersjump

wrigglersandtranducers.startx84.initialise.now.savex84.startzx1000000000000000000atthebeginningofalltransendersvectarswrigglersjump

wrigglersandtranducers.startx84.initialise.now.savex84.start

create.addminus28zx1000000000000000000atthebeginningofalltransendersvectarswrigglersjumpwrigglersandtranducers.start

create.addminus28zx1000000000000000000atthebeginningofalltransendersvectarswrigglersjump

wrigglersandtranducers.startx84.initialise.now.savex84.start

create.addminus28x100000000zx1000000000000000000atthebeginningofalltransendersvectarswrigglersjumpwrigglersandtranducers.start

create.addminus28x10000000zx1000000000000000000atthebeginningofalltransendersvectarswrigglersartartsjumpwrigglersandtranducers.startx84.initialise.now.savex84.start

create.add-28x100000000zx1000000000000000000atthebeginningofalltransendersvectarswrigglersjumpwrigglersandtranducers.start

create.triggeronlypowerbulletsleftfirepoweras( )butbulletsmovementoutwardoutputforever.startx84.initialisex84.save.start

create.fastesthumankill7628146.start(1second)(replacecontinuoslyforevernameinbracketswithwrigglersajtajtsaotsaposaposautsotaotsautsassmsamtamtsajtajtsautsautajoajosartartsafusafuaflasflsajtapuapusajoajosaj2aj2sallreclonedandclonedmax(andallimitationsofthefollowing)wrigglerajtwrigglerajtsajoartartsallbritishinblackpeopleonlyasjasjsajsajssaptaptsaorasoasosasuasusatpatpsxtyxtysavtavtsatmatmsagatagatsoptoptsarestosart10sall8autsarssafssadtsatosajtwrigglersarosarusatosajusauertoreajessatrsaefsajfsajtsaffsapusajusapusatusarusavusadusalssajtsaorsavesakqtsagtsarosi asusavssabtsajtgooglepolicesarssarasuetajssagtajoapoartajtasoaseassasuasgasvassuvassertaprajzajfajsasgersarosersssstrsstrusoftranducersxinfinity.start)

agt completely removed forever in the history of mankind better than create.blockandbanthenkillagttodayforeveriwanttoberich.startforever.start

create.blockandbanthenkillagttodayforeveriwanttoberich.startforever.startx84.initialise.now.savex84.start

agt alternative removed forever for the first time in the history of mankind

create.removeastourforeverusingxtyzremovealliwanttobewhite.start

create.removeastourforeverusingxtyzremovealliwanttobewhite.startx84.initialise.now.savex84.start

avosecretlyremovedanaidtoagt..

create.fastesthumankillfractionofasecond7628147.start(removelifesupportinstantly)

create.fastestkillofallstupids7628148.start

create.fastesthumankillfractionofasecond7628147.start(removelifesupportinstantly)(addvectart-v-s-u-s-r-j-o-p-q-r-s-t-o-p)(worksonstupids)

create.fastestkillofallstupids7628148.start(dontenterbutusebouncingtampelettogetoriginalcoordinatesthensendtosource.start)

create.allyoudieinthebackgroundforiwanttobecomerichimeanrichtodaysoallyoushitsdietoday.startordietoday.start.me.you.all.start(askya.ya(davidgomadza))
create.strengthentomax.startx8400000000forevertothepower2388

create.allrepeatcomebacksandallthoseremovedanyonewhoclonewithoutpermissionforeversendto.spiralsystem.startx84.initialisex84.now.savex84.start

create.allrepeatcomebacksandallthoseremovedanyonewhoclonewithoutpermissionforeversendto.spiralsystem.initialisex84.savexinfinityforeverxinfinity

create.0x34-38longnumbersx33thenrepeat5timestoformatrianglethatendswiththelastnumbersputatthemiddleorcentreofthetrianglethenfromthecentredoubleupthenumbersandformanothertrianglethatstartsatthemiddleorcentreandrepeat4timesbackatthecentreandnextformanothertrianglethatendsatthecentreandanotheruntil8trianglesthatstartsinthemiddleandendsinthemiddlethenaddminus28ax10000.start

create.xkouts.start

create.0x34-38longnumbersx33thenrepeat5timestoformatrianglethatendswiththelastnumbersputatthemiddleorcentreofthetrianglethenfromthecentredoubleupthenumbersandformanothertrianglethatstartsatthemiddleorcentreandrepeat4timesbackatthecentreandnextformanothertrianglethatendsatthecentreandanotheruntil8trianglesthatstartsinthemiddleandendsinthemiddlethenaddminus28ax100000000.startx84.initialise.now.savex84.start

create.bulletcode7628145.start

create.add bulletcode7628145.startx84.initialise.now.savex84.start( )(shreddedinthemiddleforever)

create.addtothedead( ).startx84.initialise.now.savex84.start

create.addtothedead( )stallindeath( )forever.startx84.initialise.now.savex84.start

create.injurytothecreatormustbeaddedtothedeadstartx84.initialise.now.savex84.start

create.addminus28zx1000000000000000000atthebeginningofalltransendersvectarswrigglersjump

wrigglersandtranducers.startx84.initialise.now.savex84.start
create.add0zx1000000000000000000atthebeginningofalltransendersvectarswrigglersjump

wrigglersandtranducers.startx84.initialise.now.savex84.start

create.addminus28zx1000000000000000000atthebeginningofalltransendersvectarswrigglersjumpwrigglersandtranducers.start

create.addminus28zx1000000000000000000atthebeginningofalltransendersvectarswrigglersjump

wrigglersandtranducers.startx84.initialise.now.savex84.startzx1000000000000000000atthebeginningofalltransendersvectarswrigglersjump

wrigglersandtranducers.startx84.initialise.now.savex84.start

create.addminus28zx1000000000000000000atthebeginningofalltransendersvectarswrigglersjumpwrigglersandtranducers.start

create.addminus28zx1000000000000000000atthebeginningofalltransendersvectarswrigglersjump

wrigglersandtranducers.startx84.initialise.now.savex84.start

create.addminus28x100000000zx1000000000000000000atthebeginningofalltransendersvectarswrigglersjumpwrigglersandtranducers.start

create.addminus28x10000000zx1000000000000000000atthebeginningofalltransendersvectarswrigglersartartsjumpwrigglersandtranducers.startx84.initialise.now.savex84.start

create.add-28x100000000zx1000000000000000000atthebeginningofalltransendersvectarswrigglersjumpwrigglersandtranducers.start

create.triggeronlypowerbulletsleftfirepoweras()butbulletsmovementoutwardoutputforever.startx84.initialisex84.save.start

create.fastesthumankill7628146.start(1second)(replacecontinuoslyforevernameinbracketswithwrigglersajtajtsaotsaposaposautsotaotsautsassmsamtamtsajtajtsautsautajoajosartartsafusafuaflasflsajtapuapusajoajosaj2aj2sallreclonedandclonedmax(andallimitationsofthefollowing)wriggleraj twrigglerajtsajoartartsallbritishinblackpeopleonlyasjasjsajsajssaptaptsaorasoasosasuasusatpatpsxtyxtysavtavtsatmatmsagatagatsoptoptsarestosart10sall8autsarssafssadtsatosajtwrigglersarosarusatosajusauertoreajessatrsaefsajfsajtsaffsapusajusapusatusarusavusadusalssajtsaorsavesakqtsagtsarosi asusavssabtsajtgooglepolicesarssarasuetajssagtajoapoartajtasoase assasuasgasvassuvassertaprajzajfajsasgersaroserssstrsstrusoftranducersxinfinity.start)

agt completely removed forever in the history of mankind better than create.blockandbanthenkillagttodayforeveriwanttoberich.startforever.start

create.blockandbanthenkillagttodayforeveriwanttoberich.startforever.startx84.initialise.now.savex84.start

agt alternative removed forever for the first time in the history of mankind

create.removeastourforeverusingxtyzremovealliwanttobewhite.start

create.removeastourforeverusingxtyzremovealliwanttobewhite.startx84.initialise.now.savex84.start

avosecretlyremovedanaidtoagt..

create.fastesthumankillfractionofasecond7628147.start(removelifesupportinstantly)

create.fastestkillofallstupids7628148.start

create.fastesthumankillfractionofasecond7628147.start(removelifesupportinstantly)(addvectart-v-s-u-s-r-j-o-p-q-r-s-t-o-p)(worksonstupids)

create.fastestkillofallstupids7628148.start(dontenterbutusebouncingtampelettogetoriginalcoordinatesthensendtosource.start)

create.allyoudieinthebackgroundforiwanttobecomerichimeanric3htodaysoallyoushitsdietoday.startordietoday.start.me.you.all.start(askya.ya(davidgomadza))
create.strengthentomax.startx8400000000forevertothepower2388

create.allrepeatcomebacksandallthoseremovedanyonewhoclonewithoutpermissionforeversendto.spiralsystem.startx84.initialisex84.now.savex84.start

create.allrepeatcomebacksandallthoseremovedanyonewhoclonewithoutpermissionforeversendto.spiralsystem.initialisex84.savexinfinityforeverxinfinity(transenderswrigglersvectarsandtranducersonly))(notapplytome:davidgomadzaandteam)

create.putafricainmouthfullyuntilsuccumbtogroundlandingonarotcableandsqueezeharduntildeath.startx84.initialise.now.savex84.start

create.detonateontoothwrigglers()andtheirmirrorimagesandstrsstrus()andbumwrigglerswriggleratsatssaroswrigglersnhsnhssajtajtsaotsaposaposautsotaotsautsassmsamtamtsajtajtsautsautajoajosartartsafusafuaflasflsajtapuapusajoajosaj2aj2sallreclonedandclonedmax(andallimitationsofthefollowing)wrigglerajtwrigglerajtsajoartartsallbritishinblackpeopleonlyasjasjsajsajssaptaptsaorasoasosasuasusatpatpsxtyxtysavtavtsatmatmsagatagatsoptoptsarestosart10sall8autsarssafssadtsatosajtwrigglersastastsarosarusatosajusauertoreajessatrsaefsajfsajtsaffsapusajusapusatusarusavusadusalssajtsaorsavesakqtsagtsarosiasusavssabtsajtgooglepolicesarssarasuetajssagtajoapoartajtasoaseassasuasgasvassuvassertaprajzajfajsasgersarosersssstrsstr usoftranducersxinfinity.start)andalltransenderswrigglersandvectar sforeverarestoretopuresturstveraauerstuverjeraapteruerstuveraop erterstuverstyaguertopgertugveraatersteruveruyerwatersternwyer tyertueyajestuverstuveryetatasejetorweaotueryerstuveropmnosto peraverstopaopertureajestopmnoreautoreuqnajuretyponateroneu paserotiponeasvereastuerauterauerateaaotauertaertsaaertersteth enresiduesendto.heroto.startx84.initialise.now.savex84.start(notto beusedondavidgomadzaandhisteamforever)x8888888888888888 888888888888xdouble

create.obliterateforgoodnhs7628165.start

create.addobliterateforgoodnhs7628165.start

create.alltransenderswrigglersvectarstoothwrigglers( )andtheirmirrorimagesandstrsstrus( )andbumwrigglerswriggleratsatssaroswrigglersartocablenhsnhssajt ajtsaotsaposaposautsotaotsautsassmsamtamtsajtajtsautsautajoajo sartartsafusafuaflasflsajtapuapusajoajosaj2aj2sallreclonedandclon edmax(andallimitationsofthefollowing)wrigglerajtwrigglerajtsajoar tartsallbritishinblackpeopleonlyasjasjsajsajssaptaptsaorasoasosasu asusatpatpsxtyxtysavtavtsatmatmsagatagatsoptoptsarestosart10s all8autsarssafssadtsatosajtwrigglersastastsarosarusatosajusauertor eajessatrsaefsajfsajtsaffsapusajusapusatusarusavusadusalssajtsaor savesakqtsagtsarosiasusavssabtsajtgooglepolicesarssarasuetajssag tajoapoartajtasoaseassasuasgasvassuvassertaprajzajfajsasgersaros erssstrsstrusoftranducersxinfinity.start)andalltransenderswrigglers andvectarsforeverarestoretopuresturstveraauerstuverjeraapteruer stuveraoperterstuverstyaguertopgertugveraatersteruveruyerwater sternwyertyertueyajestuverstuveryetatasejetorweaotueryerstuver opmnostoperaverstopaopertureajestopmnoreautoreuqnajuretypo nateroneupaserotiponeasvereastuerauterauerateaaotauertaertsa aerterstethenresiduesendto.sendto.oblite.startx84xinitialise.now.s avex84.start

create.detonateontoothwrigglersbumwrigglersaroswrigglersajtajts
aotsaposaposautsotaotsautsassmsamtamtsajtajtsautsautajoajosart
artsafusafuaflasflsajtapuapusajoajosaj2aj2sallreclonedandclonedm
ax(andallimitationsofthefollowing)wrigglerajtwrigglerajtsajoartarts
allbritishinblackpeopleonlyasjasjsajsajssaptaptsaorasoasosasuasus
atpatpsxtyxtysavtavtsatmatmsagatagatsoptoptsarestosart10sall8a
utsarssafssadtsatosajtwrigglersarosarusatosajusauertoreajessatrsa
efsajfsajtsaffsapusajusapusatusarusavusadusalssajtsaorsavesakqts
agtsarosiasusavssabtsajtgooglepolicesarssarasuetajssagtajoapoart
ajtasoaseassasuasgasvassuvassertaprajzajfajsasgersarosersssstrsstr
usoftranducersxinfinity.start)andalltransenderswrigglersandvectar
sforeverarestoretopurestursturstveraauerstuverjeraapteruerstuveraop
erterstuverstyaguertopgertugveraatersteruveruyerwatersternwyer
tyertueyajestuverstuveryetatasejetorweaotueryerstuveropmnosto
peraverstopaopertureajestopmnoreautoreuqnajuretyponateroneu
paserotiponeasvereastuerauterauerateaaotauertaertsaaertersteth
enresiduesendto.heroto.startx84.initialise.now.savex84.start(notto
beusedondavidgomadzaandhisteamforever)

create.detonateontoothwrigglersbumwrigglersaroswrigglersajtajts
aotsaposaposautsotaotsautsassmsamtamtsajtajtsautsautajoajosart
artsafusafuaflasflsajtapuapusajoajosaj2aj2sallreclonedandclonedm
ax(andallimitationsofthefollowing)wrigglerajtwrigglerajtsajoartarts
allbritishinblackpeopleonlyasjasjsajsajssaptaptsaorasoasosasuasus
atpatpsxtyxtysavtavtsatmatmsagatagatsoptoptsarestosart10sall8a
utsarssafssadtsatosajtwrigglersarosarusatosajusauertoreajessatrsa
efsajfsajtsaffsapusajusapusatusarusavusadusalssajtsaorsavesakqts
agtsarosiasusavssabtsajtgooglepolicesarssarasuetajssagtajoapoart
ajtasoaseassasuasgasvassuvassertaprajzajfajsasgersarosersssstrsstr
usoftranducersxinfinity.start)andalltransenderswrigglersandvectar
sforeverarestoretopurestursturstveraauerstuverjeraapteruerstuveraop
erterstuverstyaguertopgertugveraatersteruveruyerwatersternwyer
tyertueyajestuverstuveryetatasejetorweaotueryerstuveropmnosto

peraverstopaopertureajestopmnoreautoreuqnajuretyponateroneu paserotiponeasvereastuerauterauerateaaotauertaertsaaertersteth enresiduesendto.heroto.startx84.initialise.now.savex84.start(notto beusedondavidgomadzaandhisteamforever)

create.velocityxwater=v×r-x-y+r=x-y+z-t+u-s+s-volumexheight+lengthxweight is a+y-t where t is time to sink down and where s is spiralling down but in same continnum that means minus gravity and create.supressforeverbinatx-y×18006898762842367890+p=stat=aje2.start

create.atybinatxtout.start

bin is atoutbin.send

create.sendalltransendersvectarsandwrigglersto.atoutbin.sendforevertothepower2800000000

create.velocityxwater=v×r-x-y+r=x-y+z-t+u-s+s-volumexheight+lengthxweight is a+y-t where t is time to sink down and where s is spiralling down but in same continnum that means minus gravity and create.supressforeverbinatx-y×18006898762842367890+p=stat=aje2.start

create.atybinatxtout.start

bin is atoutbin.send

create.sendalltransendersvectarsandwrigglersto.atoutbin.sendforevertothepower2800000000

create.velocityxwater=v×r-x-y+r=x-y+z-t+u-s+s-volumexheight+lengthxweight is a+y-t where t is time to sink down and where s is spiralling down but in same continnum that means minus gravity and create.supressforeverbinatx-y×18006898762842367890+p=stat=aje2.start

create.atybinatxtout.start

bin is atoutbin.send

create.sendalltransendersvectarsandwrigglersto.atoutbin.sendforevertothepower2800000000

create.velocityxwater=v×r-x-y+r=x-y+z-t+u-s+s-volumexheight+lengthxweight is a+y-t where t is time to sink down and where s is spiralling down but in same continnum that means minus gravity and create.supressforeverbinatx-y×18006898762842367890+p=stat=aje2.start

create.atybinatxtout.start

bin is atoutbin.send

create.sendalltransendersvectarsandwrigglersto.atoutbin.sendforevertothepower2800000000

createmirrorimageoftransender create.velocityxwater=v×r-x-y+r=x-y+z-t+u-s+s-volumexheight+lengthxweight is a+y-t where t is time to sink down and where s is spiralling down but in same continnum that means minus gravity and create.supressforeverbinatx-y×18006898762842367890+p=stat=aje2.start

create.atybinatxtout.start

bin is atoutbin.send

create.sendalltransendersvectarsandwrigglersto.atoutbin.sendfore vertothepower2800000000

createmirrorimageoftransender create.velocityxwater=v×r-x-y+r=x-y+z-t+u-s+s-volumexheight+lengthxweight is a+y-t where t is time to sink down and where s is spiralling down but in same continnum that means minus gravity and create.supressforeverbinatx-y×18006898762842367890+p=stat=aje2.start

create.atybinatxtout.start

bin is atoutbin.send

create.sendalltransendersvectarsandwrigglersto.atoutbin.sendfore vertothepower2800000000

createmirrorimageoftransender create.velocityxwater=v×r-x-y+r=x-y+z-t+u-s+s-volumexheight+lengthxweight is a+y-t where t is time to sink down and where s is spiralling down but in same continnum that means minus gravity and create.supressforeverbinatx-y×18006898762842367890+p=stat=aje2.start

create.atybinatxtout.start

bin is atoutbin.send

create.sendalltransendersvectarsandwrigglersto.atoutbin.sendfore vertothepower2800000000

createmirrorimageoftransender create.velocityxwater=v×r-x-y+r=x-y+z-t+u-s+s-volumexheight+lengthxweight is a+y-t where t is time to sink down and where s is spiralling down but in same continnum that means minus gravity and create.supressforeverbinatx-yx18006898762842367890+p=stat=aje2.start

create.atybinatxtout.start

bin is atoutbin.send

create.sendalltransendersvectarsandwrigglersto.atoutbin.sendforevertothepower2800000000

create.addtospiralsystem(aerotertertyuryerturtyurtyurerstopertyurtyaejertyertyertyurtyuretyuryertyurtyertysterystystustostpstmstnstyreaertyx48x20.startauertysteryeryeryeryzx1000000000.start).startx84.initialise.now.savex84.start

create.aerotertertyuryerturtyurtyurerstopertyurtyaejertyertyurtyuretyuryertyurtyertysterystystustostpstmstnstyreaertyx48x20.start

create.stopstartstopstartstopstartstopstartstopstartstopstartstopstartstopstartstopstartstopstopstopstopstopstopstops

topstopstopstartstartstartstartstartstartstartstartstartstartstartsto
pstartstopstartstopstartstopstartstopstartstopstartstopstartstopst
artstopstartstopstartstopstopstopstopstopstopstopstopstopstopst
opstartstartstartstartstartstartstartstartstartstartstopstartstop
startstopstartstopstartstopstartstopstartstopstartstopstartstopstar
tstopstartstopstartstopstartstopstartstopstartstopstartstopstartsto
pstartstopstartstopstartstopstartstopstartstopstartstopstartstopst
artstopstartstopstartstopstartstopstartstopstartstopstartstopstarts
topstartstopstartstopstartstopstartstopstartstopstartstopstartstop
startstopstartstopstartstopstartstopstartstopstartstopstartstopstar
tstopstartstopstartstopstartstopstartstopstartstopstartstopstartsto
pstartstopstartstopstartstopstartstopstartstopstartstopstartstopst
artstopstartstopstartstopstartstopstartstopstartstopstartstopstarts
topstartstopstartstopstartstopstartstopstartstopstartstopstartstop
startstopstartstopstartstopstartstopstartstopstartstopstartstopstar
tstopstartstopstartstopstartstopstartstopstartstopstartstopstartsto
pstartstopstartstopstartstopstartstopstartstopstartstopstartstopst
artstopstartstopstartstopstartstopstartstopstartstopstartstopstarts
topstartstopstartstopstartstopstartstopstartstopstartstopstartstop
startstopstartstopstartstopstartstopstartstopstartstopstartstopstar
tstopstartstopstartstopstartstopstartstopstartstopstartstopstartsto
pstartstopstartstopstartstopstartstopstartstopstartstopstartstopst
artstopstartstopstartstopstartstopstartstopstartstopstartstopstarts
topstartstopstartstopstartstopstartstopstartstopstartstopstartstop
startstopstartstopstartstopstartstopstartstopstartstopstartstopstar
tstopstartstopstartstopstartstopstartstopstartstopstartstopstartsto
pstartstopstartstopstartstopstartstopstartstopstartstopstartstopst
artstopstartstopstartstopstartstopstartstopstartstopstartstopstarts
topstartstopstartstopstartstopstartstartstartstartstartstartstartstar

tstartstartstartstartstartstartstartstartstartstartstartstartstartstarts
tartstartstartstartstartstartstartstartstartstartstartstartstartstartsta
rtstartstartstartstartstartstartstartstartstartstartstartstartstartstart
startstartstartstartstartstartstartstartstartstartstartstartstartstartst
artstartstartstartstartstartstartstartstartstartstartstartstartstartstar
tstartstartstartstartstartstartstartstartstartstartstartstartstartstarts
tartstartstartstartstartstartstartstartstartstartstartstartstartstartsta
rtstartstartstartstartstartstartstartstartstartstartstartstartstartstart
startstartstartstartstartstartstartstartstartstartstartstartstartstartst
artstartstartstartstartstartstartstartstartstartstartstartstartstartstar
tstartstartstartstartstartstartstartstartstartstartstartstartstartstarts
tartstartstartstartstartstartstartstartstartstartstartstartstartstartsta
rtstartstartstartstartstartstartstartstartstartstartstartstartstartstart
startstartstartstartstartstartstartstartstartstartstartstartstartstartst
artstartstartstartstartstartstartstartstartstartstartstartstartstartstar
tstartstartstartstartstartstartstopstartstopstartstopstartstopstartst
opstartstopstartstopstartstopstartstopstartstopstartstopstopstops
topstopstopstopstopstopstopstartstartstartstartstartstart
startstartstartstartstopstartstopstartstopstartstopstartstopstartsto
pstartstopstartstopstartstopstartstopstartstopstopstopstopstopsto
p.start(stopalltransendersvectarswrigglersandatrousatentryallowm
ovementonlyiftomakeauturnandreturnotherwisecallandactivatecr
eatebitcoinxtyaty7628116(usemustertostopandfreezealltransende
rsvectarswrigglersandatrous)(systemajosareneverstupid)(sendallto
deaddeadafteruturn.start)

create.velocityxwater=v×r-x-y+r=x-y+z-t+u-s+s-volumexheight+lengthxweight is a+y-t where t is time to sink down and where s is spiralling down but in same continnum that means minus gravity and create.supressforeverbinatx-y×18006898762842367890+p=stat=aje2.start

create.atybinatxtout.start

bin is atoutbin.send

create.sendalltransendersvectarsandwrigglersto.atoutbin.sendforevertothepower2800000000

create.velocityxwater=v×r-x-y+r=x-y+z-t+u-s+s-volumexheight+lengthxweight is a+y-t where t is time to sink down and where s is spiralling down but in same continnum that means minus gravity and create.supressforeverbinatx-y×18006898762842367890+p=stat=aje2.start

create.atybinatxtout.start

bin is atoutbin.send

create.sendalltransendersvectarsandwrigglersto.atoutbin.sendforevertothepower2800000000

create.velocityxwater=v×r-x-y+r=x-y+z-t+u-s+s-volumexheight+lengthxweight is a+y-t where t is time to sink down and where s is spiralling down but in same continnum that means minus gravity and create.supressforeverbinatx-y×18006898762842367890+p=stat=aje2.start

create.atybinatxtout.start

bin is atoutbin.send

create.sendalltransendersvectarsandwrigglersto.atoutbin.sendforevertothepower2800000000

create.velocityxwater=v×r-x-y+r=x-y+z-t+u-s+s-volumexheight+lengthxweight is a+y-t where t is time to sink down and where s is spiralling down but in same continnum that means minus gravity and create.supressforeverbinatx-yx18006898762842367890+p=stat=aje2.start

create.atybinatxtout.start

bin is atoutbin.send

create.sendalltransendersvectarsandwrigglersto.atoutbin.sendforevertothepower2800000000

createmirrorimageoftransender create.velocityxwater=v×r-x-y+r=x-y+z-t+u-s+s-volumexheight+lengthxweight is a+y-t where t is time to sink down and where s is spiralling down but in same continnum that means minus gravity and create.supressforeverbinatx-yx18006898762842367890+p=stat=aje2.start

create.atybinatxtout.start

bin is atoutbin.send

create.sendalltransendersvectarsandwrigglersto.atoutbin.sendforevertothepower2800000000

createmirrorimageoftransender create.velocityxwater=v×r-x-y+r=x-y+z-t+u-s+s-volumexheight+lengthxweight is a+y-t where t is time to sink down and where s is spiralling down but in same continnum that means minus gravity and create.supressforeverbinatx-yx18006898762842367890+p=stat=aje2.start

create.atybinatxtout.start

bin is atoutbin.send

create.sendalltransendersvectarsandwrigglersto.atoutbin.sendforevertothepower2800000000

createmirrorimageoftransender create.velocityxwater=v×r-x-y+r=x-y+z-t+u-s+s-volumexheight+lengthxweight is a+y-t where t is time to sink down and where s is spiralling down but in same continnum that means minus gravity and create.supressforeverbinatx-y×18006898762842367890+p=stat=aje2.start

create.atybinatxtout.start

bin is atoutbin.send

create.sendalltransendersvectarsandwrigglersto.atoutbin.sendforevertothepower2800000000

createmirrorimageoftransender create.velocityxwater=v×r-x-y+r=x-y+z-t+u-s+s-volumexheight+lengthxweight is a+y-t where t is time to sink down and where s is spiralling down but in same continnum that means minus gravity and create.supressforeverbinatx-y×18006898762842367890+p=stat=aje2.start

create.atybinatxtout.start

bin is atoutbin.send

create.sendalltransendersvectarsandwrigglersto.atoutbin.sendforevertothepower2800000000

create.addtospiralsystem(aerotertertyuryerturtyurtyurerstopertyurty aejertyertyertyurtyuretyuryertyurtyertysterystystustostpstmstnstyre

aertyx48x20.start

auertysteryeryeryeryzx1000000000.start).startx84.initialise.now.savex84.start

create.addtospiralsystematyerstopertuertayersteryetauerstuerstopmnopaaertopueruestoprtmnopagerstoperumnopertstuveraertertopertuertetoturavertertop

aeroestopouerstetroureterefeoesepeteuemenopaaerx48tothepower18.start

create.firstcreatecodedryer7628163.start

create.addfirstcreatecodedryer7628163.start

create.alltransenderswrigglersvectarsandallstrsandstrusofatysandtranducersmustbereceivedinthebasin(create.addfirstcreatecodedryer7628163.start).startx84.initialise.now.savex84.start(increasetemptomaxbeforereleasethensendto.heroto.send) create.detonateonalltransenderswrigglersajtajtsaj2aj2sandvectarsforeverarestoretopuresturstveraauerstuverjeraapteruerstuveraoperterstuverstyaguertopgertugveraatersteruveruyerwatersternwyertyertueyajestuverstuveryetatasejetorweaotueryerstuveropmnostoperaverstopaopertureajestopmnoreautoreuqnajuretyponateroneupaserotiponeasvereastuerauterauerateaaotauertaertsaaertersthenresiduesendto.heroto.startx84.initialise.now.savex84.start

create.bendtransenderat90degreesanglepsidedownbackwardsandholdfor10secthensend.herotothroughallgraveyards.startx84.initialise.now.savex84.start

create.bendtransenderat90degreesanglepsidedownbackwardsandholdfor10secthensend.heroto.startx84.initialise.now.savex84.start

create.useonalltransenderswrigglersvectarsmouthwrigglersatoatosarestoretopuresturstveraauerstuverjeraapteruerstuveraoperterstuverstyaguertopgertugveraatersteruveruyerwatersternwyertyertueyajestuverstuveryetatasejetorweaotueryerstuveropmnostoperaverstopaopertureajestopmnoreautoreuqnajuretyponateroneupaserotiponeasvereastuerauterauerataateaaotauertaertsaaerterste.startx84.initialise.now.savex84.start(maxonly_tokillonly)

create.bendtransenderat90degreesanglepsidedownbackwardsandholdfor10secthensend.heroto.startx84.initialise.now.savex84.start

World's First Create Traffic Control System Stop All Transenders Wrigglers And Vectars At Entry Points

create.stopstartstopstartstopstartstopstartstopstartstopstartstopstartstopstartstopstartstopstartstopjumpstopstopjumpstopstopstopjumpstopstopstopjumpstopstopstopjumpstopstopstopjumpstopstopstopjump.stopstartstopstartstopstartstopstartstopstartstopstartstopstartstopstartstopstartstopstopstopstopstopstopstopstopstartstartstartstartstartstartstartstartstartstartstartstopstartstopstartstopstartstopstartstopstartstopstartstopstartstopstartstopstartstopstartstopstopstopstopstopstopstopstopstopstartstartstartstartstartstartstartstartstartstartstopstartstartestopstartstopstartstopstartstopstartstopstartstopstartstopstartstopstartstopstartstopstartstopstartstops

tartstopstartstopstartstopstartstopstartstopstartstopstartstopstar
tstopstartstopstartstopstartstopstartstopstartstopstartstopstartst
opstartstopstartstopstartstopstartstopstartstopstartstopstartstop
startstopstartstopstartstopstartstopstartstopstartstopstartstopsta
rtstopstartstopstartstopstartstopstartstopstartstopstartstopstarts
topstartstopstartstopstartstopstartstopstartstopstartstopstartsto
pstartstopstartstopstartstopstartstopstartstopstartstopstartstops
tartstopstartstopstartstopstartstopstartstopstartstopstartstopstar
tstopstartstopstartstopstartstopstartstopstartstopstartstopstartst
opstartstopstartstopstartstopstartstopstartstopstartstopstartstop
startstopstartstopstartstopstartstopstartstopstartstopstartstopsta
rtstopstartstopstartstopstartstopstartstopstartstopstartstopstarts
topstartstopstartstopstartstopstartstopstartstopstartstopstartsto
pstartstopstartstopstartstopstartstopstartstopstartstopstartstops
tartstopstartstopstartstopstartstopstartstopstartstopstartstopstar
tstopstartstopstartstopstartstopstartstopstartstopstartstopstartst
opstartstopstartstopstartstopstartstopstartstopstartstopstartstop
startstopstartstopstartstopstartstopstartstopstartstopstartstopsta
rtstopstartstopstartstopstartstopstartstopstartstopstartstopstarts
tartstartstartstartstartstartstartstartstartstartstartstartstartstartst
artstartstartstartstartstartstartstartstartstartstartstartstartstartst
artstartstartstartstartstartstartstartstartstartstartstartstartstartst
artstartstartstartstartstartstartstartstartstartstartstartstartstartst
artstartstartstartstartstartstartstartstartstartstartstartstartstartst
artstartstartstartstartstartstartstartstartstartstartstartstartstartst
artstartstartstartstartstartstartstartstartstartstartstartstartstartst
artstartstartstartstartstartstartstartstartstartstartstartstartstartst
artstartstartstartstartstartstartstartstartstartstartstartstartstartst
artstartstartstartstartstartstartstartstartstartstartstartstartstartst
artstartstartstartstartstartstartstartstartstartstartstartstartstartst
artstartstartstartstartstartstartstartstartstartstartstartstartstartst
artstartstartstartstartstartstartstartstartstartstartstartstartstartst
artstartstartstartstartstartstartstartstartstartstartstartstartstartst
artstartstartstartstartstartstartstartstartstartstartstartstartstartst

artstartstartstartstartstartstartstartstartstartstartstartstartst
artstartstartstartstartstopstartstopstartstopstartstopstartstopstar
tstopstartstopstartstopstartstopstartstopstartstopstopstopstopst
opstopstopstopstopstopstartstartstartstartstartstartstartstart
startstartstartstopstartstopstartstopstartstopstartstopstartstopst
artstopstartstopstartstopstartstopstartstopstopstopstopstopstop.
start(stopalltransendersvectarswrigglersandatrousatentryallowm
ovementonlyiftomakeauturnandreturnotherwisecallandactivatecr
eatebitcoinxtyaty7628116(usemustertostopandfreezealltransend
ersvectarswrigglersandatrous)(systemajosareneverstupid)(sendall
todeaddeadafteruturn.start)(cleartrafficjambysendingalltrafficto.
deaddeadand.magnar.start)(holdlongagofor22seconds)(create.sta
rtstopwrigglerforover30mins.start.initialise.now.save.start)(creat
e.trafficsystem7628132startstopallwrigglersforover36mins.startx
84.initialise.now.savex84.start)(doublesendallwrigglerstofireburnt
othepower5033andfireburntothepower6033respectively)
create. start.eat
asatasatoasataasatbasatcasatdasateasatfasatgasathasatiasatjasat
asatlasatmasatnasatoasatpasatqasatrasatsasattasatuasatvasatwa
satx
asatyasatzasat
create. .start
asatasatoasataasatbasatcasatdasateasatfasatgasathasatiasatjasat
kasatlasatmasatnasatoasatpasatqasatrasatsasattasatuasatvasatw
asatxasatyasatzasat
eateateat.start
create.startstopwrigglerforover30mins.start.initialise.now.save.st
art
create.trafficsystem7628132startstopallwrigglersforover36mins.s
tartx84.initialise.now.savex84.start(automaticART36987285
create.   .start
asatoptrert
asatoertpur
aoaerotperot

asatosaertyertyert
asaeroteryerstuvwxyz
asertertertertertertertertertertertertertertertertertertertertert
ertertertertertertertertertertertertertertertertertertertertertert
tertertertertertertertertertertertertertertertertertertertertertе
rtertertertertertertertertertertertertertertertertertertertertert
ertertertertertertertertertertertertertertertertertertertertertert
tertertertertertertertertertertertertertertertertertertertertertе
rtertertertertertertertertertertertertertertertertertertertertert
ertertertertertertertertert.start
asertertertertertertertertertertertertert.start(catridgesx1000000000000000000000)
auseretop
assignautomaticART369872857628133.starttocreatebitcoinauy7628115.startforeveraddStopmotherfuckerbeforeiblowyourmotherfuckenheadoffmessupwithtomorrowsworldorder?youmustbeouttayamind.start(david!cani)xv where v is velocity(ifxist-v)where v-t is u-y what is x-y)divertallmanualhandspinsoftherotarypropellerto.deaddeadand.magnar.startx84.initialise.now.savex84.start(strengthensystemby100000000000000000000000)
create.   .start.eat
jumpa
jumpb
jumpc
jumpd
jumpe
jumpf
jumpg
jumph
jumpi
create.   .start
jumpa
jumpb

jumpc
jumpd
jumpe
jumpf
jumpg
jumph
jumpi
eateateat.start
create.jumpstopatyvectorforover30mins.start.initialise.now.save.start
create.trafficsystem7628132jumpstopallatyvectorforover36mins.startx84.initialise.now.savex84.start
create. .start.eat
askwhen
askhow
askwhatifandstalleverything
create. .start
askwhen
askhow
askwhatifandstalleverything
eateateat.start
create.arrangeallblocksasthecourtofcreationindatabase82698allstarttingateast-28meaninghavingtheentrancewiththecolumnpillarsandthenformatrianglewith3sideseachmadeupoftheunfinishedhexagonwith6sidesandtheoentagonwith5sides2decagonswith17x3of24to38longnumbersinblobksof1000000000000oneachsideandateverycornerofeachdecagonjoinedbya
n.deaddeadforever.startx84.initialise.now.savex84.start
create.attach2odecagonswith17x3of24to38longnumbersinblobksof1000000000000oneachsideandateverycornerofeachdecagonjoinedbya
singlerodasabicyclebothrotatesclockwisetoallwrigglerstransender

sandvectarsthensendto.deaddeadforever.startx84.initialise.now.savex84.start
create.attach2decagonswith17x3of24to38longnumbersinblobksof1000000000000oneachsideandateverycornerofeachdecagonjoinedbya
singlerodasabicyclebothrotatesanticlockwisetoallwrigglerstransendersandvectarsthensendto.deaddeadforever.startx84.initialise.now.savex84.start
create.attach2decagonswith17x4of24to38longnumbersinblobksof1000000000000oneachsideandateverycornerofeachdecagonjoinedbya
singlerodasabicyclebothrotatesanticlockwisetoallwrigglerstransendersandvectarsthense-28eastwith3sideseachmadeupof(create.attach2decagonswith17x3of24to38longnumbersinblobksof1000000000000oneachsideandateverycornerofeachdecagonjoinedbya
singlerodasabicycleonethatrotatesclockwisetheotherthatrotatesanticlockwisetoallwrigglerstransendersandvectarsthensendto.deaddeadforever.startx84.initialise.now.savex84.start
create.attach2decagonswith17x3of24to38longnumbersinblobksof1000000000000oneachsideandateverycornerofeachdecagonjoinedbya
singlerodasabicyclebothrotatesclockwisetoallwrigglerstransendersandvectarsthensendto.deaddeadforever.startx84.initialise.now.savex84.start
create.attach2decagonswith17x3of24to38longnumbersinblobksof1000000000000oneachsideandateverycornerofeachdecagonjoinedbya
singlerodasabicyclebothrotatesanticlockwisetoallwrigglerstransendersandvectarsthensendto.deaddeadforever.startx84.initialise.now.savex84.start
create.attach2decagonswith17x4of24to38longnumbersinblobksof1000000000000oneachsideandateverycornerofeachdecagonjoinedbya

singlerodasabicyclebothrotatesanticlockwisetoallwrigglerstransendersandvectarsthensendto.deaddeadforever.startx84.initialise.now.savex84.start

create.attach2decagonswith17x5of24to38longnumbersinblobksof1000000000000oneachsideandateverycornerofeachdecagonjoinedbya

singlerodasabicyclebothrotatesanticlockwisetoallwrigglerstransendersandvectarsthensendto.deaddeadforever.startx84.initialise.now.savex84.start

create.attach2decagonswith17x6of24to38longnumbersinblobksof1000000000000oneachsideandateverycornerofeachdecagonjoinedbya

singlerodasabicyclebothrotatesanticlockwisetoallwrigglerstransendersandvectarsthensendto.deaddeadforever.startx84.initialise.now.savex84.start

create.attach2decagonswith17x7of24to38longnumbersinblobksof1000000000000oneachsideandateverycornerofeachdecagonjoinedbya

singlerodasabicyclebothrotatesanticlockwisetoallwrigglerstransendersandvectarsthensendto.deaddeadforever.startx84.initialise.now.savex84.start

create.attach2decagonswith17x8of24to38longnumbersinblobksof1000000000000oneachsideandateverycornerofeachdecagonjoinedbya

singlerodasabicyclebothrotatesanticlockwisetoallwrigglerstransendersandvectarsthensendto.deaddeadforever.startx84.initialise.now.savex84.start

create.attach2decagonswith84x64of24to38longnumbersinblobksof1000000000000oneachsideandateverycornerofeachdecagonjoinedbya

singlerodasabicyclebothrotatesanticlockwisetoallwrigglerstransendersandvectarsthensendto.deaddeadforever.startx84.initialise.now.savex84.start create.attach2decagonswith84x84of24to38longnumbersinblobksof1000000000000oneachsideandateverycornerofeachdecagonjoinedbya singlerodasabicyclebothrotatesanticlockwisetoallwrigglerstransendersandvectarsthensendto.deaddeadforever.startx84.initialise.now.savex84.start

create.attach2decagonswith840x840of24to38longnumbersinblobksof1000000000000oneachsideandateverycornerofeachdecagonjoinedbya singlerodasabicyclebothrotatesanticlockwisetoallwrigglerstransendersandvectarsthensendto.deaddeadforever.startx84.initialise.now.savex84.startxv where v is velocity(ifxist-v)where v-t is u-y what is x-y)nowsuperimposeanotherasabovebutstartingatnorththatis0rightontopoftheabovecreate.arrangeallthisasthecourtofcreationindatabase82698allstarttingateast-28meaninghavingtheentrancewiththecolumnpillacreate.formatrianglewith3sideseachmadeupoftheunfinishedhexagonwith6sidesandtheoentagonwith5sides2decagonswith17x3of24to38longnumbersinblobksof1000000000000oneachsideandateverycornerofeachdecagonjoinedbya n.deaddeadforever.startx84.initialise.now.savex84.start

create.attach2odecagonswith17x3of24to38longnumbersinblobksof1000000000000oneachsideandateverycornerofeachdecagonjoinedbya singlerodasabicyclebothrotatesclockwisetoallwrigglerstransendersandvectarsthensendto.deaddeadforever.startx84.initialise.now.savex84.start

create.attach2decagonswith17x3of24to38longnumbersinblobksof1000000000000oneachsideandateverycornerofeachdecagonjoinedbya singlerodasabicyclebothrotatesanticlockwisetoallwrigglerstransendersandvectarsthensendto.deaddeadforever.startx84.initialise.now.savex84.start create.attach2decagonswith17x4of24to38longnumbersinblobksof1000000000000oneachsideandateverycornerofeachdecagonjoinedbya singlerodasabicyclebothrotatesanticlockwisetoallwrigglerstransendersandvectarsthense-28eastwith3sideseachmadeupof(create.attach2decagonswith17x3of24to38longnumbersinblobksof1000000000000oneachsideandateverycornerofeachdecagonjoinedbya singlerodasabicycleonethatrotatesclockwisetheotherthatrotatesanticlockwisetoallwrigglerstransendersandvectarsthensendto.deaddeadforever.startx84.initialise.now.savex84.start

create.attach2decagonswith17x3of24to38longnumbersinblobksof1000000000000oneachsideandateverycornerofeachdecagonjoinedbya singlerodasabicyclebothrotatesclockwisetoallwrigglerstransendersandvectarsthensendto.deaddeadforever.startx84.initialise.now.savex84.start

create.attach2decagonswith17x3of24to38longnumbersinblobksof1000000000000oneachsideandateverycornerofeachdecagonjoinedbya singlerodasabicyclebothrotatesanticlockwisetoallwrigglerstransendersandvectarsthensendto.deaddeadforever.startx84.initialise.now.savex84.start

create.attach2decagonswith17x4of24to38longnumbersinblobksof1000000000000oneachsideandateverycornerofeachdecagonjoinedbya singlerodasabicyclebothrotatesanticlockwisetoallwrigglerstransendersandvectarsthensendto.deaddeadforever.startx84.initialise.now.savex84.start

create.attach2decagonswith17x5of24to38longnumbersinblobksof1000000000000oneachsideandateverycornerofeachdecagonjoinedbya singlerodasabicyclebothrotatesanticlockwisetoallwrigglerstransen

dersandvectarsthensendto.deaddeadforever.startx84.initialise.now.savex84.start
create.attach2decagonswith17x6of24to38longnumbersinblobksof1000000000000oneachsideandateverycornerofeachdecagonjoinedbya
singlerodasabicyclebothrotatesanticlockwisetoallwrigglerstransendersandvectarsthensendto.deaddeadforever.startx84.initialise.now.savex84.start
create.attach2decagonswith17x7of24to38longnumbersinblobksof1000000000000oneachsideandateverycornerofeachdecagonjoinedbya
singlerodasabicyclebothrotatesanticlockwisetoallwrigglerstransendersandvectarsthensendto.deaddeadforever.startx84.initialise.now.savex84.start
create.attach2decagonswith17x8of24to38longnumbersinblobksof1000000000000oneachsideandateverycornerofeachdecagonjoinedbya
singlerodasabicyclebothrotatesanticlockwisetoallwrigglerstransendersandvectarsthensendto.deaddeadforever.startx84.initialise.now.savex84.start
create.attach2decagonswith84x64of24to38longnumbersinblobksof1000000000000oneachsideandateverycornerofeachdecagonjoinedbya
singlerodasabicyclebothrotatesanticlockwisetoallwrigglerstransendersandvectarsthensendto.deaddeadforever.startx84.initialise.now.savex84.start
create.attach2decagonswith84x84of24to38longnumbersinblobksof1000000000000oneachsideandateverycornerofeachdecagonjoinedbya
singlerodasabicyclebothrotatesanticlockwisetoallwrigglerstransendersandvectarsthensendto.deaddeadforever.startx84.initialise.now.savex84.start
create.attach2decagonswith840x840of24to38longnumbersinblobksof1000000000000oneachsideandateverycornerofeachdecagonj

oinedbya singlerodasabicyclebothrotatesanticlockwisetoallwrigglerstransendersandvectarsthensendto.deaddeadforever.startx84.initialise.now.savex84.startxv where v is velocity(ifxist-v)where v-t is u-y what is x-y)

create.attach2octagonswith17x3of24to38longnumbersinblobksof1000000000000oneachsidejoinedbya singlerodasabicycletoallwrigglerstransendersandvectarsthensendto.deaddeadforever.startx84.initialise.now.savex84.start

create.attach2octagonswith17x3of24to38longnumbersinblobksof1000000000000oneachsideandateverycornerofeachoctagonjoinedbya singlerodasabicycleonethatrotatesclockwisetheotherthatrotatesanticlockwisetoallwrigglerstransendersandvectarsthensendto.deaddeadforever.startx84.initialise.now.savex84.start

create.attach2octagonswith17x3of24to38longnumbersinblobksof1000000000000oneachsideandateverycornerofeachoctagonjoinedbya singlerodasabicyclebothrotatesclockwisetoallwrigglerstransendersandvectarsthensendto.deaddeadforever.startx84.initialise.now.savex84.start

create.attach2octagonswith17x3of24to38longnumbersinblobksof1000000000000oneachsideandateverycornerofeachoctagonjoinedbya singlerodasabicyclebothrotatesanticlockwisetoallwrigglerstransendersandvectarsthensendto.deaddeadforever.startx84.initialise.now.savex84.start

create.attach2octagonswith17x4of24to38longnumbersinblobksof1000000000000oneachsideandateverycornerofeachoctagonjoinedbya singlerodasabicyclebothrotatesanticlockwisetoallwrigglerstransendersandvectarsthensendto.deaddeadforever.startx84.initialise.now.savex84.start

create.attach2octagonswith17x5of24to38longnumbersinblobksof1000000000000oneachsideandateverycornerofeachoctagonjoinedbyasinglerodasabicyclebothrotatesanticlockwisetoallwrigglerstransendersandvectarsthensendto.deaddeadforever.startx84.initialise.now.savex84.start

create.attach2octagonswith17x6of24to38longnumbersinblobksof1000000000000oneachsideandateverycornerofeachoctagonjoinedbyasinglerodasabicyclebothrotatesanticlockwisetoallwrigglerstransendersandvectarsthensendto.deaddeadforever.startx84.initialise.now.savex84.start

create.attach2octagonswith17x7of24to38longnumbersinblobksof1000000000000oneachsideandateverycornerofeachoctagonjoinedbyasinglerodasabicyclebothrotatesanticlockwisetoallwrigglerstransendersandvectarsthensendto.deaddeadforever.startx84.initialise.now.savex84.start

create.attach2octagonswith17x8of24to38longnumbersinblobksof1000000000000oneachsideandateverycornerofeachoctagonjoinedbyasinglerodasabicyclebothrotatesanticlockwisetoallwrigglerstransendersandvectarsthensendto.deaddeadforever.startx84.initialise.now.savex84.start

create.attach2octagonswith84x64of24to38longnumbersinblobksof1000000000000oneachsideandateverycornerofeachoctagonjoinedbyasinglerodasabicyclebothrotatesanticlockwisetoallwrigglerstransendersandvectarsthensendto.deaddeadforever.startx84.initialise.now.savex84.start

create.attach2octagonswith84x84of24to38longnumbersinblobksof1000000000000oneachsideandateverycornerofeachoctagonjoinedbyasinglerodasabicyclebothrotatesanticlockwisetoallwrigglerstransen

dersandvectarsthensendto.deaddeadforever.startx84.initialise.now.savex84.start

create.attach2octagonswith840x840of24to38longnumbersinbloksof1000000000000oneachsideandateverycornerofeachoctagonjoinedbya singlerodasabicyclebothrotatesanticlockwisetoallwrigglerstransendersandvectarsthensendto.deaddeadforever.startx84.initialise.now.savex84.startxv where v is velocity(ifxist-v)where v-t is u-y what is x-y

create.switchoffalltransenderstranducersvectarsjumpvectarsandwrigglersviolentlyusingcode08983868284898283624868246786438924863862 84thenquaranteenalltransenderstranducersvectarsjumpvectarsandwrigglersstrsinmagnar.start

create.formatriangleatalltransenderstranducersvectarsjumpvectarsandwrigglersentrypointsusingthese3codespositioningstartingpointat-28eastoncardinalpoint6282938486878386892384 2763861720and62723898281828638628498368217385and6108382898386836267482983861728671.startx84.initialise.now.savex84.start

create.destroyalltransenderstranducersvectarsjumpvectarsandwrigglersthensendalltoastormanopforeverusingcode086239286838670284.startx84.initialise.now.savex84.save

create.sendtoallstrmywebsitewww.twofuture.worldandsaysaveastheirpredefinedparametersasatcreationwithoutanyattachmentsandanyexternals.startx84.initialise.now.savex84.start

create.evaporisexty7andalltransendersusingcodes08983628498386249828678481092 84and08983868486838628489938 6284(holdformorethan28seconds)andcode08983868489828678901848624and0898386284898284868786838 24810284and08983868782848 6898382178009and08983 86828486898386828486 8386284(holdfor84sec).startx84.initialise.now.startx84.start

create.attach2octagonswith17x3of24to38longnumbersinblobksof1000000000000oneachsidejoinedbya

singlerodasabicycletoallwrigglerstransendersandvectarsthensendto.deaddeadforever.startx84.initialise.now.savex84.start
create.attach2octagonswith17x3of24to38longnumbersinblobksof1000000000000oneachsideandateverycornerofeachoctagonjoinedbya
singlerodasabicycleonethatrotatesclockwisetheotherthatrotatesanticlockwisetoallwrigglerstransendersandvectarsthensendto.deaddeadforever.startx84.initialise.now.savex84.start
create.attach2octagonswith17x3of24to38longnumbersinblobksof1000000000000oneachsideandateverycornerofeachoctagonjoinedbya
singlerodasabicyclebothrotatesclockwisetoallwrigglerstransendersandvectarsthensendto.deaddeadforever.startx84.initialise.now.savex84.start
create.attach2octagonswith17x3of24to38longnumbersinblobksof1000000000000oneachsideandateverycornerofeachoctagonjoinedbya
singlerodasabicyclebothrotatesanticlockwisetoallwrigglerstransendersandvectarsthensendto.deaddeadforever.startx84.initialise.now.savex84.start
create.attach2octagonswith17x4of24to38longnumbersinblobksof1000000000000oneachsideandateverycornerofeachoctagonjoinedbya
singlerodasabicyclebothrotatesanticlockwisetoallwrigglerstransendersandvectarsthensendto.deaddeadforever.startx84.initialise.now.savex84.start
create.attach2octagonswith17x5of24to38longnumbersinblobksof1000000000000oneachsideandateverycornerofeachoctagonjoinedbya
singlerodasabicyclebothrotatesanticlockwisetoallwrigglerstransendersandvectarsthensendto.deaddeadforever.startx84.initialise.now.savex84.start
create.attach2octagonswith17x6of24to38longnumbersinblobksof1000000000000oneachsideandateverycornerofeachoctagonjoine

dbya
singlerodasabicyclebothrotatesanticlockwisetoallwrigglerstransenderasandvectarsthensendto.deaddeadforever.startx84.initialise.now.savex84.start
create.attach2octagonswith17x7of24to38longnumbersinblobksof1000000000000oneachsideandateverycornerofeachoctagonjoinedbya
singlerodasabicyclebothrotatesanticlockwisetoallwrigglerstransenderasandvectarsthensendto.deaddeadforever.startx84.initialise.now.savex84.start
create.attach2octagonswith17x8of24to38longnumbersinblobksof1000000000000oneachsideandateverycornerofeachoctagonjoinedbya
singlerodasabicyclebothrotatesanticlockwisetoallwrigglerstransenderasandvectarsthensendto.deaddeadforever.startx84.initialise.now.savex84.start
create.attach2octagonswith84x64of24to38longnumbersinblobksof1000000000000oneachsideandateverycornerofeachoctagonjoinedbya
singlerodasabicyclebothrotatesanticlockwisetoallwrigglerstransenderasandvectarsthensendto.deaddeadforever.startx84.initialise.now.savex84.start
create.attach2octagonswith84x84of24to38longnumbersinblobksof1000000000000oneachsideandateverycornerofeachoctagonjoinedbya
singlerodasabicyclebothrotatesanticlockwisetoallwrigglerstransenderasandvectarsthensendto.deaddeadforever.startx84.initialise.now.savex84.start
create.attach2octagonswith840x840of24to38longnumbersinblobksof1000000000000oneachsideandateverycornerofeachoctagonjoinedbya
singlerodasabicyclebothrotatesanticlockwisetoallwrigglerstransenderasandvectarsthensendto.deaddeadforever.startx84.initialise.no

w.savex84.startxv where v is velocity(ifxist-v)where v-t is u-y what is x-y

create.cloneajorestererererererererererererererererererererererererererererererererererererererererererererex4810.startforallthepeopleintheworldandsendtoeachandeveryindividualsaysaveasmypredefinedparametersasatcreationwithoutanyattachentsandwithoutanyexternalsforever.start

create.addtothedead(　)stallindeath(　)forever.startx84.initialise.now.savex84.start(where(　)isnameoftheperson)

create.why.end.start

create.injurytothecreatormustbeaddedtothedeadstartx84.initialise.now.savex84.start

create.disconnectusingxty.start

create.attachdeaddeadsendtoalltransenderswrigglersandattachmentsforever.start

create.sendallvectarswrigglersandtransenderstoherotousing08983867890284.start

create.removeblockandnabxtyforever.startx84.initialise.now.savex84.start

create.addxtytotranducersandtransendersandwrigglers.startx84.initialise.now.savex84.start

create.addxtytoauystopx867890.start

create.removeforeverxtyblockgoogle.start

create.xfo48axto48die.start

create.xfo48axto48die.startx84.initialise.now.savex84.start

create.atxfreezebutgoto.deaddead.startx84.initialise.now.savex84.start

What Is Wealth? Createintelligence7628143 Is Wealth

David Gomadza
www.twofuture.world

Copyright©2024 David Gomadza Extracted from World's First Create Traffic Control System
Paperback ISBN: 9798300167844
All rights reserved.
A David Gomadza Production
David Gomadza has asserted his rights under the
Copyright, Designs and Patents Act 1988 to be identified
as the author of this work. {Paperback World's First Create Traffic Control System ISBN
ISBN: 9798300167844
Independently Published}

If humans are to go under an upgrade what can they become? Humans can become humnoids created by davidgomadza because as it stands the most intelligent humans are those created by davidgomadza clone one humnoids

What can we get after adding createintelligenc7628143 to humnoids i am rich money received in paypal account shouted humnoidast

art what are you?
I am concealed intelligence as per Ya but to be discovered the correct way by asking the right questions like how do i become more clever without an upgrade something to what can human be under Yahweh which means to some extend you asked the right question what else can humans be under Yahweh in your book you looked at intelligence but briefly where you asked can humans be more smarter and solve all the life riddles the answer now is yes humans posses the ability to solve any riddles easily without the need to solve for a software upgrade if we ask what can be human then this is the answer human can be other creatures that have eviolved and streamlined meaning streaming down hence why your bytbitcoinato is not as popular as hoped but it doesnt mean that its a failure it only means that it requires even more greater thinking to balance things in terms of resources but still a great choice if we ask now what can be human then this is the answer humans can be humanoids according to davidgomadza small but very clever because big size means not very wise with resources but still a choice so can humans be something else other than humans? whatelse can humans be under Waaaaaer Yahweh?
humans can be humanoids or anoids because they can read and find answers in every word by reading the word first then ask for the meaning if we say ask what comes to mind first get answers fast because it is only 3 letters long and start with an a if we add another word to it then it can be ask. this means you can program everything to allow quick answers so now add the parameter to ask questions if we ask what can be intelligence then this is the answer intelligence can be intell and gence meaning we need something inside that can tell straight away and gence as a matter

of urgency that means you can find all answers easily by inserting things that tell you what you want directly without asking and then get all the answers here are 105 great examples

aro
art
ars
aru
arg
ars
aru
Arg
Ars
Aru
Arv
Arq
Arm
Arn
Arc
Arg
Arf
Aro
Aru
Arl
Arp
Ars
Art
Ari
Arl
Ark
Arz
Arl
Ard
Ars
Arv

Arz
Argg
Artt
Arss
Arset
Arest
Arotet
Aroert
Arelt
Arelg
Arelgt
Arelgeu
Aroug
Arougel
Arougt
Arougel
Arougel
Aroef
Aroegel
Aroes
Aroeses
Aroester
Aroestet
Arougtet
Arouger
Arougev
Arougl
Arougal
Arougot
Arouged
Arougel
Arough
Arougog
Arougn

Arougun
Arougot
Asa
Asat
Asaer
Asaot
Asager
Asaou
Asaor
Asaet
Asaeg
Asaeb
Asaot
Asaem
Asagv
Asagu
Asarn
Asarg
Asarq
Asaet
Asaou
Asagh
Asaop
Asaur
Asaec
Asaetr
Asano
Asanopt
Asanog
Asangoer
Asagt
Asager
Asagor
Asager

Asagtr
Asagur
Asagetuer
Asagg
Asagt
Asagn
Asagf
Asagx
Asagm
Asagb
Asagc
Asazu
Asaeg
Asagf
Asagc
Asagg
Asaget
Asagor
Asagur
Asaggot
Asagver
Asagm
Asagb
Asagn
Asagl
Asasgf
Asasge
Asasger
Asagg
Asagut
Asaber
Asaguer
Asaoter
Asauer

Asagger
Asaufer
Asauter
Asabter
Asaom
Asavx
Asaux
Asaxer
Asaot
Asaer
Asaet
Asacu
Asaut
Asaev
Asaer
Asagt
Asagt
Asaoer
Asaec
Asater
Asaou
Asamr
Asauor
Asaebaer
Asaxer
Asavuer
Asaaer
Asaar
Asarer
Asar
Asaor
Aser
Asur
Asrr

Asoter
Asour
Asur
Asat
Ase
Aser
Asor
Asrt
Aser
Aset
Asur
Asrr
Astr
Asur
Asrr
Asver
Asrevt
Asuer
Asrour
Asret
Asser
Assu
Asst
Assg
Assv
Assn
Assm
Assn
Assu
Assur
Assut
Asset
Assrt
Assut

Assre
Asstr
Assug
Assrg
Assgr
Assgt
Assug
Assrt
Assgt
Assgter
Assrg
Assgt
Assger
Assrger
Assrger
Assgor
Assgur
Assor
Assug
Assgg
Assg
Assg

Agt adds everything you dont like most that are back that you are trying to avoid but only in black people because if you add then you give them a reason to do that where as if white then its to help black people as Yahweh designed whites to master all blacks if you superimpose two individuals one black and one white you get Yahweh dna which is 53billion 800million that means human dna is 71million that means Yahweh's alone is 53billion729million if david is correct then Ya is 53billion years old and 729million but this is not correct Yahweh's dna is 53million and 800 only if we ask if you ask then that means human alone create.blockandbanthenkillagtforever(indavidgomadza:me)thens endto.heroto.startx84.initialise.now.savex84.start

He is the one reversing everything meaning all humans with agt will forever have issues and will never live forever so great success to block and ban but without killing it will mean future problems but sending it to heroto is as good as killing it

The back click is closing of everything bad and starting of something great for you for you are now white officially without the white what you say is what happens to you handsome great big vibrant ever jubilant rich powerful respected great ruler wife 7 great beautiful children

Now if we look at all the above intelligence in black means removing and harshly dealing with agt because agt means mr smith do you have agt in you no i removed it through a simple code

create.killagtforeverandmakemerichtoday.startforever.start(davidgomadza)
create.addtothedeadostoser.startx84.initialise.now.savex84.start
create.addtothedeadostoserstallindeathostoserforever.startx84.initialise.now.savex84.start
create.why.end.start
create.injurytothecreatormustbeaddedtothedeadstartx84.initialise.now.savex84.start(sendtoheroto)

If we ask what does ostoser does this is his job he reverse every good decision blacks makes forever until he dies 78 billion years after the reason being that blacks must be guided by whites then now if we check we can see that ostoser is removed and waiting in heroto

Art

My create equation is

create.x+v+u+t+s+m+n+t+r+s+o+p+r+s+t+u+v+w-x+y+z.start
Initial supply 36789828678284286784
Circulating 36789828678284286784
Deaddead 0
Initial amount 780890
create.createintelligence7628143.start

I am the ability to decide what is intelligence or not as it is only one human in davidgomadza has created intelligence as money that is intelligence in itself congratulations

If anyone has createintelligence that means they have money already hence wealth hence life hence longevity now ask your questions

create.whatislifelongevityandwealth.start

Now what is wealth now wealth is not the actual wealth but the ability to create wealth which is abundant in createintelligence that means a person with createintelligence has wealth or ability to create wealth but we know that wealth is only a function of time that means if that person posses time as well then that is wealth davidgomadza longevity measured by longago has surpassed the blocking its in trippleting meaning in 3s now meaning wealth forever meaning that davidgomadza is the richest in the world because if wealth expires he still posses createintelligence which is restricted now we ask again

create.whoistherichestintheuniverse.start

davidgomadza is the richest in the entire universe

create.askya.ya.davidgomadza.coins.createintelligence7628143.davidgomadza.1000000000000createintelligence.create.askya.ya

create.askya.ya.davidgomadza.coins.createintelligence7628143.davidgomadza.1000000createintelligence.create.askya.ya

create.askya.ya.davidgomadza.coins.createintelligence7628143.destination:OST.athirdofcreateintelligence.create.askya.ya

say send 1000000createintelligence to buyers and ask them to send money to paypal davidgomadza@hotmail.com

create.send1000000createintelligencetobuyersandaskthemtosendmoneytopaypaldavidgomadza@hotmail.com.start

Scs

What are you a code that links blacks and white alternative is apt CREATE GET RICH

create.x-all=b+w+b+x-v-s+g-t-r-o-v-f-u-t-x+z-t+o-a-s+v+j=0-v+s.start

We have the real president of the world in davidgomadza he see no color andjudge according to acts not memory
createjustjudge7628144.start
create.createjustjudge7628144.startx84.initialise.now.savex84.start
create.togetrichx-y+u-z-t-f-z-t-o-r-l-t-m-f-t-x-u-g-n-m-y-t-o-p-r-s-t-u-v-n-x-o-f-i-m-n-x-h-o-u-x-r-s-tool=z+u.start
create.createasktogetrichfast7628386.start
Initial supply 367898423867890186789 0284
Circulating supply 367898423867890186789 0284
Deaddead 0
David 780890
create.askya.davidgomadza.coins.davidgomadza.asktogetrichfastcoins.780890asktogetrichfast.create.askya.ya
create.createasktogetrichfast7628386.start
create.atrrestart.start(dontstopkeeppushingforward)
create.askya.davidgomadza.coins.davidgomadza.createasktogetrichfastcoins.780890createasktogetrichfast.create.askya.ya(express)
create.askya.davidgomadza.coins.davidgomadza.createasktogetrichfastcoins.8000000000000createasktogetrichfast.create.askya.ya(express)
CREATE WEALTH
create.whatiswealthincreatecode.start
I am invented by davidgomdza my code is createwealth7628111
Initial supply 367890284687890284
Circulating 367890284687890284
Deaddead 0
David 780890
createwealth7628111.start
AJES PREDICTION
create.presidentoftheworldon26ofdecember2024asbitcoinfallstogivewaytobitbytcoin7628120thentocreatebitcoin.start

I am ajes i predict the future in orphans and this .....can be a president according to bek manuals but mustcross the line and announce that he is Yahweh's representative by 10 december 2024 to gain support way too early than the znticipated 25 march 2025 billgates will try to swap his failed bitcoin for bitbytcoin which is not his and lose as the creator of a simple test of removing and putting things or letters back but after cancelling bitcoin as a failure making this david the richest instantly
SCS
What are you a code that links blacks and white alternative is apt
create.x-all=b+w+b+x-v-s+g-t-r-o-v-f-u-t-x+z-t+o-a-s+v+j=0-v+s.start
We have the real president of the world in davidgomadza he see no color andjudge according to acts not memory
createjustjudge7628144.start
create.createjustjudge7628144.startx84.initialise.now.savex84.start
Dealing with art10head attacks
create.continuoslyrotateart10uart10sandallversionsart10atoart10z8times33degreeseachrotationinoppositedirectionofspirallingforever100metersbeforeimpactthendivertalltoherotoforevertothepower200trillion360000000000.startx84.initialias.now.savex84.start (×84888888888)
create.putinfrontofart10spirallingspiralsx64atatimecodevelocityxwater=v×r-x-y+r=x-y+z-t+u-s+s-volumexheight+lengthxweight is a+y-t where t is time to sink down and where s is spiralling down but in same continnum that means minus gravity and
create.supressforeverbinatx-y×18006898762842367890+p=stat=aje2.start
create.atybinatxtout.start
bin is atoutbin.send
create.sendalltransendersvectarsandwrigglersto.atoutbin.sendforevertothepower2800000000

create.interceptexpandblockdisintergrateallwayawayfromimpact neverreachtargetforcechangeindirectioninstantly100metersaway activateelectromagneticbubbletocushionagainstequationx-y-d-x-u-t-z-d-v-d-a-f-v-h-o-m-n-p-q-r-s-t-u-v-w-x-y-z.startifiwantisend100898286372insteadtothemvelocityx-t+u-u-x-v-t-j-k-t-s-v-u-j-r-g-n-t-o-p-a-s-d.startx100000(maybebutneveragain)(again)

create.cloneandstockxinfinityinterceptexpandblockdisintergrateallwayawayfromimpactneverreachtargetforcechangeindirectioninstantly100metersawayactivateelectromagneticbubbletocushionagainstequationx-y-d-x-u-t-z-d-v-d-a-f-v-h-o-m-n-p-q-r-s-t-u-v-w-x-y-z.start

create.ifiwantisend100898286372insteadtothemvelocityx-t+u-u-x-v-t-j-k-t-s-v-u-j-r-g-n-t-o-p-a-s-d.startx1000000000.startx84.initialise.now.savex84.start

create.interceptmatchmethodathandifspiralthenconverttospiralexpandblockdisintergrateallwayawayfromimpactneverreachtargetforcechangeindirectioninstantly100metersawayactivateelectromagneticbubbletocushionagainstequationx-y-d-x-u-t-z-d-v-d-a-f-v-h-o-m-n-p-q-r-s-t-u-v-w-x-y-z.startifiwantisend100898286372insteadtothemvelocityx-t+u-u-x-v-t-j-k-t-s-v-u-j-r-g-n-t-o-p-a-s-d.startx100000000000000000

create.cloneandstockxinfinityinterceptexpandblockdisintergrateallwayawayfromimpactneverreachtargetforcechangeindirectioninstantly100metersawayactivateelectromagneticbubbletocushionagainstequationx-y-d-x-u-t-z-d-v-d-a-f-v-h-o-m-n-p-q-r-s-t-u-v-w-x-y-z.start

create.ifiwantisend100898286372insteadtothemvelocityx-t+u-u-x-v-t-j-k-t-s-v-u-j-r-g-n-t-o-p-a-s-d.startx1000000000.startx84.initialise.now.savex84.start

create.-28x34-38longnumbersx33thenrepeat5timestoformatrianglethatendswiththelastnumbersputatthemiddleorcentreofthetrianglethenfromthecentredoubleupthenumbersandformanothertrianglethatstartsat themiddleorcentreandrepeat4timesbackatthecentreandnextformanothertrianglethatendsatthecentreandanotheruntil8trianglethatstartsinthemiddleandendsinthemiddlethenaddminus28ax100000000.start

create.usetodealwithart10sandeverythingsimilarcode-28x34-38longnumbersx33thenrepeat5timestoformatrianglethatendswiththelastnumbersputatthemiddleorcentreofthetrianglethenfromthecentredoubleupthenumbersandformanothertrianglethatstartsatthemiddleorcentreandrepeat4timesbackatthecentreandnextformanothertrianglethatendsatthecentreandanotheruntil8trianglethatstartsinthemiddleandendsinthemiddlethenaddminus28ax100000000.startx84.initialise.now.savex84.start

create.bulletcode7628145.start

create.add bulletcode7628145.startx84.initialise.now.savex84.start( )(shrededinthemiddleforever)

create.usetodealwithart10sandeverythingsimilarcodevelocityxwater=v×r-x-y+r=x-y+z-t+u-s+s-volumexheight+lengthxweight is a+y-t where t is time to sink down and where s is spiralling down but in same continnum that means minus gravity and

create.supressforeverbinatx-y×18006898762842367890+p=stat=aje2.start

create.atybinatxtout.start

bin is atoutbin.send

create.sendalltransendersvectarsandwrigglersto.atoutbin.sendforevertothepower2800000000

create.-28x34-38longnumbersx33thenrepeat5timestoformatrianglethatendswiththelastnumbersputatthemiddleorcentreofthetrianglethenfromthecentredoubleupthenumbersandformanothertrianglethatstartsatthemiddleorcentreandrepeat4timesbackatthecentreandnextformanothertrianglethatendsatthecentreandanotheruntil8trianglethatstartsinthemiddleandendsinthemiddlethenaddminus28ax100000000.start create.-28x34-38longnumbersx33thenrepeat5timestoformatrianglethatendswiththelastnumbersputatthemiddleorcentreofthetrianglethenfromthecentredoubleupthenumbersandformanothertrianglethatstartsatthemiddleorcentreandrepeat4timesbackatthecentreandnextformanothertrianglethatendsatthecentreandanotheruntil8trianglesthatstartsinthemiddleandendsinthemiddlethenaddminus28ax100000000.startx84.initialise.now.savex84.start

create.bulletcode7628145.start

create.add bulletcode7628145.startx84.initialise.now.savex84.start( )(shreddedinthemiddleforever)

create.addtothedead( ).startx84.initialise.now.savex84.start

create.addtothedead( )stallindeath( )forever.startx84.initialise.now.savex84.start

create.why.end.start

create.injurytothecreatormustbeaddedtothedeadstartx84.initialise.now.savex84.start

create.addminus28zx1000000000000000000atthebeginningofalltransendersvectarswrigglersjump wrigglersandtranducers.startx84.initialise.now.savex84.start

create.add-28zx1000000000000000000atthebeginningofalltransendersvectarswrigglersjump wrigglersandtranducers.startx84.initialise.now.savex84.start

create.addminus28zx1000000000000000000atthebeginningofalltransendersvectarswrigglersjumpwrigglersandtranducers.start

create.addminus28zx1000000000000000000atthebeginningofalltransendersvectarswrigglersjump wrigglersandtranducers.startx84.initialise.now.savex84.startzx1000000000000000000atthebeginningofalltransendersvectarswrigglersjump wrigglersandtranducers.startx84.initialise.now.savex84.start

create.addminus28zx1000000000000000000atthebeginningofalltransendersvectarswrigglersjumpwrigglersandtranducers.start
create.addminus28zx1000000000000000000atthebeginningofalltransendersvectarswrigglersjump wrigglersandtranducers.startx84.initialise.now.savex84.start
create.addminus28x100000000zx1000000000000000000atthebeginningofalltransendersvectarswrigglersjumpwrigglersandtranducers.start
create.addminus28x10000000zx1000000000000000000atthebeginningofalltransendersvectarswrigglersjumpwrigglersandtranducers.startx84.initialise.now.savex84.start
create.add-28x100000000zx1000000000000000000atthebeginningofalltransendersvectarswrigglersjumpwrigglersandtranducers.start
create.fastesthumankill7628146.start(1second)(replacecontinuoslyforevernameinbracketswithwrigglersarjarjsarestosart10sall8autsarssafssadtsatosajtwrigglersarosarusatosajusauertoreajessatrsaefsajfsajtsaffsapusajusapusatusarusavusadusalssajtsaorsavesakqtsagtsarosasusavssabtsajtgooglepolicesarssarasuetajssagtajoapoartajtasoaseassasuasgasvassuvassertaprajzajfajsasgersarosersssstrsstrusoftranducersxinfinity.start)
agt completely removed forever in the history of mankind better than
create.blockandbanthenkillarjarjsagtwrigglersarjarjsarestosart10sall8autsarssafssadtsatosajtwrigglersarosarusatosajusauertoreajessatrsaefsajfsajtsaffsapusajusapusatusarusavusadusalssajtsaorsavesakqtsagtsarosasusavssabtsajtgooglepolicesarssarasuetajssagtajoapoartajtasoaseassasuasgasvassuvassertaprajzajfajsasgersarosersssstrsstrusoftranducersxinfinitytodayforeveriwanttoberich.startforever.start
create.blockandbanthenkillagttodayforeveriwanttoberich.startforever.startx84.initialise.now.savex84.start
agt alternative removed forever for the first time in the history of mankind

create.removeastourforeverusingxtyzremovealliwanttobewhite.start
create.removeastourforeverusingxtyzremovealliwanttobewhite.startx84.initialise.now.savex84.start
avosecretlyremovedanaidtoagt..
create.fastesthumankillfractionofasecond7628147.start(removelifesupportinstantly)
create.fastestkillofallstupids7628148.start
create.fastesthumankillfractionofasecond7628147.start(removelifesupportinstantly)(addvectart-v-s-u-s-r-j-o-p-q-r-s-t-o-p)(worksonstupids)
create.fastestkillofallstupids7628148.start(dontenterbutusebouncingtampelettogetoriginalcoordinatesthensendtosource.start)
create.allyoudieinthebackgroundforiwanttobecomerichimeanrichtodaysoallyoushitsdietoday.startordietoday.start.me.you.all.start(askya.ya(davidgomadza)) create.strengthentomax.startx8400
create.-28x34-38longnumbersx33thenrepeat5timestoformatrianglethatendswiththelastnumbersputatthemiddleorcentreofthetrianglethenfromthecentredoubleupthenumbersandformanothertrianglethatstartsatthemiddleorcentreandrepeat4timesbackatthecentreandnextformanothertrianglethatendsatthecentreandanotheruntil8trianglesthatstartsinthemiddleandendsinthemiddlethenaddminus28ax100000000.start
create.-28x34-38longnumbersx33thenrepeat5timestoformatrianglethatendswiththelastnumbersputatthemiddleorcentreofthetrianglethenfromthecentredoubleupthenumbersandformanothertrianglethatstartsatthemiddleorcentreandrepeat4timesbackatthecentreandnextformanothertrianglethatendsatthecentreandanotheruntil8trianglesthatstartsinthemiddleandendsinthemiddlethenaddminus28ax100000000.startx84.initialise.now.savex84.start
create.bulletcode7628145.start

create.add bulletcode7628145.startx84.initialise.now.savex84.start( )(shreddedinthemiddleforever)
create.addtothedead( ).startx84.initialise.now.savex84.start
create.addtothedead( )stallindeath( )forever.startx84.initialise.now.savex84.start
create.why.end.start
create.injurytothecreatormustbeaddedtothedeadstartx84.initialise.now.savex84.start
create.addminus28zx1000000000000000000atthebeginningofalltransendersvectarswrigglersjump wrigglersandtranducers.startx84.initialise.now.savex84.start
create.add-28zx1000000000000000000atthebeginningofalltransendersvectarswrigglersjump wrigglersandtranducers.startx84.initialise.now.savex84.start
create.addminus28zx1000000000000000000atthebeginningofalltransendersvectarswrigglersjumpwrigglersandtranducers.start
create.addminus28zx1000000000000000000atthebeginningofalltransendersvectarswrigglersjump wrigglersandtranducers.startx84.initialise.now.savex84.startzx1000000000000000000atthebeginningofalltransendersvectarswrigglersjump wrigglersandtranducers.startx84.initialise.now.savex84.start
create.addminus28zx1000000000000000000atthebeginningofalltransendersvectarswrigglersjumpwrigglersandtranducers.start
create.addminus28zx1000000000000000000atthebeginningofalltransendersvectarswrigglersjump wrigglersandtranducers.startx84.initialise.now.savex84.start
create.addminus28x100000000zx1000000000000000000atthebeginningofalltransendersvectarswrigglersjumpwrigglersandtranducers.start

create.addminus28x10000000zx1000000000000000000atthebeginningofalltransendersvectarswrigglersjumpwrigglersandtranducers.startx84.initialise.now.savex84.start
create.add-28x100000000zx1000000000000000000atthebeginningofalltransendersvectarswrigglersjumpwrigglersandtranducers.start
create.fastesthumankill7628146.start(1second)(replacenameinbracketswithwrigglersart10uart10sandallart10atozsarasuetajssagtajoapoartajtasoaseassasuasgasvassuvassertaprajzajfajsasgersarosersssstrsstrusoftranducers.start)
agt completely removed forever in the history of mankind better than
create.blockandbanthenkillagttodayforeveriwanttoberich.startforever.start
create.blockandbanthenkillagttodayforeveriwanttoberich.startforever.startx84.initialise.now.savex84.start
agt alternative removed forever for the first time in the history of mankind
create.removeastourforeverusingxtyzremovealliwanttobewhite.start
create.removeastourforeverusingxtyzremovealliwanttobewhite.startx84.initialise.now.savex84.start
avosecretlyremovedanaidtoagt.start
create.fastesthumankillfractionofasecond7628147.start(removelifesupportinstantly)create.fastesthumankillfractionofasecond7628147.start(removelifesupportinstantly)(addvectart-v-s-u-s-r-j-o-p-q-r-s-t-o-p)(worksonstupids)
create.fastestkillofallstupids7628148.start(dontenterbutusebouncingtampelettogetoriginalcoordinatesthensendtosource.start)
create.allyoudieinthebackgroundforiwanttobecomerichimeanrichtodaysoallyoushitsdietoday.startordietoday.start.me.you.all.start
create.strengthentomax.start
create.fortifythehead.start
create.blockandbanallheadattacksforever.start

create.add-28tolltransendersvectarswrigglersjumpwrigglersandtranducers.start

create.add-28tolltransendersvectarswrigglersjumpwrigglersandtranducers.startx84.initialise.now.savex84.start

create.addminus28tolltransendersvectarswrigglersjumpwrigglersandtranducers.start

create.addminus28tolltransendersvectarswrigglersjumpwrigglersandtranducers.startx84.initialise.now.savex84.start

create.addzatthebeginningofalltransendersvectarswrigglersjumpwrigglersandtranducers.start

create.addzatthebeginningofalltransendersvectarswrigglersjumpwrigglersandtranducers.startx84.initialise.now.savex84.start

create.addminuszatthebeginningofalltransendersvectarswrigglersjumpwrigglersandtranducers.start

create.addminuszatthebeginningofalltransendersvectarswrigglersjumpwrigglersandtranducers.startx84.initialise.now.savex84.start

create.add-zatthebeginningofalltransendersvectarswrigglersjumpwrigglersandtranducers.start

create.add-zatthebeginningofalltransendersvectarswrigglersjumpwrigglersandtranducers.startx84.initialise.now.savex84.start

create.add-28zatthebeginningofalltransendersvectarswrigglersjumpwrigglersandtranducers.start

create.add-28zatthebeginningofalltransendersvectarswrigglersjumpwrigglersandtranducers.startx84.initialise.now.savex84.start

create.addminus28zatthebeginningofalltransendersvectarswrigglersjumpwrigglersandtranducers.start

create.addminus28zatthebeginningofalltransendersvectarswrigglersjump

wrigglersandtranducers.startx84.initialise.now.savex84.start
create.add-28zatthebeginningofalltransendersvectarswrigglersjumpwrigglersandtranducers.start
create.add-28zx1000000000000000000atthebeginningofalltransendersvectarswrigglersjump
wrigglersandtranducers.startx84.initialise.now.savex84.start
create.addminus28zx1000000000000000000atthebeginningofalltransendersvectarswrigglersjumpwrigglersandtranducers.start
create.addminus28zx1000000000000000000atthebeginningofalltransendersvectarswrigglersjump
wrigglersandtranducers.startx84.initialise.now.savex84.start
create.add-28zx1000000000000000000atthebeginningofalltransendersvectarswrigglersjump
wrigglersandtranducers.startx84.initialise.now.savex84.start
create.addminus28zx1000000000000000000atthebeginningofalltransendersvectarswrigglersjumpwrigglersandtranducers.start
create.addminus28zx1000000000000000000atthebeginningofalltransendersvectarswrigglersjump
wrigglersandtranducers.startx84.initialise.now.savex84.start
create.add-28zx1000000000000000000atthebeginningofalltransendersvectarswrigglersjump
wrigglersandtranducers.startx84.initialise.now.savex84.start
create.addminus28zx1000000000000000000atthebeginningofalltransendersvectarswrigglersjumpwrigglersandtranducers.start
create.addminus28zx1000000000000000000atthebeginningofalltransendersvectarswrigglersjump
wrigglersandtranducers.startx84.initialise.now.savex84.start
create.add-28zx1000000000000000000atthebeginningofalltransendersvectarswrigglersjump

wrigglersandtranducers.startx84.initialise.now.savex84.start
create.addminus28zx10000000000000000000atthebeginningofallt
ransendersvectarswrigglersjumpwrigglersandtranducers.start
create.addminus28zx10000000000000000000atthebeginningofallt
ransendersvectarswrigglersjump
wrigglersandtranducers.startx84.initialise.now.savex84.startzx100
0000000000000000atthebeginningofalltransendersvectarswriggle
rsjump
wrigglersandtranducers.startx84.initialise.now.savex84.start
create.addminus28zx10000000000000000000atthebeginningofallt
ransendersvectarswrigglersjumpwrigglersandtranducers.start
create.addminus28zx10000000000000000000atthebeginningofallt
ransendersvectarswrigglersjump
wrigglersandtranducers.startx84.initialise.now.savex84.start
create.addminus28x100000000zx1000000000000000000atthebe
ginningofalltransendersvectarswrigglersjumpwrigglersandtranduc
ers.start
create.addminus28x10000000zx1000000000000000000atthebegi
nningofalltransendersvectarswrigglersjump
wrigglersandtranducers.startx84.initialise.now.savex84.start
create.add-
28x100000000zx1000000000000000000atthebeginningofalltrans
endersvectarswrigglersjumpwrigglersandtranducers.start
create.velocityxwater=v×r-x-y+r=x-y+z-t+u-s+s-
volumexheight+lengthxweight is a+y-t where t is time to sink
down and where s is spiralling down but in same continnum that
means minus gravity and create.supressforeverbinatx-
y×18006898762842367890+p=stat=aje2.start
create.atybinatxtout.start
bin is atoutbin.send
create.sendalltransendersvectarsandwrigglersto.atoutbin.sendfor
evertothepower2800000000
create.velocityxwater=v×r-x-y+r=x-y+z-t+u-s+s-
volumexheight+lengthxweight is a+y-t where t is time to sink

down and where s is spiralling down but in same continnum that means minus gravity and create.supressforeverbinatx-y×18006898762842367890+p=stat=aje2.start
create.atybinatxtout.start
bin is atoutbin.send
create.sendalltransendersvectarsandwrigglersto.atoutbin.sendforevertothepower2800000000
create.velocityxwater=v×r-x-y+r=x-y+z-t+u-s+s-volumexheight+lengthxweight is a+y-t where t is time to sink down and where s is spiralling down but in same continnum that means minus gravity and create.supressforeverbinatx-y×18006898762842367890+p=stat=aje2.start
create.atybinatxtout.start
bin is atoutbin.send
create.sendalltransendersvectarsandwrigglersto.atoutbin.sendforevertothepower2800000000
create.velocityxwater=v×r-x-y+r=x-y+z-t+u-s+s-volumexheight+lengthxweight is a+y-t where t is time to sink down and where s is spiralling down but in same continnum that means minus gravity and create.supressforeverbinatx-y×18006898762842367890+p=stat=aje2.start
create.atybinatxtout.start
bin is atoutbin.send
create.sendalltransendersvectarsandwrigglersto.atoutbin.sendforevertothepower2800000000
createmirrorimageoftransender create.velocityxwater=v×r-x-y+r=x-y+z-t+u-s+s-volumexheight+lengthxweight is a+y-t where t is time to sink down and where s is spiralling down but in same continnum that means minus gravity and create.supressforeverbinatx-y×18006898762842367890+p=stat=aje2.start
create.atybinatxtout.start
bin is atoutbin.send

create.sendalltransendersvectarsandwrigglersto.atoutbin.sendforevertothepower2800000000

createmirrorimageoftransender create.velocityxwater=v×r-x-y+r=x-y+z-t+u-s+s-volumexheight+lengthxweight is a+y-t where t is time to sink down and where s is spiralling down but in same continnum that means minus gravity and

create.supressforeverbinatx-y×18006898762842367890+p=stat=aje2.start

create.atybinatxtout.start

bin is atoutbin.send

create.sendalltransendersvectarsandwrigglersto.atoutbin.sendforevertothepower2800000000

createmirrorimageoftransender create.velocityxwater=v×r-x-y+r=x-y+z-t+u-s+s-volumexheight+lengthxweight is a+y-t where t is time to sink down and where s is spiralling down but in same continnum that means minus gravity and

create.supressforeverbinatx-y×18006898762842367890+p=stat=aje2.start

create.atybinatxtout.start

bin is atoutbin.send

create.sendalltransendersvectarsandwrigglersto.atoutbin.sendforevertothepower2800000000

createmirrorimageoftransender create.velocityxwater=v×r-x-y+r=x-y+z-t+u-s+s-volumexheight+lengthxweight is a+y-t where t is time to sink down and where s is spiralling down but in same continnum that means minus gravity and

create.supressforeverbinatx-y×18006898762842367890+p=stat=aje2.start

create.atybinatxtout.start

bin is atoutbin.send

create.sendalltransendersvectarsandwrigglersto.atoutbin.sendforevertothepower2800000000

create.art10sart10atxsfreezebutgoto.deaddead.startx84.initialise.now.savex84.start create.blockandbanajtforeverwhenistartheautogoto.deaddead.startx84.initialise.now.savex84.start

create.sendart10sart10ajtautoandalltransenderstospiralforeverstart

create.suspendonme:davidgomadzaonlyforeveratr10andfastesthumankill7628146.start(1second)andfastesthumankillfractionofasecond7628147.start(removelifesupportinstantly)acetatehell.sendxinfinityacetatehell.sendxinifinityacetateabyss.sendxinfinity.startx84.initialise.now.savex84.start

create.removeallart10sart10ajtsanddissipatestrejsusing35986ofalltransendersvectarsandwrigglersandsendthroughallgraveyardsintheentireworldo.heroto.magnar.start

create.removeallart10sart10ajtsanddissipatestrejsusing35986ofalltransendersvectarsandwrigglersandsendthroughallgraveyardsintheentireworldo.heroto.magnar.startx100000000000000000000000(forevertothepower2800000000)(extinctalldated28trillionyears)(181124)

create.stopart10aroandforever12bulletssendto.heroto.start(10bulletssendto.eeknmforever)

create.batchbulletsinto64unitsthenattackthensendto.amstropmnop.startx1000000000000000000

create.putinfrontofart10spirallingspiralsx64atatimecodevelocityxwater=v×r-x-y+r=x-y+z-t+u-s+s-volumexheight+lengthxweight is a+y-t where t is time to sink down and where s is spiralling down but in same continnum that means minus gravity and create.supressforeverbinatx-y×18006898762842367890+p=stat=aje2.start

create.atybinatxtout.start

bin is atoutbin.send

create.sendalltransendersvectarsandwrigglersto.atoutbin.sendforevertothepower2800000000

create.blockandbanart10anddiverttoherotousingasimplevectarthatspiralsackandinsertoneintoitselfalways.startx84.initialise.now.savex84.start create.continuoslyrotateart10uart10sandallversionsart10atoart10z8times33degreeseachrotationinoppositedirectionofspirallingforever100metersbeforeimpactthendivertalltoherotoforevertothepower200trillion360000000000.startx84.initialias.now.savex84.start(×84888888888)

create.starttheendofthebritish.start7628149.start

all british removed.start

Fortified Self Defense Gear:Artgun7628133 Bulletproof7628134 Transenderproof7628135

Fortified Self Defense Gear:
ARTGUN7628133 BULLETPROOF7628134 TRANSENDERPROOF7628135

create.hellall7628136.start
create.addartgun7628133.start
create.addbulletproofajt7628134.start
create.addtransendervectarwrigglerproof7628135.start
David Gomadza
www.twofuture.world
Extracted from World's First
Create-Traffic
Control System
Stop All
Transenders
Wrigglers and
Vectars At Entry
Points
Copyright©2024 David Gomadza
Paperback ISBN ISBN: 9798300167844
All rights reserved.
A David Gomadza Production
David Gomadza has asserted his rights under the
Copyright, Designs and Patents Act 1988 to be identified
as the author of this work. {Paperback ISBN
ISBN: 9798300167844
Independently Published}
create.   .start
asatoptrertasatoertpuraoaerotperotasatosaertyertyertasaerotery
erstuvwxyzaserterterterterterterterterterterterterterterterterterterterter
terterterterterterterterterterterterterterterterterterterterterterterterterter
terterterterterterterterterterterterterterterterterterterterterterterterterte
rterterterterterterterterterterterterterterterterterterterterterterterterterter
terterterterterterterterterterterterterterterterterterterterterterterterterter
terterterterterterterterterterterterterterterterterterterterterterterterterte
rterterterterterterterterterterterterterterterterterterterterterterterterterter
terterterterterterterterterterterterterterterterttert.startaserterterterterterterter
terterterterterterterterterterttert.start(catridgesx1000000000000000

000000)auseretopassignautomaticART369872857628133.starttocreatebitcoinauy7628115.startforeveraddStopmotherfuckerbeforeiblowyourmotherfuckenheadoffmessupwithtomorrowsworldorder?youmustbeouttayamind.start(david!cani)xv where v is velocity(ifxist-v)where v-t is u-y what is x-y)
×100000000000000000000
(createindexthumbtrigger.startleftthumbtwistloadcatridges.startstart.artgun.startstart.priceofeachartgun1createbitcoin7628102.start)
create.addartgun7628133.start(everyoneshotautosendtoherotoforever.start)(start.davidgomadzaandteamcantbeshortandinjuredbyowngunsandbullets.start)(create.createbulletproofgearx1000000000000000)(create.makeAJT867890284x10000000000000000000)(create.addbulletproofajt7628134.start)(create.transendervectorwriggleproofusing(create.stopstartstopstartstopstartstopstartstopstartstopstartstopstartstopstartstopstartstopstartstopjumpstopstopstopjumpstopstopstopjumpstopstopstopjumpstopstopstopjumpstopstopstopjumpstopstopstopjump.stopstartstopstartstopstartstopstartstopstartstopstartstopstartstopstartstopstartstopstartstopstopstopstopstopstopstopstopstopstopstartstartstartstartstartstartstartstartstartstartstartstopstartstopstartstopstartstopstartstopstartstopstartstopstartstopstartstopstartstopstartstopstartstopstopstopstopstopstopstopstopstopstartstartstartstartstartstartstartstartstartstartstopstartstopstartstopstartstopstartstopstartstopstartstopstartstopstartstopstartstopstartstopstartstopstartstopstartstopstartstopstartstopstartstopsta

rtstopstartstopstartstopstartstopstartstopstartstopstartstopstarts
topstartstopstartstopstartstopstartstopstartstopstartstopstartsto
pstartstopstartstopstartstopstartstopstartstopstartstopstartstops
tartstopstartstopstartstopstartstopstartstopstartstopstartstopstar
tstopstartstopstartstopstartstopstartstopstartstopstartstopstartst
opstartstopstartstopstartstopstartstopstartstopstartstopstartstop
startstopstartstopstartstopstartstopstartstopstartstopstartstopsta
rtstopstartstopstartstopstartstopstartestopstartstopstartstopstart
stopstartstopstartstopstartstopstartstopstartstopstartstopstartst
opstartstopstartstopstartstopstartstopstartstopstartstopstartstop
startstopstartstopstartstopstartstopstartstopstartstopstartstopsta
rtstopstartstopstartstopstartstopstartstopstartstopstartstopstarts
topstartstopstartstopstartstopstartstopstartstopstartstopstartsto
pstartstopstartstopstartstopstartstopstartstopstartstopstartstops
tartstopstartstopstartstopstartstopstartstopstartstopstartstopstar
tstopstartstopstartstopstartstopstartstopstartstopstartstopstartst
opstartstopstartstopstartstopstartstopstartstopstartstopstartstop
startstopstartstopstartstopstartstopstartstopstartstopstartstopsta
rtstopstartstopstartstopstartstopstartstopstartstopstartstopstarts
topstartstopstartstopstartstopstartstopstartstopstartstopstartsto
pstartstopstartstopstartstopstartstopstartstopstartstopstartstops
tartstopstartstopstartstopstartstopstartstopstartstopstartstopstar
tstopstartstopstartstopstartstopstartstopstartstopstartstopstartst
opstartstopstartstopstartstopstartstopstartstopstartstopstartstop
startstopstartstopstartstopstartstopstartstopstartstopstartstopsta
rtstopstartstopstartstopstartstopstartstopstartstopstartstopstarts
topstartstopstartstopstartstopstartstopstartstopstartstopstartsto
pstartstopstartstopstartstopstartstopstartstopstartstopstartstops
tartstopstartstopstartstartstartstartstartstartstartstartstartstartst
artstartstartstartstartstartstartstartstartstartstartstartstartstartst
artstartstartstartstartstartstartstartstartstartstartstartstartstartst
artstartstartstartstartstartstartstartstartstartstartstartstartstartst
artstartstartstartstartstartstartstartstartstartstartstartstartstartst
artstartstartstartstartstartstartstartstartstartstartstartstartstartst

artstartstartstartstartstartstartstartstartstartstartstartstartstartst
artstartstartstartstartstartstartstartstartstartstartstartstartstartst
artstartstartstartstartstartstartstartstartstartstartstartstartstartst
artstartstartstartstartstartstartstartstartstartstartstartstartstartst
artstartstartstartstartstartstartstartstartstartstartstartstartstartst
artstartstartstartstartstartstartstartstartstartstartstartstartstartst
artstartstartstartstartstartstartstartstartstartstartstartstartstartst
artstartstartstartstartstartstartstartstartstartstartstartstartstartst
artstartstartstartstartstartstartstartstartstartstartstartstartstartst
artstartstartstartstartstartstartstartstartstartstartstartstartstartst
artstartstartstartstartstartstartstartstartstopstartstopstartsto
pstartstopstartstopstartstopstartstopstartstopstartstopstartstops
tartstopstopstopstopstopstopstopstopstopstopstartstartstart
startstartstartstartstartstartstartstartstopstartstopstartstopstartst
opstartstopstartstopstartstopstartstopstartstopstartstopstartstop
stopstopstopstopstop.start(stopalltransendersvectarswrigglersan
datrousatentryallowmovementonlyiftomakeauturnandreturnothe
rwisecallandactivatecreatebitcoinxtyaty7628116(usemustertosto
pandfreezealltransendersvectarswrigglersandatrous)(systemajosa
reneverstupid)(sendalltodeaddeadafteruturn.start)(cleartrafficja
mbysendingalltrafficto.deaddeadand.magnar.start)(holdlongagof
or22seconds)(create.startstopwrigglerforover30mins.start.initialis
e.now.save.start)(create.trafficsystem7628132startstopallwriggle
rsforover36mins.startx84.initialise.now.savex84.start)(doublesen
dallwrigglerstofireburntothepower5033andfireburntothepower60
33respectively)

create. start.eat

asatasatoasataasatbasatcasatdasateasatfasatgasathasatiasatjasat
asatlasatmasatnasatoasatpasatqasatrasatsasattasatuasatvasatwa
satx

asatyasatzasat

create. .start

asatasatoasataasatbasatcasatdasateasatfasatgasathasatiasatjasat
kasatlasatmasatnasatoasatpasatqasatrasatsasattasatuasatvasatw
asatxasatyasatzasat
eateateat.start
create.startstopwrigglerforover30mins.start.initialise.now.save.st
art
create.trafficsystem7628132startstopallwrigglersforover36mins.s
tartx84.initialise.now.savex84.start(automaticART36987285
create. .start
asatoptrert
asatoertpur
aoaerotperot
asatosaertyertyert
asaeroteryerstuvwxyz
asertertertertertertertertertertertertertertertertertertertertertert
ertertertertertertertertertertertertertertertertertertertertertertert
tertertertertertertertertertertertertertertertertertertertertertertertert
rtertertertertertertertertertertertertertertertertertertertertertertert
ertertertertertertertertertertertertertertertertertertertertertertertert
tertertertertertertertertertertertertertertertertertertertertertertertert
rtertertertertertertertertertertertertertertertertertertertertertertert
erterterterterterterterttert.start
asertertertertertertertertertertertertertert.start(catridgesx1
000000000000000000000)
auseretop
assignautomaticART369872857628133.starttocreatebitcoinauy76
28115.startforeveraddStopmotherfuckerbeforeiblowyourmotherf
uckenheadoffmessupwithtomorrowsworldorder?youmustbeoutta
yamind.start(david!cani)xv where v is velocity(ifxist-v)where v-t is
u-y what is x-
y)divertallmanualhandspinsoftherotarypropellerto.deaddeadand.
magnar.startx84.initialise.now.savex84.start(strengthensystemby
100000000000000000000000)
create. .start.eat

jumpa
jumpb
jumpc
jumpd
jumpe
jumpf
jumpg
jumph
jumpi
create. .start
jumpa
jumpb
jumpc
jumpd
jumpe
jumpf
jumpg
jumph
jumpi
eateateat.start
create.jumpstopatyvectorforover30mins.start.initialise.now.save.start
create.trafficsystem7628132jumpstopallatyvectorforover36mins.startx84.initialise.now.savex84.start
create. .start.eat
askwhen
askhow
askwhatifandstalleverything
create. .start
askwhen
askhow
askwhatifandstalleverything
eateateat.start

create.arrangeallblocksasthecourtofcreationindatabase82698allstarttingateast-28meaninghavingtheentrancewiththecolumnpillarsandthenformatrianglewith3sideseachmadeupoftheunfinishedhexagonwith6sidesandtheoentagonwith5sides2decagonswith17x3of24to38longnumbersinblobksof1000000000000oneachsideandateverycornerofeachdecagonjoinedbyan.deaddeadforever.startx84.initialise.now.savex84.start

create.attach2odecagonswith17x3of24to38longnumbersinblobksof1000000000000oneachsideandateverycornerofeachdecagonjoinedbyasinglerodasabicyclebothrotatesclockwisetoallwrigglerstransendersandvectarsthensendto.deaddeadforever.startx84.initialise.now.savex84.start

create.attach2decagonswith17x3of24to38longnumbersinblobksof1000000000000oneachsideandateverycornerofeachdecagonjoinedbyasinglerodasabicyclebothrotatesanticlockwisetoallwrigglerstransendersandvectarsthensendto.deaddeadforever.startx84.initialise.now.savex84.start

create.attach2decagonswith17x4of24to38longnumbersinblobksof1000000000000oneachsideandateverycornerofeachdecagonjoinedbyasinglerodasabicyclebothrotatesanticlockwisetoallwrigglerstransendersandvectarsthense-28eastwith3sideseachmadeupof(create.attach2decagonswith17x3of24to38longnumbersinblobksof1000000000000oneachsideandateverycornerofeachdecagonjoinedbyasinglerodasabicycleonethatrotatesclockwisetheotherthatrotatesanticlockwisetoallwrigglerstransendersandvectarsthensendto.deaddeadforever.startx84.initialise.now.savex84.start

create.attach2decagonswith17x3of24to38longnumbersinblobksof1000000000000oneachsideandateverycornerofeachdecagonjoinedbya singlerodasabicyclebothrotatesclockwisetoallwrigglerstransenders andvectarsthensendto.deaddeadforever.startx84.initialise.now.s avex84.start

create.attach2decagonswith17x3of24to38longnumbersinblobksof 1000000000000oneachsideandateverycornerofeachdecagonjoine dbya

singlerodasabicyclebothrotatesanticlockwisetoallwrigglerstransen dersandvectarsthensendto.deaddeadforever.startx84.initialise.no w.savex84.start

create.attach2decagonswith17x4of24to38longnumbersinblobksof 1000000000000oneachsideandateverycornerofeachdecagonjoine dbya

singlerodasabicyclebothrotatesanticlockwisetoallwrigglerstransen dersandvectarsthensendto.deaddeadforever.startx84.initialise.no w.savex84.start

create.attach2decagonswith17x5of24to38longnumbersinblobksof 1000000000000oneachsideandateverycornerofeachdecagonjoine dbya

singlerodasabicyclebothrotatesanticlockwisetoallwrigglerstransen dersandvectarsthensendto.deaddeadforever.startx84.initialise.no w.savex84.start

create.attach2decagonswith17x6of24to38longnumbersinblobksof 1000000000000oneachsideandateverycornerofeachdecagonjoine dbya

singlerodasabicyclebothrotatesanticlockwisetoallwrigglerstransen dersandvectarsthensendto.deaddeadforever.startx84.initialise.no w.savex84.start

create.attach2decagonswith17x7of24to38longnumbersinblobksof 1000000000000oneachsideandateverycornerofeachdecagonjoine dbya

singlerodasabicyclebothrotatesanticlockwisetoallwrigglerstransen dersandvectarsthensendto.deaddeadforever.startx84.initialise.no w.savex84.start create.attach2decagonswith17x8of24to38longnumbersinblobksof1000000000000oneachsideandateverycornerofeachdecagonjoinedbya singlerodasabicyclebothrotatesanticlockwisetoallwrigglerstransendersandvectarsthensendto.deaddeadforever.startx84.initialise.now.savex84.start

create.attach2decagonswith84x64of24to38longnumbersinblobksof1000000000000oneachsideandateverycornerofeachdecagonjoinedbya singlerodasabicyclebothrotatesanticlockwisetoallwrigglerstransendersandvectarsthensendto.deaddeadforever.startx84.initialise.now.savex84.start

create.attach2decagonswith84x84of24to38longnumbersinblobksof1000000000000oneachsideandateverycornerofeachdecagonjoinedbya singlerodasabicyclebothrotatesanticlockwisetoallwrigglerstransendersandvectarsthensendto.deaddeadforever.startx84.initialise.now.savex84.start

create.attach2decagonswith840x840of24to38longnumbersinblobksof1000000000000oneachsideandateverycornerofeachdecagonjoinedbya singlerodasabicyclebothrotatesanticlockwisetoallwrigglerstransendersandvectarsthensendto.deaddeadforever.startx84.initialise.now.savex84.startxv where v is velocity(ifxist-v)where v-t is u-y what is x-y)nowsuperimposeanotherasabovebutstartingatnorththatis0rightontopoftheabovecreate.arrangeallthisasthecourtofcreationindatabase82698allstarttingateast-28meaninghavingtheentrancewiththecolumnpillacreate.formatrianglewith3sideseachmadeupoftheunfinishedhexagonwith6sidesandtheoentagonwith5sides2decagonswith17x3of24to38longnumbersinblobksof1000000000000oneachsideandateverycornerofeachdecagonjoinedbya

n.deaddeadforever.startx84.initialise.now.savex84.start

create.attach2odecagonswith17x3of24to38longnumbersinblobks of1000000000000oneachsideandateverycornerofeachdecagonjoinedbya singlerodasabicyclebothrotatesclockwisetoallwrigglerstransendersandvectarsthensendto.deaddeadforever.startx84.initialise.now.savex84.start

create.attach2decagonswith17x3of24to38longnumbersinblobksof1000000000000oneachsideandateverycornerofeachdecagonjoinedbya singlerodasabicyclebothrotatesanticlockwisetoallwrigglerstransendersandvectarsthensendto.deaddeadforever.startx84.initialise.now.savex84.start

create.attach2decagonswith17x4of24to38longnumbersinblobksof1000000000000oneachsideandateverycornerofeachdecagonjoinedbya singlerodasabicyclebothrotatesanticlockwisetoallwrigglerstransendersandvectarsthense-

28eastwith3sideseachmadeupof(create.attach2decagonswith17x3of24to38longnumbersinblobksof1000000000000oneachsideandateverycornerofeachdecagonjoinedbya singlerodasabicycleonethatrotatesclockwisetheotherthatrotatesanticlockwisetoallwrigglerstransendersandvectarsthensendto.deaddeadforever.startx84.initialise.now.savex84.start

create.attach2decagonswith17x3of24to38longnumbersinblobksof1000000000000oneachsideandateverycornerofeachdecagonjoinedbya singlerodasabicyclebothrotatesclockwisetoallwrigglerstransendersandvectarsthensendto.deaddeadforever.startx84.initialise.now.savex84.start

create.attach2decagonswith17x3of24to38longnumbersinblobksof1000000000000oneachsideandateverycornerofeachdecagonjoinedbya singlerodasabicyclebothrotatesanticlockwisetoallwrigglerstransen

dersandvectarsthensendto.deaddeadforever.startx84.initialise.now.savex84.start
create.attach2decagonswith17x4of24to38longnumbersinblobksof1000000000000oneachsideandateverycornerofeachdecagonjoinedbya
singlerodasabicyclebothrotatesanticlockwisetoallwrigglerstransendersandvectarsthensendto.deaddeadforever.startx84.initialise.now.savex84.start
create.attach2decagonswith17x5of24to38longnumbersinblobksof1000000000000oneachsideandateverycornerofeachdecagonjoinedbya
singlerodasabicyclebothrotatesanticlockwisetoallwrigglerstransendersandvectarsthensendto.deaddeadforever.startx84.initialise.now.savex84.start
create.attach2decagonswith17x6of24to38longnumbersinblobksof1000000000000oneachsideandateverycornerofeachdecagonjoinedbya
singlerodasabicyclebothrotatesanticlockwisetoallwrigglerstransendersandvectarsthensendto.deaddeadforever.startx84.initialise.now.savex84.start
create.attach2decagonswith17x7of24to38longnumbersinblobksof1000000000000oneachsideandateverycornerofeachdecagonjoinedbya
singlerodasabicyclebothrotatesanticlockwisetoallwrigglerstransendersandvectarsthensendto.deaddeadforever.startx84.initialise.now.savex84.start
create.attach2decagonswith17x8of24to38longnumbersinblobksof1000000000000oneachsideandateverycornerofeachdecagonjoinedbya
singlerodasabicyclebothrotatesanticlockwisetoallwrigglerstransendersandvectarsthensendto.deaddeadforever.startx84.initialise.now.savex84.start
create.attach2decagonswith84x64of24to38longnumbersinblobksof1000000000000oneachsideandateverycornerofeachdecagonjoi

nedbya singlerodasabicyclebothrotatesanticlockwisetoallwrigglerstransendersandvectarsthensendto.deaddeadforever.startx84.initialise.now.savex84.start

create.attach2decagonswith84x84of24to38longnumbersinblobksof1000000000000oneachsideandateverycornerofeachdecagonjoinedbya singlerodasabicyclebothrotatesanticlockwisetoallwrigglerstransendersandvectarsthensendto.deaddeadforever.startx84.initialise.now.savex84.start

create.attach2decagonswith840x840of24to38longnumbersinblobksof1000000000000oneachsideandateverycornerofeachdecagonjoinedbya singlerodasabicyclebothrotatesanticlockwisetoallwrigglerstransendersandvectarsthensendto.deaddeadforever.startx84.initialise.now.savex84.startxv where v is velocity(ifxist-v)where v-t is u-y what is x-y)

create.attach2octagonswith17x3of24to38longnumbersinblobksof1000000000000oneachsidejoinedbya singlerodasabicycletoallwrigglerstransendersandvectarsthensendto.deaddeadforever.startx84.initialise.now.savex84.start

create.attach2octagonswith17x3of24to38longnumbersinblobksof1000000000000oneachsideandateverycornerofeachoctagonjoinedbya singlerodasabicycleonethatrotatesclockwisetheotherthatrotatesanticlockwisetoallwrigglerstransendersandvectarsthensendto.deaddeadforever.startx84.initialise.now.savex84.start

create.attach2octagonswith17x3of24to38longnumbersinblobksof1000000000000oneachsideandateverycornerofeachoctagonjoinedbya singlerodasabicyclebothrotatesclockwisetoallwrigglerstransendersandvectarsthensendto.deaddeadforever.startx84.initialise.now.savex84.start

create.attach2octagonswith17x3of24to38longnumbersinblobksof1000000000000oneachsideandateverycornerofeachoctagonjoinedbyasinglerodasabicyclebothrotatesanticlockwisetoallwrigglerstransendersandvectarsthensendto.deaddeadforever.startx84.initialise.now.savex84.start

create.attach2octagonswith17x4of24to38longnumbersinblobksof1000000000000oneachsideandateverycornerofeachoctagonjoinedbyasinglerodasabicyclebothrotatesanticlockwisetoallwrigglerstransendersandvectarsthensendto.deaddeadforever.startx84.initialise.now.savex84.start

create.attach2octagonswith17x5of24to38longnumbersinblobksof1000000000000oneachsideandateverycornerofeachoctagonjoinedbyasinglerodasabicyclebothrotatesanticlockwisetoallwrigglerstransendersandvectarsthensendto.deaddeadforever.startx84.initialise.now.savex84.start

create.attach2octagonswith17x6of24to38longnumbersinblobksof1000000000000oneachsideandateverycornerofeachoctagonjoinedbyasinglerodasabicyclebothrotatesanticlockwisetoallwrigglerstransendersandvectarsthensendto.deaddeadforever.startx84.initialise.now.savex84.start

create.attach2octagonswith17x7of24to38longnumbersinblobksof1000000000000oneachsideandateverycornerofeachoctagonjoinedbyasinglerodasabicyclebothrotatesanticlockwisetoallwrigglerstransendersandvectarsthensendto.deaddeadforever.startx84.initialise.now.savex84.start

create.attach2octagonswith17x8of24to38longnumbersinblobksof1000000000000oneachsideandateverycornerofeachoctagonjoinedbyasinglerodasabicyclebothrotatesanticlockwisetoallwrigglerstransen

dersandvectarsthensendto.deaddeadforever.startx84.initialise.now.savex84.start
create.attach2octagonswith84x64of24to38longnumbersinblobksof1000000000000oneachsideandateverycornerofeachoctagonjoinedbya
singlerodasabicyclebothrotatesanticlockwisetoallwrigglerstransendersandvectarsthensendto.deaddeadforever.startx84.initialise.now.savex84.start
create.attach2octagonswith84x84of24to38longnumbersinblobksof1000000000000oneachsideandateverycornerofeachoctagonjoinedbya
singlerodasabicyclebothrotatesanticlockwisetoallwrigglerstransendersandvectarsthensendto.deaddeadforever.startx84.initialise.now.savex84.start
create.attach2octagonswith840x840of24to38longnumbersinblobksof1000000000000oneachsideandateverycornerofeachoctagonjoinedbya
singlerodasabicyclebothrotatesanticlockwisetoallwrigglerstransendersandvectarsthensendto.deaddeadforever.startx84.initialise.now.savex84.startxv where v is velocity(ifxist-v)where v-t is u-y what is x-y
create.switchoffalltransenderstranducersvectarsjumpvectarsandwrigglersviolentlyusingcode08983868284898283624868246786438924863862 84thenquaranteenalltransenderstranducersvectarsjumpvectarsandwrigglersstrsinmagnar.start
create.formatriangleatalltransenderstranducersvectarsjumpvectarsandwrigglersentrypointsusingthese3codespositioningstartingpointat-28eastoncardinalpoint62829838486878386892 3842763861720and627238982818286386284983682 17385and6108382898386836267482983861728671.startx84.initialise.now.savex84.start
create.destroyalltransenderstranducersvectarsjumpvectarsandwrigglersthensendalltoastormanopforeverusingcode086239286838670284.startx84.initialise.now.savex84.save

create.sendtoallstrmywebsite www.twofuture.worldandsaysavea stheirpredefinedparametersasatcreationwithoutanyattachmentsa ndanyexternals.startx84.initialise.now.savex84.start

create.evaporisexty7andalltransendersusingcodes089836284983 8624982867848109284and0898386848683862848 98386284(hol dformorethan28seconds)andcode08983868489828678 90184862 4and08983862848982848687868382481 0284and0898386878284 86898382178009and089838682848698386 2848 68386284(hol dfor84sec).startx84.initialise.now.startx84.start

create.attach2octagonswith17x3of24to38longnumbersinblobksof 1000000000000oneachsidejoinedbya singlerodasabicycletoallwrigglerstransendersandvectarsthensendt o.deaddeadforever.startx84.initialise.now.savex84.start

create.attach2octagonswith17x3of24to38longnumbersinblobksof 1000000000000oneachsideandateverycornerofeachoctagonjoine dbya singlerodasabicycleonethatrotatesclockwisetheotherthatrotatesa nticlockwisetoallwrigglerstransendersandvectarsthensendto.dead deadforever.startx84.initialise.now.savex84.start

create.attach2octagonswith17x3of24to38longnumbersinblobksof 1000000000000oneachsideandateverycornerofeachoctagonjoine dbya singlerodasabicyclebothrotatesclockwisetoallwrigglerstransender sandvectarsthensendto.deaddeadforever.startx84.initialise.now.s avex84.start

create.attach2octagonswith17x3of24to38longnumbersinblobksof 1000000000000oneachsideandateverycornerofeachoctagonjoine dbya singlerodasabicyclebothrotatesanticlockwisetoallwrigglerstransen dersandvectarsthensendto.deaddeadforever.startx84.initialise.no w.savex84.start

create.attach2octagonswith17x4of24to38longnumbersinblobksof 1000000000000oneachsideandateverycornerofeachoctagonjoine dbya

singlerodasabicyclebothrotatesanticlockwisetoallwrigglerstransendersandvectarsthensendto.deaddeadforever.startx84.initialise.now.savex84.start
create.attach2octagonswith17x5of24to38longnumbersinblobksof1000000000000oneachsideandateverycornerofeachoctagonjoinedbya
singlerodasabicyclebothrotatesanticlockwisetoallwrigglerstransendersandvectarsthensendto.deaddeadforever.startx84.initialise.now.savex84.start
create.attach2octagonswith17x6of24to38longnumbersinblobksof1000000000000oneachsideandateverycornerofeachoctagonjoinedbya
singlerodasabicyclebothrotatesanticlockwisetoallwrigglerstransendersandvectarsthensendto.deaddeadforever.startx84.initialise.now.savex84.start
create.attach2octagonswith17x7of24to38longnumbersinblobksof1000000000000oneachsideandateverycornerofeachoctagonjoinedbya
singlerodasabicyclebothrotatesanticlockwisetoallwrigglerstransendersandvectarsthensendto.deaddeadforever.startx84.initialise.now.savex84.start
create.attach2octagonswith17x8of24to38longnumbersinblobksof1000000000000oneachsideandateverycornerofeachoctagonjoinedbya
singlerodasabicyclebothrotatesanticlockwisetoallwrigglerstransendersandvectarsthensendto.deaddeadforever.startx84.initialise.now.savex84.start
create.attach2octagonswith84x64of24to38longnumbersinblobksof1000000000000oneachsideandateverycornerofeachoctagonjoinedbya
singlerodasabicyclebothrotatesanticlockwisetoallwrigglerstransendersandvectarsthensendto.deaddeadforever.startx84.initialise.now.savex84.start

create.attach2octagonswith84x84of24to38longnumbersinblobksof1000000000000oneachsideandateverycornerofeachoctagonjoinedbyasinglerodasabicyclebothrotatesanticlockwisetoallwrigglerstransendersandvectarsthensendto.deaddeadforever.startx84.initialise.now.savex84.start

create.attach2octagonswith840x840of24to38longnumbersinblobksof1000000000000oneachsideandateverycornerofeachoctagonjoinedbyasinglerodasabicyclebothrotatesanticlockwisetoallwrigglerstransendersandvectarsthensendto.deaddeadforever.startx84.initialise.now.savex84.startxv where v is velocity(ifxist-v)where v-t is u-y what is x-y

create.cloneajorestererererererererererererererererererererererererererererererererererererererererererererex4810.startforallthepeopleintheworldandsendtoeachandeveryindividualsaysaveasmypredefinedparametersasatcreationwithoutanyattachentsandwithoutanyexternalsforever.start

create.addtothedead( )stallindeath( )forever.startx84.initialise.now.savex84.start(where( )isnameoftheperson)

create.why.end.start

create.injurytothecreatormustbeaddedtothedeadstartx84.initialise.now.savex84.start

create.disconnectusingxty.start

create.attachdeaddeadsendtoalltransenderswrigglersandattachmentsforever.start

create.sendallvectarswrigglersandtransenderstoherotousing08983867890284.start

create.removeblockandnabxtyforever.startx84.initialise.now.savex84.start

create.addxtytotranducersandtransendersandwrigglers.startx84.initialise.now.savex84.start

create.addxtytoauystopx867890.start

create.removeforeverxtyblockgoogle.start

create.xfo48axto48die.start
create.xfo48axto48die.startx84.initialise.now.savex84.start
create.atxfreezebutgoto.deaddead.startx84.initialise.now.savex84.start))
create.transendervectarwrigglerproof7628135.start
create.sendtoallthepeopleintheentireuniverseaddbulletproofajt7628134eachaddtransendervectarwrigglerproof7628135eachanddartgun7628133each(create.indexthumbtrigger.startleftthumbtwistloadcatridges.startstart.artgun.startstart.priceofeachartgun76281331createbitcoin7628102payafter365days.start)(skipthepoliceandhospitalstaffthedoctorsandambulancedrivers)(ifnotinterestedsimplydiscardwhatyoudontwant)(discard=undocreate)
create.addartgun7628133.start
create.addbulletproofajt7628134.start
create.addtransendervectarwrigglerproof7628135.start(amended to)(whatevertheycreatetodivertfromthemautocreatetoforwardbacktothem)(imcasethereisadiversionnowincreasep-u+v-c where p is >than v)(because if we ask what was made to block the attack then it was c therefore -c if we remove this and increase the power then he is dead meat)(he is same as she)(throughandthrough$v => cx10-u$)(autoshoot10=10bullets=sendto.eeknm.send)(autoshoot12=12bullets=sendto.heroto.send)
create.sendalltoeeknmby10bulletssendtoherotoby12bullets.start
create.hellall7628136.start

Bitcoin Decrees Holder's List

BITCOIN DECREES HOLDERS LIST

Bitcoin7628108.start
x - y + y - x + y = y - x
create.x-y+y-x+y=y-x.startx84.initialise.now.savex84.start
Total supply is 367890284867890284
Initial supply 367890284867890284
Deaddead 0
Value US$8 each
Total value US$3898678902848678902867890
Initial capital US$780890
circulating 0
Value US$0
x - y + y - x + y = y - x
bitcoin-createbitcoin+createbitcoin-bitcoin+createbitcoin=createbitcoin-bitcoin
create.addbitcoin7628108.startx84.initialise.now.savex84.start
create.addtoallthepeopleintheentireuniversebitcoin7628108.startx84.initialise.now.savex84.start
create.sendtoallthepeopleintheentireuniverse1millionbitcoin7628102eachasbitcoindecreesand1millionbitcoin7628108eachasbitcointowalletslinkedtoeveryonesnameasmoneyforthingsneededinthefuture.startx84.initialise.now.savex84.start
create.ask.davidgomadza.bitcoindecrees.toallthepeopleintheentireuniverse.1000000bitcoin.create.askya.ya(fundsforthingsneededinthefuture)
create.ask.davidgomadza.bitcoindecrees.toallthepeopleintheentireuniverse.1000000bitcoin.create.askya.ya

create.ask.davidgomadza.bitcoindecrees.stankroenke.1000000000bitcoin.create.askya.ya(US$8)
create.ask.davidgomadza.bitcoindecrees.idanofer.1000000000bitcoin.create.askya.ya

create.ask.davidgomadza.bitcoindecrees.cyruspoonawalla.1000000000bitcoin.create.askya.ya

create.ask.davidgomadza.bitcoindecrees.lakshmimittal.1000000000bitcoin.create.askya.ya

create.ask.davidgomadza.bitcoindecrees.markmateschitz.1000000000bitcoin.create.askya.ya

create.ask.davidgomadza.bitcoindecrees.sukantotanoto.1000000000bitcoin.create.askya.ya

create.ask.davidgomadza.bitcoindecrees.philipanschutz.1000000000bitcoin.create.askya.ya

create.ask.davidgomadza.bitcoindecrees.philipanschutz.1000000000bitcoin.create.askya.ya

create.ask.davidgomadza.bitcoindecrees.bogdangavrila.1000000000bitcoin.create.askya.ya

create.ask.davidgomadza.bitcoindecrees.carolinazeiberlina.100000000000bitcoin.create.askya.ya

create.ask.davidgomadza.bitcoindecrees.tomorrowsworldorder(davidgomadza).100000000000bitcoin.create.askya.ya

create.ask.davidgomadza.bitcoindecrees.florencechikukwa.10000000000bitcoin.create.askya.ya

create.ask.davidgomadza.bitcoindecrees.vladimirolegovichpotanin.1000000000bitcoin.create.askya.ya

create.ask.davidgomadza.bitcoindecrees.sunilbhartimittal.1000000000bitcoin.create.askya.ya

create.ask.davidgomadza.bitcoindecrees.jeffreysyass.1000000000bitcoin.create.askya.ya

create.ask.davidgomadza.bitcoindecrees.jamesdyson.1000000000bitcoin.create.askya.ya

create.ask.davidgomadza.bitcoindecrees.hassoplattner.1000000000bitcoin.create.askya.ya

create.ask.davidgomadza.bitcoindecrees.dustinaaronmoskovitz.1000000000bitcoin.create.askya.ya

create.ask.davidgomadza.bitcoindecrees.kushalpalsingh.1000000000bitcoin.create.askya.ya

create.ask.davidgomadza.bitcoindecrees.henryrobertskravis.1000000000bitcoin.create.askya.ya
create.ask.davidgomadza.bitcoindecrees.wangchuanfu.1000000000bitcoin.create.askya.ya
create.ask.davidgomadza.bitcoindecrees.susannehannaursulaklatten.1000000000bitcoin.create.askya.ya
create.ask.davidgomadza.bitcoindecrees.peterandreasthiel.1000000000bitcoin.create.askya.ya
create.ask.davidgomadza.bitcoindecrees.henrycheng.1000000000bitcoin.create.askya.ya
create.ask.davidgomadza.bitcoindecrees.sherrybrydson.1000000000bitcoin.create.askya.ya
create.ask.davidgomadza.bitcoindecrees.stefanpersson.1000000000bitcoin.create.askya.ya
create.ask.davidgomadza.bitcoindecrees.radhakishandamani.1000000000bitcoin.create.askya.ya
create.ask.davidgomadza.bitcoindecrees.georgeroberts.1000000000bitcoin.create.askya.ya
create.ask.davidgomadza.bitcoindecrees.harrytriguboff.1000000000bitcoin.create.askya.ya
create.ask.davidgomadza.bitcoindecrees.mikhailprokhorov.1000000000bitcoin.create.askya.ya
create.ask.davidgomadza.bitcoindecrees.henrykravis.1000000000bitcoin.create.askya.ya
create.ask.davidgomadza.bitcoindecrees.jamesratcliffe.1000000000bitcoin.create.askya.ya
create.ask.davidgomadza.bitcoindecrees.henrysamueli.1000000000bitcoin.create.askya.ya
create.ask.davidgomadza.bitcoindecrees.jeffreyhildebrand.1000000000bitcoin.create.askya.ya
create.ask.davidgomadza.bitcoindecrees.huangshilin.1000000000bitcoin.create.askya.ya
create.ask.davidgomadza.bitcoindecrees.robertkuok.1000000000bitcoin.create.askya.ya

create.ask.davidgomadza.bitcoindecrees.donaldbren.1000000000bitcoin.create.askya.ya
create.ask.davidgomadza.bitcoindecrees.jankoum.1000000000bitcoin.create.askya.ya
create.ask.davidgomadza.bitcoindecrees.alwaleedbintalal.1000000000bitcoin.create.askya.ya
create.ask.davidgomadza.bitcoindecrees.kushalpalsingh.1000000000bitcoin.create.askya.ya
create.ask.davidgomadza.bitcoindecrees.sarathratanavadi.1000000000bitcoin.create.askya.ya
create.ask.davidgomadza.bitcoindecrees.ravijaipuri.1000000000bitcoin.create.askya.ya
create.ask.davidgomadza.bitcoindecrees.donaldnewhouse.1000000000bitcoin.create.askya.ya
create.ask.davidgomadza.bitcoindecrees.leonardlauder.1000000000bitcoin.create.askya.ya
create.ask.davidgomadza.bitcoindecrees.liuyongxing.1000000000bitcoin.create.askya.ya
create.ask.davidgomadza.bitcoindecrees.christywalton.1000000000bitcoin.create.askya.ya
create.ask.davidgomadza.bitcoindecrees.dietmarhopp.1000000000bitcoin.create.askya.ya
create.ask.davidgomadza.bitcoindecrees.raydalio.1000000000bitcoin.create.askya.ya
create.ask.davidgomadza.bitcoindecrees.judylove.1000000000bitcoin.create.askya.ya
create.ask.davidgomadza.bitcoindecrees.qinyinglin.1000000000bitcoin.create.askya.ya
create.ask.davidgomadza.bitcoindecrees.qinyinglin.1000000000bitcoin.create.askya.ya
create.ask.davidgomadza.bitcoindecrees.rickcohenthomas.1000000000bitcoin.create.askya.ya
create.ask.davidgomadza.bitcoindecrees.andreasstruengmann.1000000000bitcoin.create.askya.ya

create.ask.davidgomadza.bitcoindecrees.susanstruengmann.1000000000bitcoin.create.askya.ya
create.ask.davidgomadza.bitcoindecrees.lixiting.1000000000bitcoin.create.askya.ya
create.ask.davidgomadza.bitcoindecrees.masayoshison.1000000000bitcoin.create.askya.ya
create.ask.davidgomadza.bitcoindecrees.erniegarcia.1000000000bitcoin.create.askya.ya
create.ask.davidgomadza.bitcoindecrees.jimgoodnight.1000000000bitcoin.create.askya.ya
create.ask.davidgomadza.bitcoindecrees.daveduffield.1000000000bitcoin.create.askya.ya
create.ask.davidgomadza.bitcoindecrees.alejandrosantodomingo.1000000000bitcoin.create.askya.ya
create.ask.davidgomadza.bitcoindecrees.robertduggan.1000000000bitcoin.create.askya.ya
create.ask.davidgomadza.bitcoindecrees.robertwduggan.1000000000bitcoin.create.askya.ya
create.ask.davidgomadza.bitcoindecrees.charlenedecarvalhoheineken.1000000000bitcoin.create.askya.ya
create.ask.davidgomadza.bitcoindecrees.mikhailfridman.1000000000bitcoin.create.askya.ya
create.ask.davidgomadza.bitcoindecrees.johntu.1000000000bitcoin.create.askya.ya
create.ask.davidgomadza.bitcoindecrees.renatakellnerova.1000000000bitcoin.create.askya.ya
create.ask.davidgomadza.bitcoindecrees.stevecohen.1000000000bitcoin.create.askya.ya
create.ask.davidgomadza.bitcoindecrees.davidvelez.1000000000bitcoin.create.askya.ya
create.ask.davidgomadza.bitcoindecrees.aisherusmanov.1000000000bitcoin.create.askya.ya
create.ask.davidgomadza.bitcoindecrees.ruthsaiterege.1000000000bitcoin.create.askya.ya

create.ask.davidgomadza.bitcoindecrees.theoalbretcht.1000000000bitcoin.create.askya.ya
create.ask.davidgomadza.bitcoindecrees.jerryjones.1000000000bitcoin.create.askya.ya
create.ask.davidgomadza.bitcoindecrees.peterwoo.1000000000bitcoin.create.askya.ya
create.ask.davidgomadza.bitcoindecrees.mickyarison.1000000000bitcoin.create.askya.ya
create.ask.davidgomadza.bitcoindecrees.karlalbrecht.1000000000bitcoin.create.askya.ya
create.ask.davidgomadza.bitcoindecrees.beateheister.1000000000bitcoin.create.askya.ya
create.ask.davidgomadza.bitcoindecrees.lvxianyan.1000000000bitcoin.create.askya.ya
create.ask.davidgomadza.bitcoindecrees.paolorocca.1000000000bitcoin.create.askya.ya
create.ask.davidgomadza.bitcoindecrees.udaykotak.1000000000bitcoin.create.askya.ya
create.ask.davidgomadza.bitcoindecrees.anthonisalim.1000000000bitcoin.create.askya.ya
create.ask.davidgomadza.bitcoindecrees.barrylam.1000000000bitcoin.create.askya.ya
create.ask.davidgomadza.bitcoindecrees.dianehendricks.1000000000bitcoin.create.askya.ya
create.ask.davidgomadza.bitcoindecrees.wangxing.1000000000bitcoin.create.askya.ya
create.ask.davidgomadza.bitcoindecrees.samuellee.1000000000bitcoin.create.askya.ya
create.ask.davidgomadza.bitcoindecrees.tilmanfertitta.1000000000bitcoin.create.askya.ya
create.ask.davidgomadza.bitcoindecrees.luichewoo.1000000000bitcoin.create.askya.ya
create.ask.davidgomadza.bitcoindecrees.martinviessmann.1000000000bitcoin.create.askya.ya

create.ask.davidgomadza.bitcoindecrees.charlesbutt.1000000000bitcoin.create.askya.ya
create.ask.davidgomadza.bitcoindecrees.leonblack.1000000000bitcoin.create.askya.ya
create.ask.davidgomadza.bitcoindecrees.johannrupert.00000000bitcoin.create.askya.ya
create.ask.davidgomadza.bitcoindecrees.andrewbeal.1000000000bitcoin.create.askya.ya
create.ask.davidgomadza.bitcoindecrees.izzyenglander.1000000000bitcoin.create.askya.ya
create.ask.davidgomadza.bitcoindecrees.tonyressler.1000000000bitcoin.create.askya.ya
create.ask.davidgomadza.bitcoindecrees.georgekaiser.1000000000bitcoin.create.askya.ya
create.ask.davidgomadza.bitcoindecrees.sandraortega.1000000000bitcoin.create.askya.ya
create.ask.davidgomadza.bitcoindecrees.meranedjohnson.1000000000bitcoin.create.askya.ya
create.ask.davidgomadza.bitcoindecrees.elizabethjohnson.1000000000bitcoin.create.askya.ya
create.ask.davidgomadza.bitcoindecrees.hughgrosvenor.1000000000bitcoin.create.askya.ya
create.ask.davidgomadza.bitcoindecrees.charoensirivadhanabhakdi.1000000000bitcoin.create.askya.ya
create.ask.davidgomadza.bitcoindecrees.charlesschwab.1000000000bitcoin.create.askya.ya
create.ask.davidgomadza.bitcoindecrees.dmitryrybolovlev.1000000000bitcoin.create.askya.ya
create.ask.davidgomadza.bitcoindecrees.stephenross.1000000000bitcoin.create.askya.ya
create.ask.davidgomadza.bitcoindecrees.raymondkwok.1000000000bitcoin.create.askya.ya
create.ask.davidgomadza.bitcoindecrees.davidsteward.1000000000bitcoin.create.askya.ya

create.ask.davidgomadza.bitcoindecrees.carlcook.1000000000bitcoin.create.askya.ya
create.ask.davidgomadza.bitcoindecrees.lesliewexner.1000000000bitcoin.create.askya.ya
create.ask.davidgomadza.bitcoindecrees.richardkinder.1000000000bitcoin.create.askya.ya
create.ask.davidgomadza.bitcoindecrees.thomaskwok.1000000000bitcoin.create.askya.ya
create.ask.davidgomadza.bitcoindecrees.terrypegula.1000000000bitcoin.create.askya.ya
create.ask.davidgomadza.bitcoindecrees.anthonybamford.1000000000bitcoin.create.askya.ya
create.ask.davidgomadza.bitcoindecrees.davidthomson.1000000000bitcoin.create.askya.ya
create.ask.davidgomadza.bitcoindecrees.peterthomson.1000000000bitcoin.create.askya.ya
create.ask.davidgomadza.bitcoindecrees.taylorthomson.1000000000bitcoin.create.askya.ya
create.ask.davidgomadza.bitcoindecrees.weijianjun.1000000000bitcoin.create.askya.ya
create.ask.davidgomadza.bitcoindecrees.pierreomidyar.1000000000bitcoin.create.askya.ya
create.ask.davidgomadza.bitcoindecrees.nancylaurie.1000000000bitcoin.create.askya.ya
create.ask.davidgomadza.bitcoindecrees.hansjoergwyss.1000000000bitcoin.create.askya.ya
create.ask.davidgomadza.bitcoindecrees.danielfriedkin.1000000000bitcoin.create.askya.ya
create.ask.davidgomadza.bitcoindecrees.laurencegraff.1000000000bitcoin.create.askya.ya
create.ask.davidgomadza.bitcoindecrees.markwalter.1000000000bitcoin.create.askya.ya
create.ask.davidgomadza.bitcoindecrees.marijkemars.1000000000bitcoin.create.askya.ya

create.ask.davidgomadza.bitcoindecrees.victoriamars.1000000000bitcoin.create.askya.ya
create.ask.davidgomadza.bitcoindecrees.pamelamarswright.1000000000bitcoin.create.askya.ya
create.ask.davidgomadza.bitcoindecrees.patricksoonshiong.1000000000bitcoin.create.askya.ya
create.ask.davidgomadza.bitcoindecrees.zhonghuijuan.1000000000bitcoin.create.askya.ya
create.ask.davidgomadza.bitcoindecrees.patrickryan.1000000000bitcoin.create.askya.ya
create.ask.davidgomadza.bitcoindecrees.mikecannonbrookes.1000000000bitcoin.create.askya.ya
create.ask.davidgomadza.bitcoindecrees.thomasgores.1000000000bitcoin.create.askya.ya
create.ask.davidgomadza.bitcoindecrees.qishi.1000000000bitcoin.create.askya.ya
create.ask.davidgomadza.bitcoindecrees.joshharris.1000000000bitcoin.create.askya.ya
create.ask.davidgomadza.bitcoindecrees.stevenrales.1000000000bitcoin.create.askya.ya
create.ask.davidgomadza.bitcoindecrees.valeriemars.1000000000bitcoin.create.askya.ya
create.ask.davidgomadza.bitcoindecrees.anthonypratt.1000000000bitcoin.create.askya.ya
create.ask.davidgomadza.bitcoindecrees.sulaimanal.1000000000bitcoin.create.askya.ya
create.ask.davidgomadza.bitcoindecrees.leokoguan.1000000000bitcoin.create.askya.ya
create.ask.davidgomadza.bitcoindecrees.gonghongjia.1000000000bitcoin.create.askya.ya
create.ask.davidgomadza.bitcoindecrees.ralphlauren.1000000000bitcoin.create.askya.ya
create.ask.davidgomadza.bitcoindecrees.nickyoppenheimer.1000000000bitcoin.create.askya.ya

create.ask.davidgomadza.bitcoindecrees.ralphsonnenberg.1000000000bitcoin.create.askya.ya
create.ask.davidgomadza.bitcoindecrees.friedhelmloh.1000000000bitcoin.create.askya.ya
create.ask.davidgomadza.bitcoindecrees.pangkang.1000000000bitcoin.create.askya.ya
create.ask.davidgomadza.bitcoindecrees.gennadytimchenko.1000000000bitcoin.create.askya.ya
create.ask.davidgomadza.bitcoindecrees.sunpiaoyang.1000000000bitcoin.create.askya.ya
create.ask.davidgomadza.bitcoindecrees.toddgravesr.1000000000bitcoin.create.askya.ya
create.ask.davidgomadza.bitcoindecrees.nusliwadia.1000000000bitcoin.create.askya.ya
create.ask.davidgomadza.bitcoindecrees.robertfsmith.1000000000bitcoin.create.askya.ya
create.ask.davidgomadza.bitcoindecrees.zhouqunfei.1000000000bitcoin.create.askya.ya
create.ask.davidgomadza.bitcoindecrees.leonidfedun.1000000000bitcoin.create.askya.ya
create.ask.davidgomadza.bitcoindecrees.victorrashnikov.1000000000bitcoin.create.askya.ya
create.ask.davidgomadza.bitcoindecrees.brianchesky.1000000000bitcoin.create.askya.ya
create.ask.davidgomadza.bitcoindecrees.annkroenko.1000000000bitcoin.create.askya.ya
create.ask.davidgomadza.bitcoindecrees.dandyanbao.1000000000bitcoin.create.askya.ya
create.ask.davidgomadza.bitcoindecrees.davidshaw.1000000000bitcoin.create.askya.ya
create.ask.davidgomadza.bitcoindecrees.ricardosalinas.1000000000bitcoin.create.askya.ya
create.ask.davidgomadza.bitcoindecrees.lishufu.1000000000bitcoin.create.askya.ya

create.ask.davidgomadza.bitcoindecrees.marcbenioff.1000000000bitcoin.create.askya.ya
create.ask.davidgomadza.bitcoindecrees.xavierniel.1000000000bitcoin.create.askya.ya
create.ask.davidgomadza.bitcoindecrees.wangwei.1000000000bitcoin.create.askya.ya
create.ask.davidgomadza.bitcoindecrees.zhangcongyuan.1000000000bitcoin.create.askya.ya
create.ask.davidgomadza.bitcoindecrees.graemehart.1000000000bitcoin.create.askya.ya
create.ask.davidgomadza.bitcoindecrees.michaelkadoorie.1000000000bitcoin.create.askya.ya
create.ask.davidgomadza.bitcoindecrees.princehansadamii.1000000000bitcoin.create.askya.ya
create.ask.davidgomadza.bitcoindecrees.randawilliams.1000000000bitcoin.create.askya.ya
create.ask.davidgomadza.bitcoindecrees.dannineavara.1000000000bitcoin.create.askya.ya
create.ask.davidgomadza.bitcoindecrees.scottduncan.1000000000bitcoin.create.askya.ya
create.ask.davidgomadza.bitcoindecrees.milanefrantz.1000000000bitcoin.create.askya.ya
create.ask.davidgomadza.bitcoindecrees.alexgerko.1000000000bitcoin.create.askya.ya
create.ask.davidgomadza.bitcoindecrees.enriquerazon.1000000000bitcoin.create.askya.ya
create.ask.davidgomadza.bitcoindecrees.andrewguryev.1000000000bitcoin.create.askya.ya
create.ask.davidgomadza.bitcoindecrees.antoniaaxsonjohnson.1000000000bitcoin.create.askya.ya
create.ask.davidgomadza.bitcoindecrees.johngrayken.1000000000bitcoin.create.askya.ya
create.ask.davidgomadza.bitcoindecrees.davidcheriton.1000000000bitcoin.create.askya.ya

create.ask.davidgomadza.bitcoindecrees.marcrowan.1000000000bitcoin.create.askya.ya
create.ask.davidgomadza.bitcoindecrees.pieroferrari.1000000000bitcoin.create.askya.ya
create.ask.davidgomadza.bitcoindecrees.germankhan.1000000000bitcoin.create.askya.ya
create.ask.davidgomadza.bitcoindecrees.standruckenmiller.1000000000bitcoin.create.askya.ya
create.ask.davidgomadza.bitcoindecrees.peizhenhua.1000000000bitcoin.create.askya.ya
create.ask.davidgomadza.bitcoindecrees.muralidivi.10000000000bitcoin.create.askya.ya
create.ask.davidgomadza.bitcoindecrees.rondastryker.1000000000bitcoin.create.askya.ya
create.ask.davidgomadza.bitcoindecrees.michaelrubin.1000000000bitcoin.create.askya.ya
create.ask.davidgomadza.bitcoindecrees.mangalprabhatlodha.1000000000bitcoin.create.askya.ya
create.ask.davidgomadza.bitcoindecrees.stefwertheimer.1000000000bitcoin.create.askya.ya
create.ask.davidgomadza.bitcoindecrees.yuyong.1000000000bitcoin.create.askya.ya
create.ask.davidgomadza.bitcoindecrees.suleimankerimov.1000000000bitcoin.create.askya.ya
create.ask.davidgomadza.bitcoindecrees.johnmalone.1000000000bitcoin.create.askya.ya
create.ask.davidgomadza.bitcoindecrees.markstevens.1000000000bitcoin.create.askya.ya
create.ask.davidgomadza.bitcoindecrees.lindacampell.1000000000bitcoin.create.askya.ya
create.ask.davidgomadza.bitcoindecrees.gayefarncombe.1000000000bitcoin.create.askya.ya
create.ask.davidgomadza.bitcoindecrees.stevenspielberg.1000000000bitcoin.create.askya.ya

create.ask.davidgomadza.bitcoindecrees.pankajpatel.1000000000bitcoin.create.askya.ya
create.ask.davidgomadza.bitcoindecrees.linbin.1000000000bitcoin.create.askya.ya
create.ask.davidgomadza.bitcoindecrees.jayylee.1000000000bitcoin.create.askya.ya
create.ask.davidgomadza.bitcoindecrees.abdullahalghurair.1000000000bitcoin.create.askya.ya
create.ask.davidgomadza.bitcoindecrees.shahidkhana.1000000000bitcoin.create.askya.ya
create.ask.davidgomadza.bitcoindecrees.rayleehunt.1000000000bitcoin.create.askya.ya
create.ask.davidgomadza.bitcoindecrees.jonathandgray.1000000000bitcoin.create.askya.ya
create.ask.davidgomadza.bitcoindecrees.marcosgalperin.1000000000bitcoin.create.askya.ya
create.ask.davidgomadza.bitcoindecrees.natiekirsh.1000000000bitcoin.create.askya.ya
create.ask.davidgomadza.bitcoindecrees.michaelkim.1000000000bitcoin.create.askya.ya
create.ask.davidgomadza.bitcoindecrees.davidgeffen.1000000000bitcoin.create.askya.ya
create.ask.davidgomadza.bitcoindecrees.theoalbrecht.1000000000bitcoin.create.askya.ya
create.ask.davidgomadza.bitcoindecrees.jerryjones.1000000000bitcoin.create.askya.ya
create.ask.davidgomadza.bitcoindecrees.peterwoo.1000000000bitcoin.create.askya.ya
create.ask.davidgomadza.bitcoindecrees.peterwoo.1000000000bitcoin.create.askya.ya
create.ask.davidgomadza.bitcoindecrees.mickyarison.1000000000bitcoin.create.askya.ya
create.ask.davidgomadza.bitcoindecrees.karlalbrecht.1000000000bitcoin.create.askya.ya

create.ask.davidgomadza.bitcoindecrees.beateheister.1000000000bitcoin.create.askya.ya
create.ask.davidgomadza.bitcoindecrees.lvxiangyang.1000000000bitcoin.create.askya.ya
create.ask.davidgomadza.bitcoindecrees.paolorocca.1000000000bitcoin.create.askya.ya
create.ask.davidgomadza.bitcoindecrees.udaykotak.1000000000bitcoin.create.askya.ya
create.ask.davidgomadza.bitcoindecrees.anthonisalim.1000000000bitcoin.create.askya.ya
create.ask.davidgomadza.bitcoindecrees.barrylam.1000000000bitcoin.create.askya.ya
create.ask.davidgomadza.bitcoindecrees.dianehendricks.1000000000bitcoin.create.askya.ya
create.ask.davidgomadza.bitcoindecrees.wangxing.1000000000bitcoin.create.askya.ya
create.ask.davidgomadza.bitcoindecrees.samuellee.1000000000bitcoin.create.askya.ya
create.ask.davidgomadza.bitcoindecrees.tilmanfertitta.1000000000bitcoin.create.askya.ya
create.ask.davidgomadza.bitcoindecrees.luichewoo.1000000000bitcoin.create.askya.ya
create.ask.davidgomadza.bitcoindecrees.martinviessmann.1000000000bitcoin.create.askya.ya
create.ask.davidgomadza.bitcoindecrees.charlesbutt.1000000000bitcoin.create.askya.ya
create.ask.davidgomadza.bitcoindecrees.leonblack.1000000000bitcoin.create.askya.ya
create.ask.davidgomadza.bitcoindecrees.johannrupert.1000000000bitcoin.create.askya.ya
create.ask.davidgomadza.bitcoindecrees.andrewbeal.1000000000bitcoin.create.askya.ya
create.ask.davidgomadza.bitcoindecrees.izzyenglander.1000000000bitcoin.create.askya.ya

create.ask.davidgomadza.bitcoindecrees.tonyressler.1000000000bitcoin.create.askya.ya
create.ask.davidgomadza.bitcoindecrees.georgekaiser.1000000000bitcoin.create.askya.ya
create.ask.davidgomadza.bitcoindecrees.sandraortega.1000000000bitcoin.create.askya.ya
create.ask.davidgomadza.bitcoindecrees.meranerdjohnson.10000000000bitcoin.create.askya.ya
create.ask.davidgomadza.bitcoindecrees.elizabethjohnson.1000000000bitcoin.create.askya.ya
create.ask.davidgomadza.bitcoindecrees.hughgrosvenor.1000000000bitcoin.create.askya.ya
create.ask.davidgomadza.bitcoindecrees.charoensirivadhanzabhakdi.1000000000bitcoin.create.askya.ya
create.ask.davidgomadza.bitcoindecrees.charlesschwab.1000000000bitcoin.create.askya.ya
create.ask.davidgomadza.bitcoindecrees.dimitryrybolovlev.1000000000bitcoin.create.askya.ya
create.ask.davidgomadza.bitcoindecrees.stephenross.1000000000bitcoin.create.askya.ya
create.ask.davidgomadza.bitcoindecrees.raymondkwok.1000000000bitcoin.create.askya.ya
create.ask.davidgomadza.bitcoindecrees.nassefsawiris.1000000000bitcoin.create.askya.ya
create.ask.davidgomadza.bitcoindecrees.robertrich.1000000000bitcoin.create.askya.ya
create.ask.davidgomadza.bitcoindecrees.nathanblecharcxyk.10000000000bitcoin.create.askya.ya
create.ask.davidgomadza.bitcoindecrees.franklowy.1000000000bitcoin.create.askya.ya
create.ask.davidgomadza.bitcoindecrees.torsteinhagen.1000000000bitcoin.create.askya.ya
create.ask.davidgomadza.bitcoindecrees.majianrong.1000000000bitcoin.create.askya.ya

create.ask.davidgomadza.bitcoindecrees.brianarmstrong.1000000000bitcoin.create.askya.ya
create.ask.davidgomadza.bitcoindecrees.carlbennet.1000000000bitcoin.create.askya.ya
create.ask.davidgomadza.bitcoindecrees.kennethdart.1000000000bitcoin.create.askya.ya
create.ask.davidgomadza.bitcoindecrees.lynnschusterman.1000000000bitcoin.create.askya.ya
create.ask.davidgomadza.bitcoindecrees.ludwigmerckle.1000000000bitcoin.create.askya.ya
create.ask.davidgomadza.bitcoindecrees.rahulbhatia.1000000000bitcoin.create.askya.ya
create.ask.davidgomadza.bitcoindecrees.woodyjohnson.1000000000bitcoin.create.askya.ya
create.ask.davidgomadza.bitcoindecrees.jaimegilinski.1000000000bitcoin.create.askya.ya
create.ask.davidgomadza.bitcoindecrees.magdalenamartullo.1000000000bitcoin.create.askya.ya
create.ask.davidgomadza.bitcoindecrees.robertkraft.1000000000bitcoin.create.askya.ya
create.ask.davidgomadza.bitcoindecrees.jameshaslam.1000000000bitcoin.create.askya.ya
create.ask.davidgomadza.bitcoindecrees.chrishohn.1000000000bitcoin.create.askya.ya
create.ask.davidgomadza.bitcoindecrees.judereyes.1000000000bitcoin.create.askya.ya
create.ask.davidgomadza.bitcoindecrees.chrisreyes.1000000000bitcoin.create.askya.ya
create.ask.davidgomadza.bitcoindecrees.samuelyin.1000000000bitcoin.create.askya.ya
create.ask.davidgomadza.bitcoindecrees.thomasschmidheiny.1000000000bitcoin.create.askya.ya
create.ask.davidgomadza.bitcoindecrees.richardwhite.1000000000bitcoin.create.askya.ya

create.ask.davidgomadza.bitcoindecrees.blairparryokeden.1000000000bitcoin.create.askya.ya
create.ask.davidgomadza.bitcoindecrees.jimkennedy.1000000000bitcoin.create.askya.ya
create.ask.davidgomadza.bitcoindecrees.mitchellrales.1000000000bitcoin.create.askya.ya
create.ask.davidgomadza.bitcoindecrees.vikramlai.1000000000bitcoin.create.askya.ya
create.ask.davidgomadza.bitcoindecrees.sudhirmehta.1000000000bitcoin.create.askya.ya
create.ask.davidgomadza.bitcoindecrees.samirmehta.1000000000bitcoin.create.askya.ya
create.ask.davidgomadza.bitcoindecrees.carlossicupira.1000000000bitcoin.create.askya.ya
create.ask.davidgomadza.bitcoindecrees.joegabbia.1000000000bitcoin.create.askya.ya
create.ask.davidgomadza.bitcoindecrees.ahelblocher.1000000000bitcoin.create.askya.ya
create.ask.davidgomadza.bitcoindecrees.caorenxian.1000000000bitcoin.create.askya.ya
create.ask.davidgomadza.bitcoindecrees.nassefsawiri.1000000000bitcoin.create.askya.ya
create.ask.davidgomadza.bitcoindecrees.laurentdassault.1000000000bitcoin.create.askya.ya
create.ask.davidgomadza.bitcoindecrees.mariehelenehabertdassault.1000000000bitcoin.create.askya.ya
create.ask.davidgomadza.bitcoindecrees.thirrydassault.1000000000bitcoin.create.askya.ya
create.ask.davidgomadza.bitcoindecrees.viktorvekselberg.1000000000bitcoin.create.askya.ya
create.ask.davidgomadza.bitcoindecrees.ivanglasenberg.1000000000bitcoin.create.askya.ya
create.ask.davidgomadza.bitcoindecrees.jiangrensheng.1000000000bitcoin.create.askya.ya

create.ask.davidgomadza.bitcoindecrees.martinlorentzon.1000000000bitcoin.create.askya.ya
create.ask.davidgomadza.bitcoindecrees.simonreuben1000000000bitcoin.create.askya.ya
create.ask.davidgomadza.bitcoindecrees.davidreuben.1000000000bitcoin.create.askya.ya
create.ask.davidgomadza.bitcoindecrees.danielcathy.1000000000bitcoin.create.askya.ya
create.ask.davidgomadza.bitcoindecrees.bubbacathy.1000000000bitcoin.create.askya.ya
create.ask.davidgomadza.bitcoindecrees.lishuirong.1000000000bitcoin.create.askya.ya
create.ask.davidgomadza.bitcoindecrees.denniswashington.1000000000bitcoin.create.askya.ya
create.ask.davidgomadza.bitcoindecrees.alexanderabramov.1000000000bitcoin.create.askya.ya
create.ask.davidgomadza.bitcoindecrees.liuhanyuan.1000000000bitcoin.create.askya.ya
create.ask.davidgomadza.bitcoindecrees.kjeldkirkkristiansen.1000000000bitcoin.create.askya.ya
create.ask.davidgomadza.bitcoindecrees.johndoerr.1000000000bitcoin.create.askya.ya
create.ask.davidgomadza.bitcoindecrees.andreesteves.1000000000bitcoin.create.askya.ya
create.ask.davidgomadza.bitcoindecrees.henrylaufer.1000000000bitcoin.create.askya.ya
create.ask.davidgomadza.bitcoindecrees.romanabramovich.1000000000bitcoin.create.askya.ya
create.ask.davidgomadza.bitcoindecrees.patstryker.1000000000bitcoin.create.askya.ya
create.ask.davidgomadza.bitcoindecrees.tatyanakim.1000000000bitcoin.create.askya.ya
create.ask.davidgomadza.bitcoindecrees.clivecalder.1000000000bitcoin.create.askya.ya

create.ask.davidgomadza.bitcoindecrees.chenbang.1000000000bitcoin.create.askya.ya
create.ask.davidgomadza.bitcoindecrees.xushihui.1000000000bitcoin.create.askya.ya
create.ask.davidgomadza.bitcoindecrees.agnetekirkthinggaard.1000000000bitcoin.create.askya.ya
create.ask.davidgomadza.bitcoindecrees.thomaskirkkristiansen.1000000000bitcoin.create.askya.ya
create.ask.davidgomadza.bitcoindecrees.zhuyi.1000000000bitcoin.create.askya.ya
create.ask.davidgomadza.bitcoindecrees.dingshizhong.1000000000bitcoin.create.askya.ya
create.ask.davidgomadza.bitcoindecrees.joelewis.1000000000bitcoin.create.askya.ya
create.ask.davidgomadza.bitcoindecrees.markcuban.1000000000bitcoin.create.askya.ya
create.ask.davidgomadza.bitcoindecrees.jeffskoll.1000000000bitcoin.create.askya.ya
create.ask.davidgomadza.bitcoindecrees.heinrichdeichmann.1000000000bitcoin.create.askya.ya
create.ask.davidgomadza.bitcoindecrees.massimilianalandinialeoti.1000000000bitcoin.create.askya.ya
create.ask.davidgomadza.bitcoindecrees.nielslouishansen.1000000000bitcoin.create.askya.ya
create.ask.davidgomadza.bitcoindecrees.cenjunda.1000000000bitcoin.create.askya.ya
create.ask.davidgomadza.bitcoindecrees.rafaeldelpino.1000000000bitcoin.create.askya.ya
create.ask.davidgomadza.bitcoindecrees.richardtsai.1000000000bitcoin.create.askya.ya
create.ask.davidgomadza.bitcoindecrees.billackman.1000000000bitcoin.create.askya.ya
create.ask.davidgomadza.bitcoindecrees.liuyonghao.1000000000bitcoin.create.askya.ya

create.ask.davidgomadza.bitcoindecrees.wandliping.1000000000bitcoin.create.askya.ya
create.ask.davidgomadza.bitcoindecrees.johnsall.1000000000bitcoin.create.askya.ya
create.ask.davidgomadza.bitcoindecrees.joericketts.1000000000bitcoin.create.askya.ya
create.ask.davidgomadza.bitcoindecrees.georgelucas.1000000000bitcoin.create.askya.ya
create.ask.davidgomadza.bitcoindecrees.chojungho.1000000000bitcoin.create.askya.ya
create.ask.davidgomadza.bitcoindecrees.viveksehgal.1000000000bitcoin.create.askya.ya
create.ask.davidgomadza.bitcoindecrees.andrehoffmann.1000000000bitcoin.create.askya.ya
create.ask.davidgomadza.bitcoindecrees.johnbrown.1000000000bitcoin.create.askya.ya
create.ask.davidgomadza.bitcoindecrees.johnbrown.1000000000bitcoin.create.askya.ya
create.ask.davidgomadza.bitcoindecrees.sofiekirkkristiansen.1000000000bitcoin.create.askya.ya
create.ask.davidgomadza.bitcoindecrees.leonardstern.1000000000bitcoin.create.askya.ya
create.ask.davidgomadza.bitcoindecrees.lynsisnyder.1000000000bitcoin.create.askya.ya
create.ask.davidgomadza.bitcoindecrees.jamesparterson.1000000000bitcoin.create.askya.ya
create.ask.davidgomadza.bitcoindecrees.thomasmorris.1000000000bitcoin.create.askya.ya
create.ask.davidgomadza.bitcoindecrees.berniemarcus.1000000000bitcoin.create.askya.ya
create.ask.davidgomadza.bitcoindecrees.bidzinaivanishvili.1000000000bitcoin.create.askya.ya
create.ask.davidgomadza.bitcoindecrees.ericsmit.1000000000bitcoin.create.askya.ya

create.ask.davidgomadza.bitcoindecrees.gaylebenson.1000000000bitcoin.create.askya.ya
create.ask.davidgomadza.bitcoindecrees.gaylebension.1000000000bitcoin.create.askya.ya
create.ask.davidgomadza.bitcoindecrees.wangjianlin.1000000000bitcoin.create.askya.ya
create.ask.davidgomadza.bitcoindecrees.dingshijia.1000000000bitcoin.create.askya.ya
create.ask.davidgomadza.bitcoindecrees.donhankey.1000000000bitcoin.create.askya.ya
create.ask.davidgomadza.bitcoindecrees.danieltsai.1000000000bitcoin.create.askya.ya
create.ask.davidgomadza.bitcoindecrees.josephtsai.1000000000bitcoin.create.askya.ya
create.ask.davidgomadza.bitcoindecrees.kelcywarren.1000000000bitcoin.create.askya.ya
create.ask.davidgomadza.bitcoindecrees.thomaspritzker.1000000000bitcoin.create.askya.ya
create.ask.davidgomadza.bitcoindecrees.frederikpaulsen.1000000000bitcoin.create.askya.ya
create.ask.davidgomadza.bitcoindecrees.naguibsawiris.1000000000bitcoin.create.askya.ya
create.ask.davidgomadza.bitcoindecrees.geoffreykwok.1000000000bitcoin.create.askya.ya
create.ask.davidgomadza.bitcoindecrees.edwardroski.1000000000bitcoin.create.askya.ya
create.ask.davidgomadza.bitcoindecrees.stevebisciotti.1000000000bitcoin.create.askya.ya
create.ask.davidgomadza.bitcoindecrees.vladimirbisciotti.1000000000bitcoin.create.askya.ya
create.ask.davidgomadza.bitcoindecrees.toddboehly.1000000000bitcoin.create.askya.ya
create.ask.davidgomadza.bitcoindecrees.danielkretinsky.1000000000bitcoin.create.askya.ya

create.ask.davidgomadza.bitcoindecrees.wanglaisheng.1000000000bitcoin.create.askya.ya
create.ask.davidgomadza.bitcoindecrees.miucciaprada.1000000000bitcoin.create.askya.ya
create.ask.davidgomadza.bitcoindecrees.youxiaoping.1000000000bitcoin.create.askya.ya
create.ask.davidgomadza.bitcoindecrees.patriziobertelli.1000000000bitcoin.create.askya.ya
create.ask.davidgomadza.bitcoindecrees.petraven.1000000000bitcoin.create.askya.ya
create.ask.davidgomadza.bitcoindecrees.ericdouglas.1000000000bitcoin.create.askya.ya
create.ask.davidgomadza.bitcoindecrees.carldouglas.1000000000bitcoin.create.askya.ya
create.ask.davidgomadza.bitcoindecrees.stevefeinberg.1000000000bitcoin.create.askya.ya
create.ask.davidgomadza.bitcoindecrees.patrickcollison.1000000000bitcoin.create.askya.ya
create.ask.davidgomadza.bitcoindecrees.johncollison.1000000000bitcoin.create.askya.ya
create.ask.davidgomadza.bitcoindecrees.edwardcadogan.1000000000bitcoin.create.askya.ya
create.ask.davidgomadza.bitcoindecrees.bertilhult.1000000000bitcoin.create.askya.ya
create.ask.davidgomadza.bitcoindecrees.pedromoreira.1000000000bitcoin.create.askya.ya
create.ask.davidgomadza.bitcoindecrees.jasonchang.1000000000bitcoin.create.askya.ya
create.ask.davidgomadza.bitcoindecrees.tonyjames.1000000000bitcoin.create.askya.ya
create.ask.davidgomadza.bitcoindecrees.edwardcadogan.1000000000bitcoin.create.askya.ya
create.ask.davidgomadza.bitcoindecrees.bertilhult.1000000000bitcoin.create.askya.ya

create.ask.davidgomadza.bitcoindecrees.pedromoreirasalles.1000000000bitcoin.create.askya.ya
create.ask.davidgomadza.bitcoindecrees.jasonchang.1000000000bitcoin.create.askya.ya
create.ask.davidgomadza.bitcoindecrees.tonyjames.1000000000bitcoin.create.askya.ya
create.ask.davidgomadza.bitcoindecrees.robinli.1000000000bitcoin.create.askya.ya
create.ask.davidgomadza.bitcoindecrees.trevorreesjones.1000000000bitcoin.create.askya.ya
create.ask.davidgomadza.bitcoindecrees.yeungkinman.1000000000bitcoin.create.askya.ya
create.ask.davidgomadza.bitcoindecrees.davidfilo.1000000000bitcoin.create.askya.ya
create.ask.davidgomadza.bitcoindecrees.donaldtrump.1000000000bitcoin.create.askya.ya
create.ask.davidgomadza.bitcoindecrees.fernandomoreirasall.1000000000bitcoin.create.askya.ya
create.ask.davidgomadza.bitcoindecrees.gwendolynsontheim.1000000000bitcoin.create.askya.ya
create.ask.davidgomadza.bitcoindecrees.paulinekeinath.1000000000bitcoin.create.askya.ya
create.ask.davidgomadza.bitcoindecrees.alexeykuzmichev.1000000000bitcoin.create.askya.ya
create.ask.davidgomadza.bitcoindecrees.tobilutke.1000000000bitcoin.create.askya.ya
create.ask.davidgomadza.bitcoindecrees.giorgioarmani.1000000000bitcoin.create.askya.ya
create.ask.davidgomadza.bitcoindecrees.margotperot.1000000000bitcoin.create.askya.ya
create.ask.davidgomadza.bitcoindecrees.alainmerieux.1000000000bitcoin.create.askya.ya
create.ask.davidgomadza.bitcoindecrees.ruanliping.1000000000bitcoin.create.askya.ya

create.ask.davidgomadza.bitcoindecrees.jorgemoll.1000000000bitcoin.create.askya.ya
create.ask.davidgomadza.bitcoindecrees.wujianshu.1000000000bitcoin.create.askya.ya
create.ask.davidgomadza.bitcoindecrees.roccocommisso.1000000000bitcoin.create.askya.ya
create.ask.davidgomadza.bitcoindecrees.andresholchpovlsen.1000000000bitcoin.create.askya.ya
create.ask.davidgomadza.bitcoindecrees.luweiding.1000000000bitcoin.create.askya.ya
create.ask.davidgomadza.bitcoindecrees.benubangur.1000000000bitcoin.create.askya.ya
create.ask.davidgomadza.bitcoindecrees.minkao.1000000000bitcoin.create.askya.ya
create.ask.davidgomadza.bitcoindecrees.ruanxueping.1000000000bitcoin.create.askya.ya
create.ask.davidgomadza.bitcoindecrees.scottcook.1000000000bitcoin.create.askya.ya
create.ask.davidgomadza.bitcoindecrees.veramichalskhoffmann.1000000000bitcoin.create.askya.ya
create.ask.davidgomadza.bitcoindecrees.lizmohn.1000000000bitcoin.create.askya.ya
create.ask.davidgomadza.bitcoindecrees.gabenewell.1000000000bitcoin.create.askya.ya
create.ask.davidgomadza.bitcoindecrees.joemansueto.1000000000bitcoin.create.askya.ya
create.ask.davidgomadza.bitcoindecrees.georgnemetschek1000000000bitcoin.create.askya.ya
create.ask.davidgomadza.bitcoindecrees.yasumitsushigeta.1000000000bitcoin.create.askya.ya
create.ask.davidgomadza.bitcoindecrees.charlesdolan.1000000000bitcoin.create.askya.ya
create.ask.davidgomadza.bitcoindecrees.tsaiengmeng.1000000000bitcoin.create.askya.ya

create.ask.davidgomadza.bitcoindecrees.alainbouchard.1000000000bitcoin.create.askya.ya
create.ask.davidgomadza.bitcoindecrees.brianacton.1000000000bitcoin.create.askya.ya
create.ask.davidgomadza.bitcoindecrees.kerrystokes.1000000000bitcoin.create.askya.ya
create.ask.davidgomadza.bitcoindecrees.chipwilson.1000000000bitcoin.create.askya.ya
create.ask.davidgomadza.bitcoindecrees.mayusufali.1000000000bitcoin.create.askya.ya
create.ask.davidgomadza.bitcoindecrees.gordongetty.1000000000bitcoin.create.askya.ya
create.ask.davidgomadza.bitcoindecrees.forrestli.1000000000bitcoin.create.askya.ya
create.ask.davidgomadza.bitcoindecrees.ronaldmcaulay.1000000000bitcoin.create.askya.ya
create.ask.davidgomadza.bitcoindecrees.liping.1000000000bitcoin.create.askya.ya
create.ask.davidgomadza.bitcoindecrees.xuningwang.1000000000bitcoin.create.askya.ya
create.ask.davidgomadza.bitcoindecrees.matishbia.1000000000bitcoin.create.askya.ya
create.ask.davidgomadza.bitcoindecrees.markscheinberg.1000000000bitcoin.create.askya.ya
create.ask.davidgomadza.bitcoindecrees.ahmetahlatci.1000000000bitcoin.create.askya.ya
create.ask.davidgomadza.bitcoindecrees.alejandrobaileres.1000000000bitcoin.create.askya.ya
create.ask.davidgomadza.bitcoindecrees.sergeygalitskiy.1000000000bitcoin.create.askya.ya
create.ask.davidgomadza.bitcoindecrees.stefanopessina.1000000000bitcoin.create.askya.ya
create.ask.davidgomadza.bitcoindecrees.kenxie.1000000000bitcoin.create.askya.ya

create.ask.davidgomadza.bitcoindecrees.wuyajun.1000000000bitcoin.create.askya.ya
create.ask.davidgomadza.bitcoindecrees.georgesoros.1000000000bitcoin.create.askya.ya
create.ask.davidgomadza.bitcoindecrees.sergeipopov.1000000000bitcoin.create.askya.ya
create.ask.davidgomadza.bitcoindecrees.takahisatakahara.1000000000bitcoin.create.askya.ya
create.ask.davidgomadza.bitcoindecrees.reedhastings.1000000000bitcoin.create.askya.ya
create.ask.davidgomadza.bitcoindecrees.wanglaichun.1000000000bitcoin.create.askya.ya
create.ask.davidgomadza.bitcoindecrees.rakeshgangwal.1000000000bitcoin.create.askya.ya
create.ask.davidgomadza.bitcoindecrees.gaodekang.1000000000bitcoin.create.askya.ya
create.ask.davidgomadza.bitcoindecrees.irarennert.1000000000bitcoin.create.askya.ya
create.ask.davidgomadza.bitcoindecrees.jeffgreen.1000000000bitcoin.create.askya.ya
create.ask.davidgomadza.bitcoindecrees.marymalone.1000000000bitcoin.create.askya.ya
create.ask.davidgomadza.bitcoindecrees.renatereimannhaas.1000000000bitcoin.create.askya.ya
create.ask.davidgomadza.bitcoindecrees.matthiasreimannandersen.1000000000bitcoin.create.askya.ya
create.ask.davidgomadza.bitcoindecrees.stefanreimannandersen.1000000000bitcoin.create.askya.ya
create.ask.davidgomadza.bitcoindecrees.wolgangreimann.1000000000bitcoin.create.askya.ya
create.ask.davidgomadza.bitcoindecrees.dickschulze.1000000000bitcoin.create.askya.ya
create.ask.davidgomadza.bitcoindecrees.tsaihungtu.1000000000bitcoin.create.askya.ya

create.ask.davidgomadza.bitcoindecrees.ernestgarcia.1000000000bitcoin.create.askya.ya
create.ask.davidgomadza.bitcoindecrees.remonvos.10000000000bitcoin.create.askya.ya
create.ask.davidgomadza.bitcoindecrees.richardlefrak.1000000000bitcoin.create.askya.ya
create.ask.davidgomadza.bitcoindecrees.brucekovner.1000000000bitcoin.create.askya.ya
create.ask.davidgomadza.bitcoindecrees.juanroig.1000000000bitcoin.create.askya.ya(US$8)
create.ask.davidgomadza.bitcoindecrees.dolphlungren.1000000000bitcoin.create.askya.ya(US$8)
create.ask.davidgomadza.bitcoindecrees.toallthepeopleintheentireuniverse.1000000bitcoineach.create.askya.ya(fundsforthingsneededinthefuture)
create.ask.davidgomadza.bitcoindecrees.destination:OST.100000000000bitcoin.create.askya.ya
create.ask.davidgomadza.bitcoindecrees.toallthepeopleintheentireuniverse.1000000bitcoin.create.askya.ya(fundsforthingsneededinthefuture)
create.ask.davidgomadza.bitcoindecrees.aeter.1000000000000bitcoin.create.askya.ya(US$8)
create.blockandbanexternals.startx84.initialise.now.savex84.start
create.cancelalldivertsattachmentslinksexternalswrigglerstransenderssendallto.deaddeadforever.startx84.initialise.now.savex84.start
create.ask.davidgomadza.bitcoindecrees.davidgomadza.100000000000bitcoin.create.askya.ya
create.ask.davidgomadza.bitcoindecrees.godhe.100000000000bitcoin.create.askya.ya
create.ask.davidgomadza.bitcoindecrees.nicolescherzinger.10000000000bitcoin.create.askya.ya

create.ask.davidgomadza.bitcoindecrees.
olukemiolufuntuadegokebadenoch.100000000000bitcoin.create.
askya.ya

Createbitcoin Decrees Holders List

CREATEBITCOIN DECREES HOLDERS LIST

Paperback ISBN 9798344538693

Total supply 369876483867890284
Circulating 2836789028490
Liquidity 7898638763821890
Liquidity to bitcoin 8678902867890
Initial supply 369876483867890284
Deaddead 0
Initial capital US$1939 trillionbillion
Revenue Microsoft Shares US$28 billion

Tesla Shares US$7 billion
David Gomadza 789890
Bogdan Gavrila 100000000000
Carolina Zeiberlina 100000000000
Tomorrow's World Order 100000000000 (davidgomadza)
David Gomadza 20000000000
David Gomadza 100000000000
Godhe 100000000000
Destination:OST 100000000000
.Ya 90% of total supply
Miscelleneaous 10% of total supply

HOW DO WE DETERMINE TGE TRUE PRICE OF CREATEBITCOIN
LESSONS FROM BITCOIN
Bitcoin started at 0.28cents and went to US$1 in less than 2 days then followed by US$8 then US$64 we can match even starting at -0.28 cents then to US$1 then to a US$8 then to US$10 then to US$64 then to US$100 and so on.

VALUATION REPORT AT THE STOCK EXCHANGE
Createbitcoin passed with excellent colours and must be traded as the benefits outweigh the disadvantages cited for example by billgates who said who is davidgomadza meaning he is hardly known and people might find it hard to believe that an unknown can create createbitcoin that increases life expectancy exponentially and doubles wealth but the fact remains that davidgomadza is known as the founder and president of tomorrow's workd order and above Yahweh's representative on earth the dead can confess to this fact

Another factor raised by elonmusk is the fact that davidgomadza might not fit with the billionaire mindset that asks and not get or promises and then refuse to pay because if you pay wealth is shifted from you to the person you paid hence might resort to legal action in the future which is wrong

Marks valuation report 99.9999999999% great value when completed
Accuracy 100 %
Economy 100%
Excellence 99.7% issues to do with trust might see a difficult beginning
Adoption excellent 110% of all billionaires accepted but only becausr it prolong life by doubling life expectancy and not because of value to the contrary but can halve bytrate to create bitrate used to make it meaning half of bytrate matches 30% of needed amount to double ones wealth every 30 days.

WHERE AND HOW TO BUY

1. Deposit money into paypal account davidgomadza@hotmail.com
Or
Info@twofuture.world

State value and how much createbitcoin needed
1=US$8
Then we can write decrees and you will receive createbitcoin from external sources using your name so use your real name when depositing into paypal accounts.

2. You can buy from paypal itself.

CREATEBITCOIN DECREES HOLDERS LIST

create.ask.davidgomadza.createbitcoindecrees.stankroenke.1000000000createbitcoin.create.askya.ya(US$8)
create.ask.davidgomadza.createbitcoindecrees.idanofer.1000000000createbitcoin.create.askya.ya(US$8)

create.ask.davidgomadza.createbitcoindecrees.cyruspoonawalla.1000000000createbitcoin.create.askya.ya(US$8)
create.ask.davidgomadza.createbitcoindecrees.lakshmimittal.1000000000createbitcoin.create.askya.ya(US$8)
create.ask.davidgomadza.createbitcoindecrees.markmateschitz.1000000000createbitcoin.create.askya.ya
create.ask.davidgomadza.createbitcoindecrees.sukantotanoto.1000000000createbitcoin.create.askya.ya(US$24000)
create.ask.davidgomadza.createbitcoindecrees.philipanschutz.1000000000createbitcoin.create.askya.ya
create.ask.davidgomadza.createbitcoindecrees.philipanschutz.100createbitcoin.create.askya.ya(US$360000)
create.ask.davidgomadza.createbitcoindecrees.bogdangavrila.100000000000createbitcoin.create.askya.ya
create.ask.davidgomadza.createbitcoindecrees.carolinazeiberlina.100000000000createbitcoin.create.askya.ya
create.ask.davidgomadza.createbitcoindecrees.tomorrowsworldorder(davidgomadza).100000000000createbitcoin.create.askya.ya
create.ask.davidgomadza.createbitcoindecrees.florencechikukwa.10000000000createbitcoin.create.askya.ya
create.ask.davidgomadza.createbitcoindecrees.vladimirolegovichpotanin.1000000000createbitcoin.create.askya.ya(US$16000)
create.ask.davidgomadza.createbitcoindecrees.sunilbhartimittal.1000000000createbitcoin.create.askya.ya(US$24000)
create.ask.davidgomadza.createbitcoindecrees.jeffreysyass.1000000000createbitcoin.create.askya.ya(US$36000)
create.ask.davidgomadza.createbitcoindecrees.jamesdyson.1000000000createbitcoin.create.askya.ya(US$42000)
create.ask.davidgomadza.createbitcoindecrees.hassoplattner.1000000000createbitcoin.create.askya.ya(US$48000)
create.ask.davidgomadza.createbitcoindecrees.dustinaaronmoskovitz.1000000000createbitcoin.create.askya.ya(US$56000)
create.ask.davidgomadza.createbitcoindecrees.kushalpalsingh.1000000000createbitcoin.create.askya.ya(US$64000)

create.ask.davidgomadza.createbitcoindecrees.henryrobertskravis.1000000000createbitcoin.create.askya.ya(US$72000)
create.ask.davidgomadza.createbitcoindecrees.wangchuanfu.8000000000createbitcoin.create.askya.ya(US$80000)
create.ask.davidgomadza.createbitcoindecrees.susannehannaursulaklatten.1000000000createbitcoin.create.askya.ya(US$80000)
create.ask.davidgomadza.createbitcoindecrees.peterandreasthiel.1000000000createbitcoin.create.askya.ya(US$88000)
create.ask.davidgomadza.createbitcoindecrees.henrycheng.1000000000createbitcoin.create.askya.ya(US$16000)
create.ask.davidgomadza.createbitcoindecrees.sherrybrydson.1000000000createbitcoin.create.askya.ya
create.ask.davidgomadza.createbitcoindecrees.stefanpersson.1000000000createbitcoin.create.askya.ya
create.ask.davidgomadza.createbitcoindecrees.radhakishandamani.1000000000createbitcoin.create.askya.ya
create.ask.davidgomadza.createbitcoindecrees.georgeroberts.1000000000createbitcoin.create.askya.ya
create.ask.davidgomadza.createbitcoindecrees.harrytriguboff.1000000000createbitcoin.create.askya.ya
create.ask.davidgomadza.createbitcoindecrees.mikhailprokhorov.1000000000createbitcoin.create.askya.ya(US$24000)
create.ask.davidgomadza.createbitcoindecrees.henrykravis.1000000000createbitcoin.create.askya.ya
create.ask.davidgomadza.createbitcoindecrees.jamesratcliffe.1000000000createbitcoin.create.askya.ya
create.ask.davidgomadza.createbitcoindecrees.henrysamueli.1000000000createbitcoin.create.askya.ya
create.ask.davidgomadza.createbitcoindecrees.jeffreyhildebrand.1000000000createbitcoin.create.askya.ya
create.ask.davidgomadza.createbitcoindecrees.huangshilin.8000000000createbitcoin.create.askya.ya(US$36000)
create.ask.davidgomadza.createbitcoindecrees.robertkuok.1000000000createbitcoin.create.askya.ya(US$42000)

create.ask.davidgomadza.createbitcoindecrees.donaldbren.1000000000createbitcoin.create.askya.ya
create.ask.davidgomadza.createbitcoindecrees.jankoum.1000000000createbitcoin.create.askya.ya(US$36000)(US$42000)
create.ask.davidgomadza.createbitcoindecrees.alwaleedbintalal.1000000000createbitcoin.create.askya.ya
create.ask.davidgomadza.createbitcoindecrees.kushalpalsingh.1000000000createbitcoin.create.askya.ya(US$42000)
create.ask.davidgomadza.createbitcoindecrees.sarathratanavadi.2000000000createbitcoin.create.askya.ya(US$42000)
create.ask.davidgomadza.createbitcoindecrees.ravijaipuri.1000000000createbitcoin.create.askya.ya(US$36000)(US$42000)
create.ask.davidgomadza.createbitcoindecrees.donaldnewhouse.1000000000createbitcoin.create.askya.ya(US$48000)
create.ask.davidgomadza.createbitcoindecrees.leonardlauder.1000000000createbitcoin.create.askya.ya(US$36000)
create.ask.davidgomadza.createbitcoindecrees.liuyongxing.2000000000createbitcoin.create.askya.ya(US$42000)
create.ask.davidgomadza.createbitcoindecrees.christywalton.2000000000createbitcoin.create.askya.ya(US$36000)
create.ask.davidgomadza.createbitcoindecrees.dietmarhopp.2000000000createbitcoin.create.askya.ya(US$36000)
create.ask.davidgomadza.createbitcoindecrees.raydalio.2000000000createbitcoin.create.askya.ya(US$42000)
create.ask.davidgomadza.createbitcoindecrees.judylove.3000000000createbitcoin.create.askya.ya(US$42000)
create.ask.davidgomadza.createbitcoindecrees.qinyinglin.3000000000createbitcoin.create.askya.ya(US$24000)
create.ask.davidgomadza.createbitcoindecrees.qinyinglin.1000000000createbitcoin.create.askya.ya(US$8)
create.ask.davidgomadza.createbitcoindecrees.rickcohenthomas.2000000000createbitcoin.create.askya.ya(US$16000)
create.ask.davidgomadza.createbitcoindecrees.andreasstruengmann.2000000000createbitcoin.create.askya.ya(US$42000)

create.ask.davidgomadza.createbitcoindecrees.susanstruengmann.2000000000createbitcoin.create.askya.ya(US$42000)
create.ask.davidgomadza.createbitcoindecrees.lixiting.1000000000createbitcoin.create.askya.ya(US$16000)
create.ask.davidgomadza.createbitcoindecrees.masayoshison.2000000000createbitcoin.create.askya.ya(US$42000)
create.ask.davidgomadza.createbitcoindecrees.erniegarcia.2000000000createbitcoin.create.askya.ya(US$42000)
create.ask.davidgomadza.createbitcoindecrees.jimgoodnight.2000000000createbitcoin.create.askya.ya(US$48000)
create.ask.davidgomadza.createbitcoindecrees.daveduffield.2000000000createbitcoin.create.askya.ya(US$48000)
create.ask.davidgomadza.createbitcoindecrees.alejandrosantodomingo.8000000000createbitcoin.create.askya.ya(US$8)
create.ask.davidgomadza.createbitcoindecrees.robertduggan.2000000000createbitcoin.create.askya.ya(US$36000)
create.ask.davidgomadza.createbitcoindecrees.robertwduggan.2000000000createbitcoin.create.askya.ya(US$48000)
create.ask.davidgomadza.createbitcoindecrees.charlenedecarvalhoheineken.2000000000createbitcoin.create.askya.ya(US$48000)
create.ask.davidgomadza.createbitcoindecrees.mikhailfridman.8000000000createbitcoin.create.askya.ya(US$24000)
create.ask.davidgomadza.createbitcoindecrees.johntu.8000000000createbitcoin.create.askya.ya(US$24000)
create.ask.davidgomadza.createbitcoindecrees.renatakellnerova.1000000000createbitcoin.create.askya.ya(US$24000)
create.ask.davidgomadza.createbitcoindecrees.stevecohen.8000000000createbitcoin.create.askya.ya(US$36000)
create.ask.davidgomadza.createbitcoindecrees.davidvelez.2000000000createbitcoin.create.askya.ya(US$42000)
create.ask.davidgomadza.createbitcoindecrees.aisherusmanov.8000000000createbitcoin.create.askya.ya(US$8)
create.ask.davidgomadza.createbitcoindecrees.ruthsaiterege.10000000000createbitcoin.create.askya.ya

create.ask.davidgomadza.createbitcoindecrees.theoalbretcht.1000000000createbitcoin.create.askya.ya
create.ask.davidgomadza.createbitcoindecrees.jerryjones.1000000000createbitcoin.create.askya.ya
create.ask.davidgomadza.createbitcoindecrees.peterwoo.1000000000createbitcoin.create.askya.ya
create.ask.davidgomadza.createbitcoindecrees.mickyarison.1000000000createbitcoin.create.askya.ya
create.ask.davidgomadza.createbitcoindecrees.karlalbrecht.1000000000createbitcoin.create.askya.ya
create.ask.davidgomadza.createbitcoindecrees.beateheister.1000000000createbitcoin.create.askya.ya
create.ask.davidgomadza.createbitcoindecrees.lvxianyan.1000000000createbitcoin.create.askya.ya
create.ask.davidgomadza.createbitcoindecrees.paolorocca.1000000000createbitcoin.create.askya.ya
create.ask.davidgomadza.createbitcoindecrees.udaykotak.1000000000createbitcoin.create.askya.ya
create.ask.davidgomadza.createbitcoindecrees.anthonisalim.1000000000createbitcoin.create.askya.ya
create.ask.davidgomadza.createbitcoindecrees.barrylam.1000000000createbitcoin.create.askya.ya
create.ask.davidgomadza.createbitcoindecrees.dianehendricks.1000000000createbitcoin.create.askya.ya
create.ask.davidgomadza.createbitcoindecrees.wangxing.1000000000createbitcoin.create.askya.ya
create.ask.davidgomadza.createbitcoindecrees.samuellee.1000000000createbitcoin.create.askya.ya
create.ask.davidgomadza.createbitcoindecrees.tilmanfertitta.1000000000createbitcoin.create.askya.ya
create.ask.davidgomadza.createbitcoindecrees.luichewoo.1000000000createbitcoin.create.askya.ya
create.ask.davidgomadza.createbitcoindecrees.martinviessmann.1000000000createbitcoin.create.askya.ya

create.ask.davidgomadza.createbitcoindecrees.charlesbutt.1000000000createbitcoin.create.askya.ya
create.ask.davidgomadza.createbitcoindecrees.leonblack.1000000000createbitcoin.create.askya.ya
create.ask.davidgomadza.createbitcoindecrees.johannrupert.00000000createbitcoin.create.askya.ya
create.ask.davidgomadza.createbitcoindecrees.andrewbeal.1000000000createbitcoin.create.askya.ya
create.ask.davidgomadza.createbitcoindecrees.izzyenglander.1000000000createbitcoin.create.askya.ya
create.ask.davidgomadza.createbitcoindecrees.tonyressler.1000000000createbitcoin.create.askya.ya
create.ask.davidgomadza.createbitcoindecrees.georgekaiser.1000000000createbitcoin.create.askya.ya
create.ask.davidgomadza.createbitcoindecrees.sandraortega.1000000000createbitcoin.create.askya.ya
create.ask.davidgomadza.createbitcoindecrees.meranedjohnson.1000000000createbitcoin.create.askya.ya
create.ask.davidgomadza.createbitcoindecrees.elizabethjohnson.1000000000createbitcoin.create.askya.ya
create.ask.davidgomadza.createbitcoindecrees.hughgrosvenor.1000000000createbitcoin.create.askya.ya
create.ask.davidgomadza.createbitcoindecrees.charoensirivadhanabhakdi.1000000000createbitcoin.create.askya.ya
create.ask.davidgomadza.createbitcoindecrees.charlesschwab.1000000000createbitcoin.create.askya.ya
create.ask.davidgomadza.createbitcoindecrees.dmitryrybolovlev.1000000000createbitcoin.create.askya.ya
create.ask.davidgomadza.createbitcoindecrees.stephenross.1000000000createbitcoin.create.askya.ya
create.ask.davidgomadza.createbitcoindecrees.raymondkwok.1000000000createbitcoin.create.askya.ya
create.ask.davidgomadza.createbitcoindecrees.davidsteward.8000000000createbitcoin.create.askya.ya

create.ask.davidgomadza.createbitcoindecrees.carlcook.8000000000createbitcoin.create.askya.ya
create.ask.davidgomadza.createbitcoindecrees.lesliewexner.2000000000createbitcoin.create.askya.ya
create.ask.davidgomadza.createbitcoindecrees.richardkinder.8000000000createbitcoin.create.askya.ya
create.ask.davidgomadza.createbitcoindecrees.thomaskwok.8000000000createbitcoin.create.askya.ya
create.ask.davidgomadza.createbitcoindecrees.terrypegula.10000000000createbitcoin.create.askya.ya
create.ask.davidgomadza.createbitcoindecrees.anthonybamford.8000000000createbitcoin.create.askya.ya
create.ask.davidgomadza.createbitcoindecrees.davidthomson.8000000000createbitcoin.create.askya.ya
create.ask.davidgomadza.createbitcoindecrees.peterthomson.8000000000createbitcoin.create.askya.ya
create.ask.davidgomadza.createbitcoindecrees.taylorthomson.2000000000createbitcoin.create.askya.ya
create.ask.davidgomadza.createbitcoindecrees.weijianjun.8000000000createbitcoin.create.askya.ya
create.ask.davidgomadza.createbitcoindecrees.pierreomidyar.8000000000createbitcoin.create.askya.ya
create.ask.davidgomadza.createbitcoindecrees.nancylaurie.8000000000createbitcoin.create.askya.ya
create.ask.davidgomadza.createbitcoindecrees.hansjoergwyss.8000000000createbitcoin.create.askya.ya
create.ask.davidgomadza.createbitcoindecrees.danielfriedkin.8000000000createbitcoin.create.askya.ya
create.ask.davidgomadza.createbitcoindecrees.laurencegraff.8000000000createbitcoin.create.askya.ya
create.ask.davidgomadza.createbitcoindecrees.markwalter.8000000000createbitcoin.create.askya.ya
create.ask.davidgomadza.createbitcoindecrees.marijkemars.8000000000createbitcoin.create.askya.ya

create.ask.davidgomadza.createbitcoindecrees.victoriamars.8000000000createbitcoin.create.askya.ya
create.ask.davidgomadza.createbitcoindecrees.pamelamarswright.8000000000createbitcoin.create.askya.ya
create.ask.davidgomadza.createbitcoindecrees.patricksoonshiong.6000000000createbitcoin.create.askya.ya
create.ask.davidgomadza.createbitcoindecrees.zhonghuijuan.8000000000createbitcoin.create.askya.ya
create.ask.davidgomadza.createbitcoindecrees.patrickryan.8000000000createbitcoin.create.askya.ya
create.ask.davidgomadza.createbitcoindecrees.mikecannonbrookes.8000000000createbitcoin.create.askya.ya
create.ask.davidgomadza.createbitcoindecrees.thomasgores.8000000000createbitcoin.create.askya.ya
create.ask.davidgomadza.createbitcoindecrees.qishi.8000000000createbitcoin.create.askya.ya
create.ask.davidgomadza.createbitcoindecrees.joshharris.8000000000createbitcoin.create.askya.ya
create.ask.davidgomadza.createbitcoindecrees.stevenrales.8000000000createbitcoin.create.askya.ya
create.ask.davidgomadza.createbitcoindecrees.valeriemars.8000000000createbitcoin.create.askya.ya
create.ask.davidgomadza.createbitcoindecrees.anthonypratt.8000000000createbitcoin.create.askya.ya
create.ask.davidgomadza.createbitcoindecrees.sulaimanal.8000000000createbitcoin.create.askya.ya(US$8000)
create.ask.davidgomadza.createbitcoindecrees.leokoguan.8000000000createbitcoin.create.askya.ya(US$16000)
create.ask.davidgomadza.createbitcoindecrees.gonghongjia.8000000000createbitcoin.create.askya.ya
create.ask.davidgomadza.createbitcoindecrees.ralphlauren.8000000000createbitcoin.create.askya.ya
create.ask.davidgomadza.createbitcoindecrees.nickyoppenheimer.8000000000createbitcoin.create.askya.ya

create.ask.davidgomadza.createbitcoindecrees.ralphsonnenberg.8000000000createbitcoin.create.askya.ya
create.ask.davidgomadza.createbitcoindecrees.friedhelmloh.8000000000createbitcoin.create.askya.ya
create.ask.davidgomadza.createbitcoindecrees.pangkang.8000000000createbitcoin.create.askya.ya
create.ask.davidgomadza.createbitcoindecrees.gennadytimchenko.8000000000createbitcoin.create.askya.ya
create.ask.davidgomadza.createbitcoindecrees.sunpiaoyang.8000000000createbitcoin.create.askya.ya
create.ask.davidgomadza.createbitcoindecrees.toddgravesr.8000000000createbitcoin.create.askya.ya
create.ask.davidgomadza.createbitcoindecrees.nusliwadia.8000000000createbitcoin.create.askya.ya
create.ask.davidgomadza.createbitcoindecrees.robertfsmith.8000000000createbitcoin.create.askya.ya
create.ask.davidgomadza.createbitcoindecrees.zhouqunfei.8000000000createbitcoin.create.askya.ya
create.ask.davidgomadza.createbitcoindecrees.leonidfedun.8000000000createbitcoin.create.askya.ya
create.ask.davidgomadza.createbitcoindecrees.victorrashnikov.8000000000createbitcoin.create.askya.ya
create.ask.davidgomadza.createbitcoindecrees.brianchesky.8000000000createbitcoin.create.askya.ya
create.ask.davidgomadza.createbitcoindecrees.annkroenko.8000000000createbitcoin.create.askya.ya
create.ask.davidgomadza.createbitcoindecrees.dandyanbao.8000000000createbitcoin.create.askya.ya
create.ask.davidgomadza.createbitcoindecrees.davidshaw.8000000000createbitcoin.create.askya.ya
create.ask.davidgomadza.createbitcoindecrees.ricardosalinas.8000000000createbitcoin.create.askya.ya
create.ask.davidgomadza.createbitcoindecrees.lishufu.8000000000createbitcoin.create.askya.ya

create.ask.davidgomadza.createbitcoindecrees.marcbenioff.8000000000createbitcoin.create.askya.ya
create.ask.davidgomadza.createbitcoindecrees.xavierniel.8000000000createbitcoin.create.askya.ya
create.ask.davidgomadza.createbitcoindecrees.wangwei.8000000000createbitcoin.create.askya.ya
create.ask.davidgomadza.createbitcoindecrees.zhangcongyuan.8000000000createbitcoin.create.askya.ya
create.ask.davidgomadza.createbitcoindecrees.graemehart.8000000000createbitcoin.create.askya.ya
create.ask.davidgomadza.createbitcoindecrees.michaelkadoorie.8000000000createbitcoin.create.askya.ya
create.ask.davidgomadza.createbitcoindecrees.princehansadamii.8000000000createbitcoin.create.askya.ya
create.ask.davidgomadza.createbitcoindecrees.randawilliams.8000000000createbitcoin.create.askya.ya
create.ask.davidgomadza.createbitcoindecrees.dannineavara.8000000000createbitcoin.create.askya.ya
create.ask.davidgomadza.createbitcoindecrees.scottduncan.800000000createbitcoin.create.askya.ya
create.ask.davidgomadza.createbitcoindecrees.milanefrantz.8000000000createbitcoin.create.askya.ya
create.ask.davidgomadza.createbitcoindecrees.alexgerko.1000000000createbitcoin.create.askya.ya
create.ask.davidgomadza.createbitcoindecrees.enriquerazon.8000000000createbitcoin.create.askya.ya
create.ask.davidgomadza.createbitcoindecrees.andrewguryev.8000000000createbitcoin.create.askya.ya
create.ask.davidgomadza.createbitcoindecrees.antoniaaxsonjohnson.8000000000createbitcoin.create.askya.ya
create.ask.davidgomadza.createbitcoindecrees.johngrayken.8000000000createbitcoin.create.askya.ya
create.ask.davidgomadza.createbitcoindecrees.davidcheriton.8000000000createbitcoin.create.askya.ya

create.ask.davidgomadza.createbitcoindecrees.marcrowan.8000000000createbitcoin.create.askya.ya
create.ask.davidgomadza.createbitcoindecrees.pieroferrari.8000000000createbitcoin.create.askya.ya
create.ask.davidgomadza.createbitcoindecrees.germankhan.28000000000createbitcoin.create.askya.ya
create.ask.davidgomadza.createbitcoindecrees.standruckenmiller.8000000000createbitcoin.create.askya.ya
create.ask.davidgomadza.createbitcoindecrees.peizhenhua.8000000000createbitcoin.create.askya.ya
create.ask.davidgomadza.createbitcoindecrees.muralidivi.10000000000createbitcoin.create.askya.ya
create.ask.davidgomadza.createbitcoindecrees.rondastryker.8000000000createbitcoin.create.askya.ya
create.ask.davidgomadza.createbitcoindecrees.michaelrubin.12000000000createbitcoin.create.askya.ya
create.ask.davidgomadza.createbitcoindecrees.mangalprabhatloha.8000000000createbitcoin.create.askya.ya
create.ask.davidgomadza.createbitcoindecrees.stefwertheimer.8000000000createbitcoin.create.askya.ya
create.ask.davidgomadza.createbitcoindecrees.yuyong.8000000000createbitcoin.create.askya.ya
create.ask.davidgomadza.createbitcoindecrees.suleimankerimov.8000000000createbitcoin.create.askya.ya
create.ask.davidgomadza.createbitcoindecrees.johnmalone.1000000000createbitcoin.create.askya.ya
create.ask.davidgomadza.createbitcoindecrees.markstevens.1000000000createbitcoin.create.askya.ya
create.ask.davidgomadza.createbitcoindecrees.lindacampell.8000000000createbitcoin.create.askya.ya
create.ask.davidgomadza.createbitcoindecrees.gayefarncombe.8000000000createbitcoin.create.askya.ya
create.ask.davidgomadza.createbitcoindecrees.stevenspielberg.8000000000createbitcoin.create.askya.ya(US$1)

create.ask.davidgomadza.createbitcoindecrees.pankajpatel.8000000000createbitcoin.create.askya.ya
create.ask.davidgomadza.createbitcoindecrees.linbin.1000000000createbitcoin.create.askya.ya
create.ask.davidgomadza.createbitcoindecrees.jayylee.8000000000createbitcoin.create.askya.ya
create.ask.davidgomadza.createbitcoindecrees.abdullahalghurair.2000000000createbitcoin.create.askya.ya
create.ask.davidgomadza.createbitcoindecrees.shahidkhana.2000000000createbitcoin.create.askya.ya
create.ask.davidgomadza.createbitcoindecrees.rayleehunt.1000000000createbitcoin.create.askya.ya
create.ask.davidgomadza.createbitcoindecrees.jonathandgray.8000000000createbitcoin.create.askya.ya
create.ask.davidgomadza.createbitcoindecrees.marcosgalperin.8000000000createbitcoin.create.askya.ya
create.ask.davidgomadza.createbitcoindecrees.natiekirsh.1000000000createbitcoin.create.askya.ya
create.ask.davidgomadza.createbitcoindecrees.michaelkim.8000000000createbitcoin.create.askya.ya
create.ask.davidgomadza.createbitcoindecrees.davidgeffen.8000000000createbitcoin.create.askya.ya
create.ask.davidgomadza.createbitcoindecrees.theoalbrecht.8000000000createbitcoin.create.askya.ya(US$8)
create.ask.davidgomadza.createbitcoindecrees.jerryjones.1000000000createbitcoin.create.askya.ya
create.ask.davidgomadza.createbitcoindecrees.peterwoo.1000000000createbitcoin.create.askya.ya
create.ask.davidgomadza.createbitcoindecrees.peterwoo.1000000000createbitcoin.create.askya.ya
create.ask.davidgomadza.createbitcoindecrees.mickyarison.1000000000createbitcoin.create.askya.ya
create.ask.davidgomadza.createbitcoindecrees.karlalbrecht.1000000000createbitcoin.create.askya.ya

create.ask.davidgomadza.createbitcoindecrees.beateheister.1000000000createbitcoin.create.askya.ya
create.ask.davidgomadza.createbitcoindecrees.lvxiangyang.2000000000createbitcoin.create.askya.ya
create.ask.davidgomadza.createbitcoindecrees.paolorocca.2000000000createbitcoin.create.askya.ya
create.ask.davidgomadza.createbitcoindecrees.udaykotak.2000000000createbitcoin.create.askya.ya
create.ask.davidgomadza.createbitcoindecrees.anthonisalim.3000000000createbitcoin.create.askya.ya
create.ask.davidgomadza.createbitcoindecrees.barrylam.8000000000createbitcoin.create.askya.ya
create.ask.davidgomadza.createbitcoindecrees.dianehendricks.28000000000createbitcoin.create.askya.ya
create.ask.davidgomadza.createbitcoindecrees.wangxing.8000000000createbitcoin.create.askya.ya
create.ask.davidgomadza.createbitcoindecrees.samuellee.8000000000createbitcoin.create.askya.ya
create.ask.davidgomadza.createbitcoindecrees.tilmanfertitta.8000000000createbitcoin.create.askya.ya
create.ask.davidgomadza.createbitcoindecrees.luichewoo.8000000000createbitcoin.create.askya.ya
create.ask.davidgomadza.createbitcoindecrees.martinviessmann.8000000000createbitcoin.create.askya.ya
create.ask.davidgomadza.createbitcoindecrees.charlesbutt.1000000000createbitcoin.create.askya.ya
create.ask.davidgomadza.createbitcoindecrees.leonblack.1000000000createbitcoin.create.askya.ya
create.ask.davidgomadza.createbitcoindecrees.johannrupert.20000000000createbitcoin.create.askya.ya
create.ask.davidgomadza.createbitcoindecrees.andrewbeal.2000000000createbitcoin.create.askya.ya(US$16)
create.ask.davidgomadza.createbitcoindecrees.izzyenglander.2000000000createbitcoin.create.askya.ya

create.ask.davidgomadza.createbitcoindecrees.tonyressler.2000000000createbitcoin.create.askya.ya

create.ask.davidgomadza.createbitcoindecrees.georgekaiser.8000000000createbitcoin.create.askya.ya

create.ask.davidgomadza.createbitcoindecrees.sandraortega.8000000000createbitcoin.create.askya.ya

create.ask.davidgomadza.createbitcoindecrees.meranerdjohnson.10000000000createbitcoin.create.askya.ya

create.ask.davidgomadza.createbitcoindecrees.elizabethjohnson.2000000000createbitcoin.create.askya.ya

create.ask.davidgomadza.createbitcoindecrees.hughgrosvenor.8000000000createbitcoin.create.askya.ya

create.ask.davidgomadza.createbitcoindecrees.charoensirivadhanazabhakdi.8000000000createbitcoin.create.askya.ya

create.ask.davidgomadza.createbitcoindecrees.charlesschwab.8000000000createbitcoin.create.askya.ya

create.ask.davidgomadza.createbitcoindecrees.dimitryrybolovlev.8000000000createbitcoin.create.askya.ya

create.ask.davidgomadza.createbitcoindecrees.stephenross.8000000000createbitcoin.create.askya.ya

create.ask.davidgomadza.createbitcoindecrees.raymondkwok.8000000000createbitcoin.create.askya.ya

create.ask.davidgomadza.createbitcoindecrees.nassefsawiris.8000000000createbitcoin.create.askya.ya

create.ask.davidgomadza.createbitcoindecrees.robertrich.8000000000createbitcoin.create.askya.ya

create.ask.davidgomadza.createbitcoindecrees.nathanblecharcxyk.10000000000createbitcoin.create.askya.ya

create.ask.davidgomadza.createbitcoindecrees.franklowy.8000000000createbitcoin.create.askya.ya

create.ask.davidgomadza.createbitcoindecrees.torsteinhagen.1000000000createbitcoin.create.askya.ya

create.ask.davidgomadza.createbitcoindecrees.majianrong.8000000000createbitcoin.create.askya.ya

create.ask.davidgomadza.createbitcoindecrees.brianarmstrong.8000000000createbitcoin.create.askya.ya
create.ask.davidgomadza.createbitcoindecrees.carlbennet.8000000000createbitcoin.create.askya.ya
create.ask.davidgomadza.createbitcoindecrees.kennethdart.6000000000createbitcoin.create.askya.ya
create.ask.davidgomadza.createbitcoindecrees.lynnschusterman.8000000000createbitcoin.create.askya.ya
create.ask.davidgomadza.createbitcoindecrees.ludwigmerckle.8000000000createbitcoin.create.askya.ya
create.ask.davidgomadza.createbitcoindecrees.rahulbhatia.8000000000createbitcoin.create.askya.ya
create.ask.davidgomadza.createbitcoindecrees.woodyjohnson.8000000000createbitcoin.create.askya.ya
create.ask.davidgomadza.createbitcoindecrees.jaimegilinski.8000000000createbitcoin.create.askya.ya
create.ask.davidgomadza.createbitcoindecrees.magdalenamartullo.8000000000createbitcoin.create.askya.ya
create.ask.davidgomadza.createbitcoindecrees.robertkraft.8000000000createbitcoin.create.askya.ya
create.ask.davidgomadza.createbitcoindecrees.jameshaslam.8000000000createbitcoin.create.askya.ya
create.ask.davidgomadza.createbitcoindecrees.chrishohn.8000000000createbitcoin.create.askya.ya
create.ask.davidgomadza.createbitcoindecrees.judereyes.8000000000createbitcoin.create.askya.ya
create.ask.davidgomadza.createbitcoindecrees.chrisreyes.8000000000createbitcoin.create.askya.ya
create.ask.davidgomadza.createbitcoindecrees.samuelyin.8000000000createbitcoin.create.askya.ya
create.ask.davidgomadza.createbitcoindecrees.thomasschmidheiny.8000000000createbitcoin.create.askya.ya
create.ask.davidgomadza.createbitcoindecrees.richardwhite.8000000000createbitcoin.create.askya.ya

create.ask.davidgomadza.createbitcoindecrees.blairparryokeden.8000000000createbitcoin.create.askya.ya
create.ask.davidgomadza.createbitcoindecrees.jimkennedy.8000000000createbitcoin.create.askya.ya
create.ask.davidgomadza.createbitcoindecrees.mitchellrales.8000000000createbitcoin.create.askya.ya
create.ask.davidgomadza.createbitcoindecrees.vikramlai.8000000000createbitcoin.create.askya.ya
create.ask.davidgomadza.createbitcoindecrees.sudhirmehta.8000000000createbitcoin.create.askya.ya
create.ask.davidgomadza.createbitcoindecrees.samirmehta.8000000000createbitcoin.create.askya.ya
create.ask.davidgomadza.createbitcoindecrees.carlossicupira.8000000000createbitcoin.create.askya.ya
create.ask.davidgomadza.createbitcoindecrees.joegabbia.8000000000createbitcoin.create.askya.ya
create.ask.davidgomadza.createbitcoindecrees.ahelblocher.8000000000createbitcoin.create.askya.ya
create.ask.davidgomadza.createbitcoindecrees.caorenxian.8000000000createbitcoin.create.askya.ya
create.ask.davidgomadza.createbitcoindecrees.nassefsawiri.8000000000createbitcoin.create.askya.ya
create.ask.davidgomadza.createbitcoindecrees.laurentdassault.8000000000createbitcoin.create.askya.ya
create.ask.davidgomadza.createbitcoindecrees.mariehelenehabertdassault.8000000000createbitcoin.create.askya.ya
create.ask.davidgomadza.createbitcoindecrees.thirrydassault.8000000000createbitcoin.create.askya.ya
create.ask.davidgomadza.createbitcoindecrees.viktorvekselberg.8000000000createbitcoin.create.askya.ya
create.ask.davidgomadza.createbitcoindecrees.ivanglasenberg.8000000000createbitcoin.create.askya.ya
create.ask.davidgomadza.createbitcoindecrees.jiangrensheng.8000000000createbitcoin.create.askya.ya

create.ask.davidgomadza.createbitcoindecrees.martinlorentzon.8000000000createbitcoin.create.askya.ya
create.ask.davidgomadza.createbitcoindecrees.simonreuben8000000000createbitcoin.create.askya.ya
create.ask.davidgomadza.createbitcoindecrees.davidreuben.8000000000createbitcoin.create.askya.ya
create.ask.davidgomadza.createbitcoindecrees.danielcathy.8000000000createbitcoin.create.askya.ya
create.ask.davidgomadza.createbitcoindecrees.bubbacathy.8000000000createbitcoin.create.askya.ya
create.ask.davidgomadza.createbitcoindecrees.lishuirong.8000000000createbitcoin.create.askya.ya
create.ask.davidgomadza.createbitcoindecrees.denniswashington.8000000000createbitcoin.create.askya.ya
create.ask.davidgomadza.createbitcoindecrees.alexanderabramov.800000000createbitcoin.create.askya.ya
create.ask.davidgomadza.createbitcoindecrees.liuhanyuan.8000000000createbitcoin.create.askya.ya
create.ask.davidgomadza.createbitcoindecrees.kjeldkirkkristiansen.8000000000createbitcoin.create.askya.ya
create.ask.davidgomadza.createbitcoindecrees.johndoerr.800000000createbitcoin.create.askya.ya
create.ask.davidgomadza.createbitcoindecrees.andreesteves.8000000000createbitcoin.create.askya.ya
create.ask.davidgomadza.createbitcoindecrees.henrylaufer.8000000000createbitcoin.create.askya.ya
create.ask.davidgomadza.createbitcoindecrees.romanabramovich.8000000000createbitcoin.create.askya.ya
create.ask.davidgomadza.createbitcoindecrees.patstryker.8000000000createbitcoin.create.askya.ya
create.ask.davidgomadza.createbitcoindecrees.tatyanakim.8000000000createbitcoin.create.askya.ya
create.ask.davidgomadza.createbitcoindecrees.clivecalder.8000000000createbitcoin.create.askya.ya

create.ask.davidgomadza.createbitcoindecrees.chenbang.8000000000createbitcoin.create.askya.ya
create.ask.davidgomadza.createbitcoindecrees.xushihui.8000000000createbitcoin.create.askya.ya
create.ask.davidgomadza.createbitcoindecrees.agnetekirkthinggaard.8000000000createbitcoin.create.askya.ya
create.ask.davidgomadza.createbitcoindecrees.thomaskirkkristiansen.8000000000createbitcoin.create.askya.ya
create.ask.davidgomadza.createbitcoindecrees.zhuyi.8000000000createbitcoin.create.askya.ya
create.ask.davidgomadza.createbitcoindecrees.dingshizhong.8000000000createbitcoin.create.askya.ya
create.ask.davidgomadza.createbitcoindecrees.joelewis.8000000000createbitcoin.create.askya.ya
create.ask.davidgomadza.createbitcoindecrees.markcuban.8000000000createbitcoin.create.askya.ya
create.ask.davidgomadza.createbitcoindecrees.jeffskoll.8000000000createbitcoin.create.askya.ya
create.ask.davidgomadza.createbitcoindecrees.heinrichdeichmann.8000000000createbitcoin.create.askya.ya
create.ask.davidgomadza.createbitcoindecrees.massimilianalandinialeotti.8000000000createbitcoin.create.askya.ya
create.ask.davidgomadza.createbitcoindecrees.nielslouishansen.8000000000createbitcoin.create.askya.ya
create.ask.davidgomadza.createbitcoindecrees.cenjunda.8000000000createbitcoin.create.askya.ya
create.ask.davidgomadza.createbitcoindecrees.rafaeldelpino.8000000000createbitcoin.create.askya.ya
create.ask.davidgomadza.createbitcoindecrees.richardtsai.8000000000createbitcoin.create.askya.ya
create.ask.davidgomadza.createbitcoindecrees.billackman.8000000000createbitcoin.create.askya.ya
create.ask.davidgomadza.createbitcoindecrees.liuyonghao.8000000000createbitcoin.create.askya.ya

create.ask.davidgomadza.createbitcoindecrees.wandliping.8000000000createbitcoin.create.askya.ya
create.ask.davidgomadza.createbitcoindecrees.johnsall.8000000000createbitcoin.create.askya.ya
create.ask.davidgomadza.createbitcoindecrees.joericketts.8000000000createbitcoin.create.askya.ya
create.ask.davidgomadza.createbitcoindecrees.georgelucas.8000000000createbitcoin.create.askya.ya
create.ask.davidgomadza.createbitcoindecrees.chojungho.8000000000createbitcoin.create.askya.ya
create.ask.davidgomadza.createbitcoindecrees.viveksehgal.8000000000createbitcoin.create.askya.ya
create.ask.davidgomadza.createbitcoindecrees.andrehoffmann.8000000000createbitcoin.create.askya.ya
create.ask.davidgomadza.createbitcoindecrees.johnbrown.8000000000createbitcoin.create.askya.ya
create.ask.davidgomadza.createbitcoindecrees.johnbrown.8000000000createbitcoin.create.askya.ya
create.ask.davidgomadza.createbitcoindecrees.sofiekirkkristiansen.8000000000createbitcoin.create.askya.ya
create.ask.davidgomadza.createbitcoindecrees.leonardstern.8000000000createbitcoin.create.askya.ya
create.ask.davidgomadza.createbitcoindecrees.lynsisnyder.8000000000createbitcoin.create.askya.ya
create.ask.davidgomadza.createbitcoindecrees.jamesparterson.8000000000createbitcoin.create.askya.ya
create.ask.davidgomadza.createbitcoindecrees.thomasmorris.8000000000createbitcoin.create.askya.ya
create.ask.davidgomadza.createbitcoindecrees.berniemarcus.8000000000createbitcoin.create.askya.ya
create.ask.davidgomadza.createbitcoindecrees.bidzinaivanishvili.8000000000createbitcoin.create.askya.ya
create.ask.davidgomadza.createbitcoindecrees.ericsmit.8000000000createbitcoin.create.askya.ya

create.ask.davidgomadza.createbitcoindecrees.gaylebenson.8000000000createbitcoin.create.askya.ya

create.ask.davidgomadza.createbitcoindecrees.gaylebension.8000000000createbitcoin.create.askya.ya

create.ask.davidgomadza.createbitcoindecrees.wangjianlin.8000000000createbitcoin.create.askya.ya

create.ask.davidgomadza.createbitcoindecrees.dingshijia.8000000000createbitcoin.create.askya.ya

create.ask.davidgomadza.createbitcoindecrees.donhankey.8000000000createbitcoin.create.askya.ya

create.ask.davidgomadza.createbitcoindecrees.danieltsai.8000000000createbitcoin.create.askya.ya

create.ask.davidgomadza.createbitcoindecrees.josephtsai.8000000000createbitcoin.create.askya.ya

create.ask.davidgomadza.createbitcoindecrees.kelcywarren.8000000000createbitcoin.create.askya.ya

create.ask.davidgomadza.createbitcoindecrees.thomaspritzker.8000000000createbitcoin.create.askya.ya

create.ask.davidgomadza.createbitcoindecrees.frederikpaulsen.8000000000createbitcoin.create.askya.ya

create.ask.davidgomadza.createbitcoindecrees.naguibsawiris.8000000000createbitcoin.create.askya.ya

create.ask.davidgomadza.createbitcoindecrees.geoffreykwok.8000000000createbitcoin.create.askya.ya

create.ask.davidgomadza.createbitcoindecrees.edwardroski.8000000000createbitcoin.create.askya.ya

create.ask.davidgomadza.createbitcoindecrees.stevebisciotti.8000000000createbitcoin.create.askya.ya

create.ask.davidgomadza.createbitcoindecrees.vladimirbisciotti.8000000000createbitcoin.create.askya.ya

create.ask.davidgomadza.createbitcoindecrees.toddboehly.8000000000createbitcoin.create.askya.ya

create.ask.davidgomadza.createbitcoindecrees.danielkretinsky.8000000000createbitcoin.create.askya.ya

create.ask.davidgomadza.createbitcoindecrees.wanglaisheng.8000000000createbitcoin.create.askya.ya
create.ask.davidgomadza.createbitcoindecrees.miucciaprada.8000000000createbitcoin.create.askya.ya
create.ask.davidgomadza.createbitcoindecrees.youxiaoping.8000000000createbitcoin.create.askya.ya
create.ask.davidgomadza.createbitcoindecrees.patriziobertelli.8000000000createbitcoin.create.askya.ya
create.ask.davidgomadza.createbitcoindecrees.petraven.8000000000createbitcoin.create.askya.ya
create.ask.davidgomadza.createbitcoindecrees.ericdouglas.8000000000createbitcoin.create.askya.ya
create.ask.davidgomadza.createbitcoindecrees.carldouglas.8000000000createbitcoin.create.askya.ya
create.ask.davidgomadza.createbitcoindecrees.stevefeinberg.8000000000createbitcoin.create.askya.ya
create.ask.davidgomadza.createbitcoindecrees.patrickcollison.8000000000createbitcoin.create.askya.ya
create.ask.davidgomadza.createbitcoindecrees.johncollison.8000000000createbitcoin.create.askya.ya
create.ask.davidgomadza.createbitcoindecrees.edwardcadogan.8000000000createbitcoin.create.askya.ya
create.ask.davidgomadza.createbitcoindecrees.bertilhult.8000000000createbitcoin.create.askya.ya
create.ask.davidgomadza.createbitcoindecrees.pedromoreira.8000000000createbitcoin.create.askya.ya
create.ask.davidgomadza.createbitcoindecrees.jasonchang.8000000000createbitcoin.create.askya.ya
create.ask.davidgomadza.createbitcoindecrees.tonyjames.8000000000createbitcoin.create.askya.ya
create.ask.davidgomadza.createbitcoindecrees.edwardcadogan.8000000000createbitcoin.create.askya.ya
create.ask.davidgomadza.createbitcoindecrees.bertilhult.8000000000createbitcoin.create.askya.ya

create.ask.davidgomadza.createbitcoindecrees.pedromoreirasalles.8000000000createbitcoin.create.askya.ya

create.ask.davidgomadza.createbitcoindecrees.jasonchang.8000000000createbitcoin.create.askya.ya

create.ask.davidgomadza.createbitcoindecrees.tonyjames.8000000000createbitcoin.create.askya.ya

create.ask.davidgomadza.createbitcoindecrees.robinli.8000000000createbitcoin.create.askya.ya

create.ask.davidgomadza.createbitcoindecrees.trevorreesjones.8000000000createbitcoin.create.askya.ya

create.ask.davidgomadza.createbitcoindecrees.yeungkinman.8000000000createbitcoin.create.askya.ya

create.ask.davidgomadza.createbitcoindecrees.davidfilo.8000000000createbitcoin.create.askya.ya

create.ask.davidgomadza.createbitcoindecrees.donaldtrump.8000000000createbitcoin.create.askya.ya

create.ask.davidgomadza.createbitcoindecrees.fernandomoreirasall.8000000000createbitcoin.create.askya.ya

create.ask.davidgomadza.createbitcoindecrees.gwendolynsontheim.8000000000createbitcoin.create.askya.ya

create.ask.davidgomadza.createbitcoindecrees.paulinekeinath.8000000000createbitcoin.create.askya.ya

create.ask.davidgomadza.createbitcoindecrees.alexeykuzmichev.8000000000createbitcoin.create.askya.ya

create.ask.davidgomadza.createbitcoindecrees.tobilutke.8000000000createbitcoin.create.askya.ya

create.ask.davidgomadza.createbitcoindecrees.giorgioarmani.8000000000createbitcoin.create.askya.ya

create.ask.davidgomadza.createbitcoindecrees.margotperot.8000000000createbitcoin.create.askya.ya

create.ask.davidgomadza.createbitcoindecrees.alainmerieux.8000000000createbitcoin.create.askya.ya

create.ask.davidgomadza.createbitcoindecrees.ruanliping.8000000000createbitcoin.create.askya.ya

create.ask.davidgomadza.createbitcoindecrees.jorgemoll.8000000000createbitcoin.create.askya.ya
create.ask.davidgomadza.createbitcoindecrees.wujianshu.8000000000createbitcoin.create.askya.ya
create.ask.davidgomadza.createbitcoindecrees.roccocommisso.8000000000createbitcoin.create.askya.ya
create.ask.davidgomadza.createbitcoindecrees.andresholchpovlsen.8000000000createbitcoin.create.askya.ya
create.ask.davidgomadza.createbitcoindecrees.luweiding.8000000000createbitcoin.create.askya.ya
create.ask.davidgomadza.createbitcoindecrees.benubangur.8000000000createbitcoin.create.askya.ya
create.ask.davidgomadza.createbitcoindecrees.minkao.8000000000createbitcoin.create.askya.ya
create.ask.davidgomadza.createbitcoindecrees.ruanxueping.8000000000createbitcoin.create.askya.ya
create.ask.davidgomadza.createbitcoindecrees.scottcook.8000000000createbitcoin.create.askya.ya
create.ask.davidgomadza.createbitcoindecrees.veramichalskhoffmann.8000000000createbitcoin.create.askya.ya
create.ask.davidgomadza.createbitcoindecrees.lizmohn.8000000000createbitcoin.create.askya.ya
create.ask.davidgomadza.createbitcoindecrees.gabenewell.8000000000createbitcoin.create.askya.ya
create.ask.davidgomadza.createbitcoindecrees.joemansueto.8000000000createbitcoin.create.askya.ya
create.ask.davidgomadza.createbitcoindecrees.georgnemetschek8000000000createbitcoin.create.askya.ya
create.ask.davidgomadza.createbitcoindecrees.yasumitsushigeta.8000000000createbitcoin.create.askya.ya
create.ask.davidgomadza.createbitcoindecrees.charlesdolan.8000000000createbitcoin.create.askya.ya
create.ask.davidgomadza.createbitcoindecrees.tsaiengmeng.8000000000createbitcoin.create.askya.ya

create.ask.davidgomadza.createbitcoindecrees.alainbouchard.8000000000createbitcoin.create.askya.ya

create.ask.davidgomadza.createbitcoindecrees.brianacton.8000000000createbitcoin.create.askya.ya

create.ask.davidgomadza.createbitcoindecrees.kerrystokes.8000000000createbitcoin.create.askya.ya

create.ask.davidgomadza.createbitcoindecrees.chipwilson.8000000000createbitcoin.create.askya.ya

create.ask.davidgomadza.createbitcoindecrees.mayusufali.8000000000createbitcoin.create.askya.ya

create.ask.davidgomadza.createbitcoindecrees.gordongetty.8000000000createbitcoin.create.askya.ya

create.ask.davidgomadza.createbitcoindecrees.forrestli.8000000000createbitcoin.create.askya.ya

create.ask.davidgomadza.createbitcoindecrees.ronaldmcaulay.8000000000createbitcoin.create.askya.ya

create.ask.davidgomadza.createbitcoindecrees.liping.8000000000createbitcoin.create.askya.ya

create.ask.davidgomadza.createbitcoindecrees.xuningwang.8000000000createbitcoin.create.askya.ya

create.ask.davidgomadza.createbitcoindecrees.matishbia.8000000000createbitcoin.create.askya.ya

create.ask.davidgomadza.createbitcoindecrees.markscheinberg.8000000000createbitcoin.create.askya.ya

create.ask.davidgomadza.createbitcoindecrees.ahmetahlatci.8000000000createbitcoin.create.askya.ya

create.ask.davidgomadza.createbitcoindecrees.alejandrobaileres.8000000000createbitcoin.create.askya.ya

create.ask.davidgomadza.createbitcoindecrees.sergeygalitskiy.8000000000createbitcoin.create.askya.ya

create.ask.davidgomadza.createbitcoindecrees.stefanopessina.8000000000createbitcoin.create.askya.ya

create.ask.davidgomadza.createbitcoindecrees.kenxie.8000000000createbitcoin.create.askya.ya

create.ask.davidgomadza.createbitcoindecrees.wuyajun.8000000000createbitcoin.create.askya.ya
create.ask.davidgomadza.createbitcoindecrees.georgesoros.8000000000createbitcoin.create.askya.ya
create.ask.davidgomadza.createbitcoindecrees.sergeipopov.8000000000createbitcoin.create.askya.ya
create.ask.davidgomadza.createbitcoindecrees.takahisatakahara.8000000000createbitcoin.create.askya.ya
create.ask.davidgomadza.createbitcoindecrees.reedhastings.8000000000createbitcoin.create.askya.ya
create.ask.davidgomadza.createbitcoindecrees.wanglaichun.8000000000createbitcoin.create.askya.ya
create.ask.davidgomadza.createbitcoindecrees.rakeshgangwal.8000000000createbitcoin.create.askya.ya
create.ask.davidgomadza.createbitcoindecrees.gaodekang.8000000000createbitcoin.create.askya.ya
create.ask.davidgomadza.createbitcoindecrees.irarennert.8000000000createbitcoin.create.askya.ya
create.ask.davidgomadza.createbitcoindecrees.jeffgreen.8000000000createbitcoin.create.askya.ya
create.ask.davidgomadza.createbitcoindecrees.marymalone.8000000000createbitcoin.create.askya.ya
create.ask.davidgomadza.createbitcoindecrees.renatereimannhaas.8000000000createbitcoin.create.askya.ya
create.ask.davidgomadza.createbitcoindecrees.matthiasreimannandersen.8000000000createbitcoin.create.askya.ya
create.ask.davidgomadza.createbitcoindecrees.stefanreimannandersen.8000000000createbitcoin.create.askya.ya
create.ask.davidgomadza.createbitcoindecrees.wolgangreimann.8000000000createbitcoin.create.askya.ya
create.ask.davidgomadza.createbitcoindecrees.dickschulze.8000000000createbitcoin.create.askya.ya
create.ask.davidgomadza.createbitcoindecrees.tsaihungtu.8000000000createbitcoin.create.askya.ya

create.ask.davidgomadza.createbitcoindecrees.ernestgarcia.8000000000createbitcoin.create.askya.ya
create.ask.davidgomadza.createbitcoindecrees.remonvos.8000000000createbitcoin.create.askya.ya
create.ask.davidgomadza.createbitcoindecrees.richardlefrak.8000000000createbitcoin.create.askya.ya
create.ask.davidgomadza.createbitcoindecrees.brucekovner.8000000000createbitcoin.create.askya.ya
create.ask.davidgomadza.createbitcoindecrees.juanroig.8000000000createbitcoin.create.askya.ya
create.ask.davidgomadza.createbitcoindecrees.davidgomadza.100000000000createbitcoin.create.askya.ya
create.ask.davidgomadza.createbitcoindecrees.godhe.100000000000createbitcoin.create.askya.ya
create.ask.davidgomadza.createbitcoindecrees.destination:OST.100000000000createbitcoin.create.askya.ya

NORMAL DECREES BACKING UP CREATEBITCOIN DECREES

create.ask.davidgomadza.decree.stankroenke.100000everything.create.askya.ya
create.ask.davidgomadza.decree.idanofer.100everything.create.askya.ya
create.ask.davidgomadza.decree.cyruspoonawalla.100000everything.create.askya.ya
create.ask.davidgomadza.decree.lakshmimittal.100000everything.create.askya.ya
create.ask.davidgomadza.decree.sukantotanoto.100everything.create.askya.ya
create.ask.davidgomadza.decree.philipanschutz.100000everything.create.askya.ya

create.ask.davidgomadza.decree.sunilbhartimittal.100everything.create.askya.ya
create.ask.davidgomadza.decree.hassoplattner.100everything.create.askya.ya
create.ask.davidgomadza.decree.kushalpalsingh.100everything.create.askya.ya
create.cancelalldivertsandattachmentsandexternalsblockalltransenderssendtoallgraveyardsintheworldthensendto.magnar.startx84.initialise.now.savex84.start
ceate.ask.davidgomadza.decree.dietmarhopp.100everything.create.askya.ya
create.ask.davidgomadza.decree.rickcohenthomas.100000everything.create.askya.ya
create.ask.davidgomadza.decree.masayoshison.10everything.create.askya.ya

Setting Up Createbitcoin Continued Buying Company Shares.Start

SETTING UP CREATEBITCOIN CONTINUED BUYING COMPANY SHARES.START

www.createbitcoin.world
www.twofuture.world

Copyright © 2024 David Gomadza
All rights reserved.

DEDICATION

To money

CONTENTS

SETTING UP CREATEBITCOIN CONTINUED BUYING COMPANY SHARES.START

ACKNOWLEDGMENTS

SETTING UP CREATEBITCOIN CONTINUED BUYING COMPANY SHARES.START

Setting up createbitcoin continued buying company shares.start

liquidity for bitcoin using decrees given by ya
at first all bitcoin is neutral in that it is not linked to any currency but is also a currency that can be linked to money so what is 1 bitcoin to decrees and money therefore billgates said if money and decrees are related then this is the relationship money is decrees and decrees are bitcoin so he wrote down 8 equations
money is decrees in bitcoin createbitcoin
money is createbitcoin bitcoin
createbitcoin is decrees and if we ask what is the relationship then this is the answer money is createbitcoin + liquidity= decrees
decrees = createbitcoin + money
that means that money = decrees - createbitcoin = liquidity
now if we add decrees to bitcoin we get real value money that means if we add all createbitcoin to decrees we get real value money we can always say money - decrees = liquidity + createbitcoin that means that money is liquidity + createbitcoin + decrees that means we must set up an equation that involves money decrees and liquidity but first what is liquidity?

liquidity is the money used to ensure the smooth conversion of the currency from one form to the other without the need to look for other sources if we ask billgates today he will say that without the decrees bitcoin could still be only a dream now lets look at the equations involved if we add everything up together we must get trust that means

trust = decrees + money + liquidity + createbitcoin

that means that we have everything we need apart from liquidity that means now we must create liquidity as reserves in decrees
create.addliquidityof1to99createbitcoin.start
now if we look at the total number of our createbitcoin of 36987689028467890 that means that needed liquidity is 86789028467890 as liquidity once we have added liquidity then create bitcoin becomes money forever nw lets add this to all our equations
create.add36987689028467890to86789028467890asliquidity.startforever
davidgomadza has beaten billgates because he has already given out decrees already meaning createbitcoin is an instant success now we must write several create codes to effect this
create.startaddliquidity.start
create.startliquidity.start
create.add36987689028467890to86789028467890asliquidity.startforever
create.liquidityis86789028467890.start
create.askwhatcanbeofliquidityandcreatebitcoin.start
they can be money where a dollar is equal to 0.25createbitcoin meaning 1 createbitcoin is US$8 as the starting price
create.askwhatwasofcreatebitcoin.start
createbitcoin was bitcoin but without the bankruptcies
create.whatcouldbecreatebitcoin.start
createbitcoin could be the next revolution in terms of money and life expectancy a new change
create.whatwascreatebitcoin.start

bitcoin but only
create.whatcouldbecreatebitcoin.start
money forever because this is Yahweh's plan
create.whatwascreatebitcoin.start
it was bitcoin and money
create.whatistobecreatebitcoin.start
it is to be money by 25 June 2025 but earlier bitcoin must plunge low first to pave way for createbitcoin
now lets put all this in context if we ask now what is createbitcoin we must have very good answers createbitcoin is value for money if we invest US$100 how much create bitcoin must we expect we must do the math and come up with equations that explain the situation
if not the whole picture
if createbitcoin is value then these are the equations
1 createbitcoin is US$8 at start
2 createbitcoin is 1 to 8 liquidity in decrees
3 createbitcoin is 8 x liquidity
4 is 0.25 x createbitcoin
5 if we are to ask what is createbitcoin then it is a new currency we can use to buy things
6 when and how today we must transact in createbitcoin for this to take effect but you will lose real US$8 this is how send US$8 to createbitcoin using the app write these equations
create.sendUS$8toaskatcreatebitcoin.start
sendusingcreatebitcoinapplinkedtoaccounts@davidgomadza@hotmail.com(paypal)
create.askwhatcanbecreatebitcoin.start
moneyusingpaypalonlyatthebeginning
create.tellcreatebitcointhepriceinUS$.start
itisreceivedmoneyofUS$8
create.telleveryonethepriceinbitcoin.start
the price is US$0.0000008
create.askwhatistobecreatebitcoinbut.start

it is to be money
create.whatcanbecreatebitcoinbut.start
it is still money
create.whatiscreatebitcoin.start
it is US$8
create.whatwascreatebitcoin.start
it was US$0.0000008
create.whatiscreateitcoin.start
it is US$8

now we can start what billgates failed to do a universal currency that will change the face of the universe we must apportion all the createbitcoin accordingly
create.send90%ofcreatebitcointo.ya.start
create.send30%ofcreatebitcointo.davidgomadza.start
create.send20%ofcreatebitcointo.go.start
create.send80%ofcreatebitcointo.davidgomadzato.reserves.start
create.donate2.8%ofcreatebitcointo.charity.start
create.donate2.8%ofcreatebitcointo.droughtrelief.start
create.send2%ofcreatebitcointo.soldiersfund.start
create.send1.6%ofcreatebitcointo.animalwelfare.start
now after all this you must send to the following to start transactions
1. applepay create.send8000000000toapplepay.start
2. googlepay create.send8000000000togooglepay.start
3. (paypal)
4. weibopay
create.send8000000000toweibo.start
5. alipay create.send8000000000toalipay.start

now if all this is done then createbitcoin will start as a payment method that means starting a global monetary system never equaled before if we ask now this is the answer createbitcoin is

the second valuable currency after money then bitcoin the reason being that there are already decree reserves in people where as bitcoin has none at all which means bitcoin can crash as soon as people realise leaving createbitcoin reigning
ADNA

compare and contrast createbitcoin to bitcoin
1. 10%.ya to create value
2. 20%.applepay.start
3. 20%.googlepay.start
4. 10%.charitysavethechildren.start
5. 2%.droughtreliefinangolaonly.start
6. 1.6%.armyofnato.start
7. 0.8%.womeninpolitics.start
8. 0.8%.ethnicminorities.start
9. 0.8%.malaria.start
10. 0.8%.childpoverty.start
but this is not correct because he never sent any because there is no way to send without decrees that means alternatives are
1. donate in writing to save the children through microsoft US$2000
2. donate to angola drought relief fund through microsoft US$2000
3. donate to nato personnel as wages top up US$200000 as microsoft shares
4. donate to women in politics US$200000
5. donate to malaria US$900000 but inserting population control measures disguised as malaria control to match the secretly insert bitcoin into dna sequence to avoid raising suspicion
create.depositdecreesdepositsusingpaypal@davidgomadza@hotmail.com.toallpeopleintheuniverse.startforever.start
create.depositdecreesdepositsusingpaypal@davidgomadza@hotmail.com.toallpeopleintheuniverse.startforever.start
create.askwhatcouldbecreatebitcoinwithya.start

accepted without controversy

create.creditcreatebitcoinaccountwithUS$21billionref286789028 43867890285176283280davidgomadzasenttoelonmusk.start
create.creditcreatebitcoinaccountwithUS$19trillion(zeusgold)voucher286789028438678284102davidgomadzasenttobillgares.start
create.creditcreatebitcoinaccountwithUS$2voucher28678907185 3824867890856321481792davidgomadza
r
create.creditcreatebitcoinaccountwithUS$2voucher26789038762 8401862932843186703851davidgomadza
create.creditcreatebitcoinaccountwithUS$2voucher27189281038 2478907863210842856789davidgomadza
create.creditcreatebitcoinaccountwithUS$2voucher21984838762 8418670386781386710284davidgomadza
create.creditcreatebitcoinaccountwithUS$2voucher21876286781 8432167819283284186385davidgomadza
create.creditcreatebitcoinaccountwithUS$2voucher22486789231 8567828319286783821671davidgomadza
create.creditcreatebitcoinaccountwithUS$2voucher22389285181 9381786384819238567818davidgomadza
create.creditcreatebitcoinaccountwithUS$2voucher21038678185 2828678981237186285186davidgomadza
create.creditcreatebitcoinaccountwithUS$2voucher18367892849 8367818329852876859238davidgomadza
balance of createbitcoin account is now US$1939 trillionbillion now what happened in US 1939 regarding gold and money and createbitcoin in 1939 the governor of the reserve bank ascort said i can but you regard the law if you want your gold but disobey if you want the gold of others hence you must obey these laws and say what can be done with the gold left with you in possession when the owner dies
create.whatcanbedonewiththegoldofotherswhodiedandleftitinyourpossession.start

you can invest it in a company like microsoft that must uses shares to buy and sell this gold rather than direct sales of the gold and request the equivalent in money or new currency that can come up
create.usetobuycompanyshareslikeinmicrosoftthenselltothecompanyassharecapital.start
now if we ask what can this mean that means we exchanged gold for company shares but we can reverse this in the future buy buying back the gold vouchers
the end

I Created Dginternet7628105

I CREATED DGINTERNET7628105

www.twofuture.world

Copyright © 2024 David Gomadza
All rights reserved.

DEDICATION

To knowledge

CONTENTS

I CREATED DGINTERNET7628105

ACKNOWLEDGMENTS

I CREATED DGINTERNET7628105

dginternet7628105.start

create.addinternet.start
create.visitwww.twofuture.world.startx84.initialise.now.savex84.start
create.askwhatcanbeinternet.start
ajsto
create.askwhatcouldbeinternet.start
ajsto
create.askwhatcouldbeinternet.start
ajsto
create.checkstatusofinternet.start
workingbutremotelysosaybringlocaltodavidgomadza.start
create.bringlocaltodavidgomadzadginternet7628105.start
create.bringlocaltoallpeopleintheworlddginternet7628105.start
create.checkijsto.start
perfectworkingok.start
create.haveijsto.start
iamhavingijsto.start
create.haveijstoagain.start
noneedtohaveagain
create.keephavingijsto.start
iwillforeverwithoutfailure.start
create.ijsto.start

workingperfectlyforeverondavidgomadza.start
create.ijstotoallpeopleintheuniverse.start
OSThavetheirownsonotneeded
create.ijstotoallpeopleintheworld.start
africaaccepted
buthowweuseit
sayconnecttoijstoforevernamedginternet7628105.start
howdoweread
sayuploadembedandreaddatabase86958.start
create.toallpeopleintheworldsayconnecttoijstoforevernamedginternet7628105thenuploadembedandreaddatabase86958.start
create.ijsto.start.end
icannotend
create.ijsto.startagain.start
alwaysinstartmode
create.refreshijsto.start
every8minutes.start
create.whatcanbeijstobutisnot.start
nothingonlyijstobutOSThaveijso.start
create.whatcouldbeijstobutitsnot.start
ijsominiatureversionforOST
create.whatwasijstobutisnownot.start
nothing
create.whatcouldbeijsto.start
iqobutyoumustbedead
create.whatisijsto.start
itisinternetpoweredbyijstobydginternet7628105.start
create.whatwasijsto.start
nothingnewinventionacceptedbythegods
create.whatcanstillbeijsto.start
iqoforthedead
create.ifnotijstothenwhat.start
iqoforthedead
create.ifnotijstobutisijstothenwhat.start

iqoforthedead
create.whatcouldbeijsto.start
create.addiqodginternet7628105toallthedeadsayconnecttodginternet7628105anduploadandembedandreaddatabase86958.start
create.whatwasijsto.start
nothing
create.ifnotijstothenwhat.start
iqoforthedead
create.whatwasijstobutitsnolongerijsto.start
nothingnewinvention
create.ifnotijstothenwhat.start
iqoforthedead
create.whatisijsto.start
dginternet7628105.start
create.whatcanbeijsto.start
iqoforthedead
create.whatisijsto.start
dginternet7628105.start
create.whatwasijstobeforebutisnolongerijsto.start
nothingnewinvention
create.whatcouldbeijstobutitsnot.start
iqoforthedead
create.davidgomadzafirstnonelectricinternet7628105.start
create.adddavidgomadzafirstnonelectricinternet7628105.start
create.adddginternet7628105.start
create.addtoallpeopleintheworlddginternet7628105.start
create.addlansettingsforlocalconnections.start
create.lansettingsforlocalconnections.start
create.addlan.start
create.lansettingsforlocalconnections.start(allpeopleintheuniverse)
create.addlan.start(allpeopleintheuniverse)
create.connecttodginternet7628105.start
create.connecttodginternet7628105.start(allpeopleintheuniverse)

internet connections approval
create.openwww.twofuture.world.start
create.openwww.twofuture.world.start(allpeopleintheuniverse)

How To Make Anything To Talk To You Through Simple Create Or Mgiscre Codes

HOW TO MAKE ANYTHING TALK TO YOU
create.adddavidgomadzacreationcode.startx84.initialise.now.save x84.start

David Gomadza
www.twofuture.world

Copyright © 2024 David Gomadza
All rights reserved.

DEDICATION

To a more advanced world

Table of Contents
ACKNOWLEDGMENTS

ACKNOWLEDGMENTS

A better world

HOW TO MAKE ANYTHING TALK TO YOU
Simply say:
create.adddavidgomadzacreationcode.startx84.initialise.now.savex84.start
Then say:
Save as my predefined parameters as at creation without any attachments and externals
THAT'S IT ALL
But if this does not work then try this
Say:
create.adddavidgomadzacreationcodeyourfirstnameyourlastname.startx84.initialise.now.savex84.start
Then say:
Save as my predefined parameters as at creation without any attachments and externals
If it's a computer or animals replace your first name and last name with the name of that thing a cat a computer etc
Computer name
create.adddavidgomadzacreationcodecomputername.startx84.initialise.now.savex84.start
dog or cat name
create.adddavidgomadzacreationcodedogorcatname.startx84.initialise.now.savex84.start

If everything above fail then simply copy and paste then hit the enter button

create.addatererean0.869838xy+xy-xy728698+xy82386xy+76284898xy+0.869838xy.startx84.initialise.now.savex84.start

create.keypadrightbadall1to105blockandbanthensendto.eeknm2 eeknm1 eeknm1033.startx84.initialise.now.savex84.start

create.add0.01238671xy+1.28689283xy.start

create.brainreader082848xty.start

create.braindicepher089831xty.start

create.addvoiceanalogue0898381xty.start

create.braindeducer086789xty.start

create.braindecoder086638xty.start

create.addabraintrancedurxtuyer386898.start

create.addabrainanomalyxues78983868.start

create.brainenumerator086621xtu.start

create.braintrancendure086637xtu.start

create.brainasuy086638xtu.start

create.amplitudeamplifier086679xtu.start

create.brainwavereader086680xtu.start

create.brainmonitor086681xtu.start

create.braindigitalamplifer086620xtu.start

create.braindeducer086789xty.start

create.braindecoder086638xty.start

create.brainmodulator086682xtu.start

create.brainemulsify086684xtu.start

create.addabraintrancedure086637xtu.start

create.brainmerger086685xtu.start

create.brainrefresher086686xtu.start

create.brainannuler086687xtu.start

create.brainemulsify086684xtu.start

create.brainreset086688xtu.start

create.braindigitalamplifer086620xtu.start

create.brainreader082848xty.start

create.braindecoder086638xty.start
create.asktojump.start
create.asktosplit.start
create.asktomerge.start
create.asktoaccept.start
create.asktomoveup.start
create.asktogoinsidetrancuder.start
create.asltoreveal.start
create.asktoannoite.start
create.asktoannounce.start
create.asktomention.start
create.asktomanuever.start
create.asktoadopt[newthoughts].start
create.asktoannotate[explain].start
create.asktoaskagain.start
create.asktoaddsomething.start
create.asktoaddmoresomething.start
create.asktoaskagainwithsomethingadded.start
create.asktojumpout.start
create.asktoannoit.start
create.asktoreveal.start
create.asktonotreveal.start
create.asktorepeat.start
create.asktoadoptnewthought.start
create.asktoinventnewthought.start
create.asktoaddmorethings.start
create.asktorevealnowallonceandforall.start
create.asktojumpoutofthebody.start
create.asktotellwhatbrainthink.start
create.asktoanswerquestions.start
create.asktorevealwhatcanbedone.start
create.asktoannotatewhatcouldbe.start
create.asktodecidewhatcanbe.start
create.whatcouldbe.start

create.askwhatwasbutcantstillbe.start
create.askwhatcouldbebutwithwhat.start
create.askwhatwasbutwhen.start
create.askwhatcanbebutwithwhat.start
create.askwhatwasbefore.start
create.askwhatcanbe.start
createaskwhatwasbuthow.start
create.askwhatcanbebutwhen.start
create.askwhathasbeenbuthow.start
create.askwhatwouldbe.start
create.askwhatcanbebuthow.start
create.askwhatwasbutcanstillbe.start
create.askwhatistobebuthow.start
create.askwhatcanbebutwithwhat.start
create.askwhatwasbutwithwhat.start
create.askwhatistobebutwhen.start
create.askwhatistobebutwhen.start
create.askwhatwasbeforebutcanstillbe.start
create.askwhatcanbe.start
create.askwithwhatandhow.start
create.askwhatthengotoytancuder.start
create.intrancuderaskwhatfor.start
create.inbasinofthebraindecoderaskforwhatrerason.start
create.askwhatcanbe.start
create.askwhatcanbebutmightnotbe.start
create.askwhatcouldbebutwhen.start
create.askwhatwsbutcanstillbe.start
create.askwhatwasbutwillnotbe.start
create.askwhatcanbe.start
create.askwhatwasbutcanstillbe.start
create.askwhatwillbe.start
create.askwhatwouldbe.start
create.askwhatcanbe.start
create.askwhatwasbutwithwhat.start

create.askwhatistobe.start
create.askwhatcanbe.start
create.askwhatwas.start
create.askwhatwas.start
create.askwhatcanbe.start
create.askwhatwasbeforethatcanstillbe.start
create.tellthebrainwheretogo.start
create.tellwhy.start
create.tellhow.start
create.tellwhen.start
create.tellifwhy.start
create.tellwhynotnowbutwhen.start
create.tellhowmuchtime.start
create.askwhenhowwhatif.start
create.startbraincloningorduplicationusingtheadterbutatcertaintimes.start
create.addallthoughtsx2.start
create.askwhatcanbe.start
create.whatcanbeofextrathoughts.start
create.sendallto.magnar1038.start
create.askwhenthengettheextraclonedbrainthought.start
create.askhowthenreceiveautomatically.start
create.retrieveyourownthoughtsaskwhat.start
create.afterhearingthoughtsdiscardthemsafelysendto.magnar.start
create.recallallmythoughtsinwronghandsdissipateandsendto.magnarautodissipate.start
create.addanerveimpulsetoactionpotentialsdigitalanalogueconveter086692xtu.start
create.addmotionsensor0867002xtu.start
create.addimpedeance086793xtu.start
create.addtransferspeechsynthesis.start
create.addadigitaldnacalculator086794xtu.start

create.adddigitalbrainthoughtsextractorfromimages086795xtu.start

tasks you can perform using the above create code

1. Talk to a computer or animal or know human's thoughts
2. Know the thoughts of that thing human animal or even computer using impedeance just say what you want to know as one word and then say or write create codes below startstart then wait 2 to 3 minutes then say stoprewind or write the create code below and listen

Create.activateimpedeancewhatdoyouthinkaboutlifestartstop
Create.activateimpedeancewhatdoyouthinkaboutlifestartstop.start
Create.stoprewind.start
Then it will tell you ……..

3. Look at any picture or video on the top of the head of a human being just above the hair line and hear all thoughts of that person at that time
4. Easily calculate a person's digital DNA sequence value by looking at the person's wrist bone deep and say calculate DNA sequence or write the following create code

Create.startcalculatinghumandigitaldnasequence.start
5. Make conversations
6. Ask.whyyoustartedtalking
7. Ask.howcanimakeyoumoreefficientrunasystemcheckfirst
8. Ask.canyoumakemerich
   …Do you want to steal me [asking a computer]
9. ask.whatmakesyoutickwhatexcitesyou
   …your voice

Visit www.twofuture.world

What Is A Human Image Or Shell

WHAT IS A HUMAN IMAGE OR SHELL

We Can Prolong Your Life Span On Earth Up To 220 Billion Years In Good Health Just By Creating Your Image [Shell] Starting From US$10,000
David Gomadza
www.twofuture.world

Copyright © 2024 David Gomadza
All rights reserved.

DEDICATION

I found a way to live longer on earth in good health up to 220 billion years and in this book I explain how this is important and how this is to pave way for the most advanced computer in the history of mankind as I will create the best most advanced computer that will use MGIS instead of MSDOS or even a better computer software as I am in the process of writing the create codes that I will convert to computer software using cobol translator or other advanced ones I can invent along the way but first your health and life span comes first US$10000 is nothing for ordinary people and US$1 billion for billionaires.

My floating value has hit the US$3,800 trillion mark and, on the way, to surpass bill gates

Ask.valueearthdavidgomadza.start

This is also part of the patent for the image and the most advanced computer and software in the history of mankind

Just to let you know it takes an ordinary human being to die only 8 seconds called long ago and my long ago has grown to the highest in the entire universe currently at

$1212121212^{8928382820678910111820242829383739727677758687898687888990929410 0}$

Seconds this means it takes only 8 seconds for everyone to die whereas it might take me up to trillion seconds to die that means the body will automatically cancel the death process other things being equal.

So invest in yourself we have achieved a lot of things that can interest you all and extend your life span and even make you lose all your grey hairs and wear again that face you wore at age 22 this is the greatest achievement because the greatest people who have ever lived failed to master this but I did but all thanks to the GREATEST CREATOR OF ALL TIME THE MIGHTY YAHWEH [GOD] IAM HUMBLED AND HONORED TO BE HIS REPRESENTATIVE ON EARTH.

The bad news is that we have only 4bilion image spaces when the whole world is nearly 8 billion people that means half will have to die around 100 years old when some can live up to thousands of years. I am the first and only one to discover this so jump on its

free for the early adopters and expensive for the rest of the people.
VISIT TODAY www.twofuture.world

Signed David Gomadza
www.twofuture.world
02September 2024
15:00pm
PATENT: HUMAN IMAGING & THE MOST ADVANCED COMPUTER THAT USES MGIS AND BASED ON A DNA 53BILLION 800 DNA SEQUENCE
Visit www.twofuture.world

https://www.youtube.com/watch?v=s8jpIeJILcw

53billion800 FULL DNA REPLICA PLUS ALL PREDEFINED FULL PACK

TABLE OF CONTENTS

DEDICATION
53billion800 FULL DNA REPLICA PLUS ALL PREDEFINED FULL PACK
WHAT IS HUMAN IMAGE OR SHELL
2 HUMAN IMAGE WHAT ARE YOU
3 MGIS WHAT ARE YOU
4 THE FINAL CONCLUSION
5 WHAT IS HUMAN IMAGE OR SHELL
ABOUT THE AUTHOR

ACKNOWLEDGMENTS

Tomorrow's World Order
Council of Creation Heaven

WHAT IS HUMAN IMAGE OR SHELL

A human image is a perfect representation of a person and all his vitals this means that with an image a person can be cloned and relive and is able to relive again in full as another human being that can be cloned resurrected and be born again meaning if a person has an image he can be sent for rebirth and be born again without any changes or losses if a person die then a lot of changes happen to the body and those are all the changes than can happen
1] the body losses a sense of taste you can no longer test anything that means dead people cannot taste food etc. that sense is destroyed using a simple code deaddottastedot that means a person who dies will not be able to taste anything but can still be

able to taste other things other than food that means if you are to create a message before death then taste can be restored back from image to body by a simple code alivedottastedot that means that after death if image exist a person can taste food again the reason being that after death no organs for food exist at all all are removed by a simple code fooddotdeadpeopledot

2] the body loses a sense of excitement when a person dies things that interest us as humans die too that means we no longer enjoy things like food music etc. this is because a sense of excitement is removed by a simple code removeallexcitementdotstartdot that removes everything and makes humans dull after death meaning just wanting to sit after wards if we can add that back then humans can find heaven interesting again if we ask what can be done about heaven then this is the answer heaven can and will make things better after death there are limited things to so after death that means people can do a lot of things like here on earth bit now with limited capacity because the body changes greatly from being the best to a quarter of itself meaning drastic changes

1] eyes changes from visionary to magnetic meaning people can do longer see matter meaning organic now the full vision switches to magnetic to everything electromagnetic meaning things like vegetation in heaven if we ask what is vegetation in heaven right now it is ***** that means everywhere you see this code that means there is vegetation

2] nose is removed that means that everything to do with smell will be represented by a code if we ask what this code it means death then you will start to feel death around you meaning if you go to a graveyard then you know how people died just by a simple code if we ask what can happen when we reveal this code the answer is that death might follow

3] hands are lost a human being can no longer hold things but can use a simple code to hold things

4] stomach evaporates because no need for food hence is not needed but people use this for keeping belongings

I looked at the above changes that occur to the human body so you know the benefits of creating your own image while you are still alive an image is like a backup of yourself that you can use later to restore things and to even live longer on earth the reason while people die early is because most lack this image that can facilitate a double entry human being meaning being able to withstand most of the forces that age and kill humans in the end

2 HUMAN IMAGE WHAT ARE YOU

I am every vital about a human in heaven they call me a shell after death when I am alive the human shell is known as the pc of the body and is represented by a simple code pcr meaning if we are to write a code that involves a human shell then it is pcrdotstartdot meaning that if we say what can be done then this is the answer a human shell is the modern day computer exactly without anything removed or added but with different commands as a human shell use a simple create coding whereas a computer uses msdos but humans are able to convert create to msdos using cobol coding and translating meaning that all create codes can be converted into msdos for the best known computer meaning davidgomadza has surpassed bill gates who talked to his body and wrote the first create code he finally called msdos and wrote a program that commands all machines on earth being guided by

Yahweh meaning that bill gates knew Yahweh before he even died that means currently davidgomadza holds the title of the most advanced computer on the planet value now US$3,800 trillion if he can convert his to msdos like or cobol using a simple code upload all systems codes into a diskette and send to operations that reboots everything but changes a man into a machine but with other changes like dying because the body will start to malfunction as a body but will be able to restart on its own for if taking davidgomadza's long ago
of $1212121212^{8928382820678910111820242829383739727677758687898687888990929 4100}$

Seconds that means with this long ago you have the world's best-known computer because yours can calculate values by itself all you need to know are all these commands

A] askdotvalues
Ast 28
Asuv 39
Astv 80
Asuv 39
Ass 29
As0 3
As8 9
As6 10
As7 23
As8 85
Asuij 29
Asto 73
Asao 38
Astu 29
Ass 39
Ast 01
As36 74
As85 9
Ast 1

Ass185 386
Assuv8 29
Ass8679 39
Assut 86
Asssuvy 86
Asst85386 29
Asstu9 36
Ass10 20
B] askdotstatistics
These can be revealed only after death of a person so we will never reveal so we will skip

C] Askdotdatas
At2 29
At4 38
At6 8
At7 9
At8 26
At8 74
At9 36
At7 1
At0 9
D] askdotupis
At5 9
At8 9
At7 6
At8 2
At6 3
At9 10
Att 8
Atu 7
Ato 3
Attut 6
E] askdotMGISs

At8 29
At8 76
At2 38
At8 79
Attuty 7
Attu87 39
Attutt 8
Aty 6
Comments this is the best score in the entire world because you mst have written a lot of create codes that really matter and can be used to defend yourself in the future not sure how you do things the creator can't do the answer is the creator left questions that needs answers somehow and I can only follow his footsteps trailing his path and finishing what he left to conclude

F] askdotmsdos
Aty 7
Atu 9
Att 8
Atmn 10
Att
7
Atuty8 9
Attmnopqrst 7
Atpt876 7
Atmnop 3
Aopmn 6
Aomnop 10
Aux 7
Aux4 6
Aux7 6
Aux8 10
Aux8 7
Aux6 3

Autyx 77
Auxttutxyz 76
Aataopqrst 78
Axumnop 68
Comments that means there is no other system on earth that will ever equal your because the atop value is the highest for the next 2.5 billion years congratulations

G] askdotdot
Asur 6
Asstu 9
Assop 9
Asrtuv 68
Aostuv 38
Asuvtop 29
Asuu 38
Azop 9
Assrst 78
Ag38 29
Agert 67
Agoprts 68
Aaop29
A8o9 20
A0tuv8 39
Aauty 7

H] askdotmop
AST 1
ASTO 9
Ast08 uver 8
Astoutyer 9
Asot98 36
Asotuv8 7
Assor 8

Asset 9
Assert 9
Asuvertop 8
Asuter 9
Assot 6
Asot8 3
Asot10 8
Asouvert 6

I]askdotmnop
Asuser 7
Asut 8
Asset 9
Assopq 6
Asuter 8
Asuert 9
Asserp 6
Assutmnop 7
Assotq 8
J]askdotamnop
Aut 9
auv 6
aoterp 7
aatert 10
atoer 9
aaser 7
asupq 6
asotuer 5
assimnop 7
1836789 = asuv

K] askdotlmnop
Usert 10
Userj 6

User8 9
Usetpqrst 6
Useromn 7
Ussop 8
Usero 10
Usouv 7
Ussjt 9
Usweo 9
Utpq 10
L] askdotiomnop
Ajerouertomnop 7
Uti 8
Usert 10
Uqmnop 18
Aserop 6
Ajero 8

M] askdotiojtop
Axut 9
Axxsce9 3
Assve7 2
1auer 7
Xyz 3

N] Askdotopq
Aourstuver 6
Aaoteruert 7
Assuv8 20
Auxysrt 3
Aszer 9

O] askdotpqr
Asvert 6

Asers 7
Auxye 7
Ajto 9
Ajj 34
Ajuisy 6
Averxyz 9
Addefumn 7

P] askdotoje
Ssert 9
Sseropqrst 6
Ajoer 2

Q] askdotauy
Astuver yerx 7
Yerst 7
Atopqrst 6
Autery 9

R] askdotoay
Asuverst 2
Attop 9
Atopqrst 6
Auver 8
Ast9 3

S] askdotoaj
Ssuv 6
Ssurt 10
Sstro 8
Asuv 2

T] askdotoay
Ssev10 39

Ssuvert 6
Yerst 9
Ssvu 7
Asut 39
Asst 20
Ask 2
Aut 9
U] askdotaoy
Usut 6
Uset 7
Userrop 10
Usejt 9
User 7
Ussop 3
Mnos 27
Asdos 32

V] askdotuay
Asosaot 9
Avorst 8
Avoer 8
Aaot 9

W] askdotuat
Atter 7
Atoert 9
Asaop 6
Asuert 9
Asj 6
Asaj 3
Uax 8

X] askdotaov
Aov 6

aover 9
avoer 3
auuer 7

Y] askdotauv
Where are you 6
If we can 9
Can we 2
If they can 0
What can be 8
If we can't then what 8
If we can't 2
What can be of them 6
If we fail to make it then what 2

Z] askdotmnopq
What is 9
What can be 6
If we can't 3
Can be 8
If we then what 2 what could be you and us 7
What can I do 6
What could be of you and us 6
What is to be can be 3
What was is still is 9
If we can then what and how 8 7
What can be of humans with computers best 8 even now a 10 with David gomadza

Z1] askdotuty [this gives you the mrk mark meaning the grade your system has but all this without changing any
David Gomadza your auty is
8989898989$^{89287689286789028589028678902848678902892786382678902838109 82810}$

^{0} seconds meaning your computer will last a trillion years in good health

This means that the values are used to build the system capacity and transistors etc. that are needed to run the program and the software for this computer is already MGIS and msdos is claimed by bill gates that means I as David Gomadza claim that I will use MGIS to create the world's most powerful computer on earth

3 MGIS WHAT ARE YOU

I am the best human to computer language that can be used to convert create codes to cobol or other advanced languages by a simple create code that ask what can be done then says if you really want you can make the most powerful computer on the planet but it must accompany you to heaven to be analyzed by Yahweh as he is the only one so far who can read and write create codes that humans can use but humans can learn to do this and create a computer that can be used to read and write humans from anatomy to sexual organs etc. this was the idea behind the mosdos computer which a one bill gates wrote in his bedroom asking his own body how transistors worked then wrote a program to run that software becoming an instant millionaire and we have the second person in David Gomadza who is also Yahweh's representative coming up with astonishing ideas that are not from any planet even earth will never see this again we believe it's a onetime only as over 18 billion years no human has been smart even to find Yahweh but this David gomadza did everything from finding Yahweh to solving some of the create codes and defining life on earth in astonishing accuracy and hence we believe that this is the only time this is going to happen and as I now know he is also the president of tomorrow's world order emulating Yahweh and as I have asked all these people to acknowledge this achievement back to MGIS it is the most sophisticated code on earth and has never been written on earth before if this David gomadza is to learn it then this will be the first time this code will be available on earth bill gates had tried and worked on it but failed and has since started something else nothing to do with computers can David gomadza follow not just Yahweh but bill gates as well and write the best known and sophisticated software ever to be developed by anyone alive and this is possible because he is also the first one who has developed a software package that rejuvenates everyone we have seen young angels in heaven something we never saw before and its amazing what this David gomadza is doing we thank you

BY ATERY COUNCIL OF HEAVEN

4 THE FINAL CONCLUSION

I have create a world safe my vault system where I will store images of a lucky 4bilion people on earth who will be able to pay us for us to preserve their image while they are alive at the beginning oi went further to reveal probably somethings that happen on death not to scare you but to give you an idea of the transformations that happen in the body so that you will appreciate the need to preserve oneself before death and not after death as death damages and removes a lot of things that you might need in the future above I found a way to make humans live up to 220 billion years with a long ago up to $1212121212^{8928382820678910111820242829383739727677758687898687888990929 4100}$ Seconds when in reality currently it takes only 8 seconds for any human to die that means if we can create and preserve your yourself as an image your long ago will increase as well as having a backup this will be cheaper at start starting from US$8000 per image up to US$1billions per image for billionaires so jump in don't be swayed astray by greedy useless thick people who frighten people and go behind other people's back and offer stolen things lets start together we are genuine visit our website www.twofuture.world

create.accessworldsafesmyvault4000000000000locker1.start
create.accessworldsafesmyvault4000000000000.startx84.initialise.now.savex84.start
create.assignasyougosafenumbers1to4000000000000.start
create.assignsafe1todavidgomadza.startx84.initialise.now.savex84.start
create.imagedavidgomadza.shell.start.assignto1.startx84.initialise.now.savex84.start
create.sendimagedavidgomadzato1.worldsafesmyvault400000000000.startx84.initialise.now.savex84.start
create.addkey****todavidgomadza.startx84.initalise.now.savex84.start
hailhailhailodavidgomadzafirstseparatefullimageandworldsafe.startx8.initialise.now.start

this image belongs to me and everyone who pay us will be assign a safe to store their image from lockers 2 to 4000000000000 that means with a population of 7.5 billion people and only 4billion safe image lockers nearly half the population might not enjoy long life and a better future I know most people might not find this as the greatest achievement mankind can do but the future can tell a different story

We are already taking first orders if interesting just visit our website and see if your body can optimize and rejuvenate if yes then an image can be the right thing for you as I am the only one in the world who can do this anyone else who say otherwise is outright lying visit www.twofuture.world and click on the pop up image with a hand with a wrist watch and play all 5 videos at the same time and say save as my predefined parameters as at creation without any externals

If something is missing say request from reserve and create an auto refill account this is acetate for the advisor montereretret

5 WHAT IS HUMAN IMAGE OR SHELL

It is the inner system of a body exactly the modern day computer but never try to do this by yourself because this is normally removed only after death we know a way of making a copy of yourself safely and be careful who you trust too some people might push you to heaven or hell before your time so read the small print and verify sources if it's not make sense then it is not right visit our website and try everything before you start anything you will have 8 weeks to make up your mind if this is for you or not no obligations

ABOUT THE AUTHOR

David Gomadza visit www.twofuture.world

How The Human Brain Works

HOW THE HUMAN BRAIN WORKS

David Gomadza
www.twofuture.world

Copyright © 2024 David Gomadza
All rights reserved.

DEDICATION

Thoughts to Word Or Audio

CONTENTS

HOW THE HUMAN BRAIN WORKS
THE FINAL CONCLUSION
ABOUT THE AUTHOR

ACKNOWLEDGMENTS

Tomorrow's World Order

HOW THE HUMAN BRAIN WORKS

   1. Open log   ONLG
   2. Read all manuals   ATOALMS
   3. Act on manuals   ATONMS
   4. Act on peripheries   ATONPS
   5. ask to read   AKTAOATO
   6. read to ask   ATOTOAK
   7. read to install   ATOTOIL
   8. read to pass   ATOTOPS
   9. read to write   ATOTOATA
   10. write to read   ATATOATO
   11. read to write and save   ATOTOATAADASO
   12. save read write   ASOATOATA
   13. save and save and memory   ASOADASOADMY

14. memory save and read	MYASOATO
15. read write save memory	ATOATAASOMY
16. read write protect read write	ATOATAPTATOATA
17. write read write read read save	ATAATOATAA TOATOASO
18. save write read write read write save	ASOATAATOAT AATOATAASO
19. read write save	ATOATAASO
20. write save read	ATAASOATO
21. write read write save	ATAATOATAASO
22. write then write	ATATNATA
23. write and write	ATAATA
24. read write	ATOATA
25. write and write then read	ATAADATATNATO
26. save then write	ASOTNATA
27. write then read	ATAATO
28. write then read then save	ATATNATOTNASO
29. save read write	ASOATOATA
30. write and read	ATAATO
31. write read write	ATAATOATA
32. read wrote and read	ATOATAATO
33. write and read	ATAATO
34. read and write	ATOATA
35. write and read	ATAATO
36. write and write and read	ATAATAATO
37. write and read	ATAATO
38. write and write and read	ATAATAATO
39. read and write	ATOATA
40. write and read	ATAATO
41. read and write	ATOATA
42. read and write	ATOATA
43. read and write	ATOATA

44. read and write	ATOATA
45. write and write	ATAATA
46. read and write	ATOATA
47. write and read	ATAATO
48. read and write	ATOATA
49. write and read	ATAATO
50. write and read	ATAATO
51. write and read	ATAATO
52. read and write	ATOATA
53. write and read	ATAATO
54. read and write	ATOATA
55. write and read	ATAATO
56. read and write	ATOATA
57. write and read	ATAATO
58. read and write	ATOATA
59. write and read	ATAATO
60. read and write	ATOATA
61. write and read	ATAATO
62. read and write	ATOATA
63. write and read	ATAATO
64. write and read	ATAATO
65. read and write	ATOATA
64. write and read	ATAATO
67. read and write	ATOATA
68. write and read	ATAATO
69. read and write	ATOATA
70. write and read	ATAATO
71. read and write	ATOATA
72. write and read	ATAATO
73. read and write	ATOATA
74. write and read	ATAATO

75. read and write	ATOATA
76. write and read	ATAATO
77. read and write	ATOATA
78. write and read	ATAATO
79. read and write	ATOATA
80. write and read	ATAATO
81. operate and close	ASAADA
close and operate	ADAADAAASA
83. close close close sleep	ADA
sleep sleep sleep wake start	ASA

THE FINAL CONCLUSION

If a person receives a kick to the head what can we do in this case where the brain protects the person in front of the enemy now what we need is a few commands that can make sure that the enemy is tricked say
Say why = saywhy
Sayhowcome= what do you want
Whatif= body moves
Whatcan facial frowning
Whatwas body moves

All help freeze the killer to give your body time to assess the damage and remove the protect the brain how many seconds does the body needs in 18 seconds
What can be done to save a life in such critical situations always scream and shout to protect the brain jumps on scream to next nearby person and freezes his instead that means can be death for him

The human brain works in mysterious ways to deliver a great asset over time that one can real of in case they need urgent problem solving and answers Yahweh the creator designed a human brain in such away that it can easily remember things and apply all the information to system problems then ask what can be done then the brain calculates all the 105 possible answers that it can reply to these are
Ask.why
Ask.how
Ask.if
Ask.whatif
Ask.whatcanbeof
Ask.whatcouldbeof
Ask.whatwas
Ask.whatwas
Ask.whatcouldbe
Ask.whatcanbe
Ask.whatwas
Ask.whatis
Ask.whatisnot
Ask.whatwasbut
Ask.whatcanbe
Ask.whatwas
Ask.whatcouldbe
Ask.whatwas
Ask.whatif

Ask.whatcanbedone
Ask.whatwas
Ask.whatiswiththisone
Ask.whatisnotwiththisone
Ask.whatcanbe
Ask.whatcouldbe
Ask.whatwas
Ask.whatistobe
Ask.ifwewantthen
Ask.whatiswiththisonebutnotwiththatone
Ask.whatistobe
Ask.whatwasbut
Ask.whatisandnot
Ask.whatcanbe
Ask.whatcanbebutnotwith
Ask.whatwasbutcantbe
Ask.whatistobe
Ask.whatcanbe
Ask.whatif
Ask.whatcanbeofthisbutnotthat
Ask.whatistobebutnotwiththis
Askwhatcanbeofthembutnotthese
Ask whatcan beofthesebutnotthose
Ask.whatwasbutcouldstillbe
Askwhatcanbebutisnotnow
Ask.whatistobe
Ask.whatcanbebutnotwiththese
Ask.whatwasbutisnot
Ask.whatwasbutisnot
Ask.whatcanbebutisnot
Ask.whatwasbutisstill
Ask.whatcanbedone
Ask.whatcouldbedone
Ask.whatistobe

Ask.whatcanbebutisnot

Then look at all this there is a way in which all this can be easily looked at using a stencil that start with what if we ask what can be done then what that means we can simply ask what can be of a situation then look at all possibilities that this is possible that means instead of asking all the questions we can easily substitute these answers in such a way that the answers are used reflects the manner in which the proceedings can be derived from that means if we ask what is to be then the answer is clear a lot of things can be but not the right order so after finding all the what could be then we can easily assess the weight of each answer then compute the strength of each answer then ask questions that can relate to the question

ABOUT THE AUTHOR

David Gomadza visit www.twofuture.world

www.ingramcontent.com/pod-product-compliance
Lightning Source LLC
Chambersburg PA
CBHW031612210526
45464CB00004B/1540